Jesus, the Prophets,
and the
End of the World

Jesus, the Prophets,
and the
End of the World

An Introduction to Biblical Eschatology

Trevor Bucknell

WIPF & STOCK · Eugene, Oregon

JESUS, THE PROPHETS, AND THE END OF THE WORLD
An Introduction to Biblical Eschatology

Copyright © 2016 Trevor Bucknell. All rights reserved. Except for brief quotations in critical publications or reviews, no part of this book may be reproduced in any manner without prior written permission from the publisher. Write: Permissions, Wipf and Stock Publishers, 199 W. 8th Ave., Suite 3, Eugene, OR 97401.

Wipf & Stock
An Imprint of Wipf and Stock Publishers
199 W. 8th Ave., Suite 3
Eugene, OR 97401

www.wipfandstock.com

PAPERBACK ISBN: 978-1-4982-2326-3
HARDCOVER ISBN: 978-1-4982-2328-7
EBOOK ISBN: 978-1-4982-2327-0

Manufactured in the U.S.A.   07/19/16

To my Mum and Dad with deep gratitude for everything, and to my family—my wife Judy, my children Julia and Arun, Luke and Anastasia. You bring great joy into my life.

CONTENTS

Foreword | ix
Preface | xi
Introduction | xv
Glossary | xix

Part One: THE PROPHETS

Chapter One
AN INTRODUCTION TO THE PROPHETS | 3

Chapter Two
PROPHETS AND THE HISTORY OF ISRAEL | 22

Chapter Three
UNDERSTANDING THE PROPHETS | 31

Chapter Four
ESCHATOLOGICAL THEMES IN THE PROPHETS | 41

Chapter Five
THE GREATEST PROPHET OF ALL | 58

Part Two: JESUS

Chapter Six
KING JESUS | 71

Chapter Seven
KINGDOM STORIES | 79

Chapter Eight
JESUS AND HIS ACTS OF POWER | 91

Chapter Nine
JESUS AND THE FATHER | 103

Chapter Ten
JESUS AND THE SPIRIT | 112

Chapter Eleven
THE KINGDOM ON EARTH | 127

Part Three: THE END OF THE WORLD

Chapter Twelve
LISTENING TO REVELATION | 143

Chapter Thirteen
READING REVELATION | 152

Chapter Fourteen
THE TIME OF DISTRESS | 159

Chapter Fifteen
THE END AND THE BEGINNING | 177

Chapter Sixteen
GARDEN AND CITY | 190

Final Word
EVERLASTING JOY | 201

Bibliography | 205

FOREWORD

In the beginning, the Bible declares in its opening sentence, God created the heavens and the earth—one creation. On the earth God then fashioned a stunningly beautiful home for himself, bursting with light and life, in which he planted a garden temple. In the garden temple he placed an image of himself—a man and woman fashioned from the earth itself and infused with his life—to serve as his stewards. Their privilege and responsibility was to rule over his earth and to serve him in his temple, kings and priests. So it was, and so it should have remained. It was very good.

The stewards, however, were persuaded to rebel against the creator, annexing the earth for themselves and consigning and confining him to "heaven," some indeterminate and distant location where he was free to do whatever God does. So the creation was separated into two realms—heaven and earth. The one was given to God and the other claimed for the independent human beings.

It was determined that God should remain in heaven where he belongs and only interfere in the earth, if at all, to benefit human beings in some way in what they are doing with their earth. He should perform beneficial miracles, for instance, when asked and be available to help whenever needed. But he should not interfere with the way his stewards are running the earth. Some of the stewards even began to declare that he, the creator, no longer existed. He was just a myth, a psychological construct of weak human beings. Human reason could explain how everything came into being.

But *"the earth is the Lord's, and everything in it"* (Ps 24:1). He will not be confined and he will not remain in a distant heaven. He has always continued to intervene in the lives of those made by him and he has always had his prophetic representatives among them, as we will see in the following pages. The image bearers are still responsible to him. The story has not changed.

Though heaven and earth are divided by human beings, it was not like that in the beginning and it will not be like that in the end. The earth is still God's and he has a plan to take it back and renew it. He has a plan to rescue the image bearers from the consequences of their own foolishness and to demonstrate to all creation the depths of his wisdom, power, and love. The center of that plan—the place where heaven and earth come together again fully and forever—is in his son Jesus Christ.

> He made known to us the mystery of his will according to his good pleasure, which he purposed in Christ, to be put into effect when the times will have reached their fulfillment—to bring all things in heaven and on earth together under one head, even Christ. (Eph 1:9–10)

God has a plan, and the Bible tells the story of how he put that plan into action at an incomprehensible cost to himself. The prophets have always played a central role within that plan, declaring his good will to their own generations and declaring his good will for the future, speaking it into being. We are now nearing the end of the story, and the end—as was the beginning—will be very good. God will be back.

> Lift up your heads, O you gates; and be lifted up you ancient doors, that the king of glory may come in . . . (Ps 24:7)

PREFACE

This book began life as a course of lectures prepared for Harvest Bible College in Melbourne on the topic of prophetic literature, which dealt primarily with the study of the Old Testament prophets. I have taught variations of the course several times in Australia and overseas. As I have studied, prepared, and lectured, I have been continually struck by the interconnections between the prophetic material and the content of the New Testament. Specifically, the huge impact that the prophetic books had on the development of the theology of the late Second Temple period, preparing the way for the ministry of Jesus in the gospels and the early church in the book of Acts. In fact, I am persuaded that in some ways the gospels and Acts belong with the Old Testament more than the New in the sense that they present the completion of Israel's story, which has no proper ending apart from them. The focus of the Old Testament story, from the "offspring" promised to Eve (Gen 3:15) to the "offspring" promised to Abraham (Gen 12:7) and David (2 Sam 7:12–13), on to the messiah and "suffering servant" predicted in the prophets—all of this and more arrives at its fulfillment in Jesus and the kingdom of God coming on earth. The stories about him in the gospels and then the stories about the Spirit-filled—and thus prophetic—church in Acts, present the outworking of all the Old Testament promises and types.

Continued study led in turn to an appreciation of the close connection between the Old Testament prophetic material and the book of Revelation. The author of Revelation, in fact, sees himself as one with the prophets, and his revelation as summing up the prophetic promises and predictions, bringing them to completion and fulfillment.

The Prophetic Literature course has always been very well received by students, and many have commented that it should be more widely available. Also, the further pursuit of these connections between the Old Testament prophetic material and the gospels/Revelation lay outside the parameters of the course I was teaching, so the idea of this book was born, both to make the material available to a wider range of people and as an avenue to allow me to pursue these other ideas. This has also resulted in the development of a different course, one that can now be called "prophetic eschatology," or "biblical eschatology." I taught this as an intensive in a Bible College in India and the students were greatly appreciative.

I have discovered that it takes a lot of time and thought and plain hard work to write a book. The tale grew in the telling, and it has filled my thoughts day and night for months and years on end. It has meant long hours of my "spare time" sitting at the computer, writing and checking, revising and revising again. It has been worth it for me personally as I have come, I feel, to a deeper understanding of the Bible story. I hope it brings a similar pleasure to those who might read it.

I have myself read a great number of books over the course of my life, and I have absorbed from these a good many ideas and insights from many people. My thinking is an anthology of all of these plus, hopefully, a few original ideas and insights of my own. From some authors I have gained a lot, from others a gem or two. I am grateful to them all and I have attempted to acknowledge the contribution of other authors to my thinking whenever I could. I apologize in advance for any seeming attempt to pass their ideas off as my own. This has been a concern for me in writing this book. After a lifetime of reading, study, and writing, it is not always possible to remember the source of every idea or concept. I am indebted to all of those who have given me illumination and understanding.

This started as a seriously "academic" book with many more citations from "erudite" (or learned) scholars, obviously chosen to lend weight to my theses and filled with wonderful words like "praxis" and "pericope" which roll so wonderfully off the tongue. But I teach often in developing nations and I would like to make the book available to that wider audience for whom English is not the first language. So I have simplified. What is the good of a book that is only going to be read by a few select people?

It is still a serious book, a book about issues that deserve the effort needed to understand and appreciate them. I believe that some of what I write about here has been previously misunderstood by many Christians, so I have provided supporting Scriptural references whenever I could in an attempt to anchor the book firmly within the biblical text.

The book is written in three sections. The first one deals with the Old Testament prophets and lays the necessary foundation for what follows, as the prophets themselves do for the later biblical eschatology. The second section focuses on various aspects of the life and ministry of Jesus as fulfilling the Old Testament expectations and prophecies, albeit with an unexpected twist. The final section focuses on the book of Revelation, bringing all the prophecies and the various elements of this book to their conclusion. What binds the three sections together is the contention that there is an underlying and unifying story that flows through each, a "prophetic eschatology," if I can put it that way.

This is not, of course, a completely comprehensive coverage of these topics. Each chapter, or at least each section, could form the basis of a separate book by itself. I have tried to produce at least an introduction to the eschatology of the prophets and the Bible. It could be much improved on, I know but maybe that's true of all books. I believe it's an improvement on much of what passes for eschatology in certain sections of the church at present. I am aware that the book contains some big holes. It includes, for instance, very little comment on the covenants, which form the background for the development of the prophetic eschatology, and it does not include more than a passing comment on the prophetic material found in the Psalms. That material is, in some ways again, a different kind of prophetic literature, but it would be very helpful to integrate it with the prophetic literature proper. Maybe a future book.

There are several people I need to thank: My wife Judy, daughter Julia, and friend Dr. Nabil Yassi were early reviewers and pointed out areas that needed correction and improvement. Dr. Jon Newton kindly reviewed an early version of the book and gave several valuable suggestions which necessitated a major rewrite. My friends Andrew Groza, Phil Kennedy, and Len Wrennall also gave valuable feedback. Roger Branford made suggestions that meant another major revision. I am grateful to each one for their helpful suggestions.

INTRODUCTION

THE BOOK IS WRITTEN within certain parameters. Firstly, I take a canonical approach to the biblical material. It has been the norm lately in academic circles to dissect the Bible in search of understanding—to study it analytically; to break up books into multiple parts, attributing them to multiple authors; and to divide the text up into smaller and smaller sections. Then opinions are given and evidence produced to show which portions are original or authentic and which are not. There may be validity and value, of course, in this kind of analysis if the motive is indeed to seek understanding that leads to obedience. But while these questions of authorship and originality are interesting—and may have some bearing on the interpretation of some passages—they do not lie within the scope of this book and they are also, necessarily, matters of conjecture, debate, and opinion. We have to deal in the end with the text in the form we have received it.

There is, secondly, a difference between doing theology "systematically" and doing it "biblically." Systematic theology asks the question, "what does the text say *about* . . . (insert any subject, e.g., "sin")." Most introductory courses on theology are studies in systematics. Again, there is obvious value in such an approach.

Biblical theology on the other hand, as I use it here, looks for the big picture and asks the question "what does the text *say*?" This is an entirely different enquiry, as it allows the text to speak for itself. It also recognizes that every biblical writer was a theologian in his own right and had, therefore, something to say, a particular theological point to make. This is the approach I take in the following pages.

I also make the assumption, thirdly, that a divine mind somehow guided the writing and composition of the biblical material and that, therefore, though the Bible is a collection of many books and several genres, one divinely guided storyline runs through and unites them all in a grand revelation of God and his eschatological purpose for those made in his image. The Old and New Testaments, therefore, are bound together, each providing an essential context for the interpretation and full understanding of the other. Certainly the New Testament authors regarded the things they were experiencing to be a fulfillment of Old Testament expectations and prophecies.

The Bible is a strange book. Some of my other favourite books I have read many times and each time I read them they get "smaller" in a sense as the story becomes more familiar. But the Bible is entirely different, it gets *bigger* the more it is read and studied. New kaleidoscopic interconnections are constantly discovered between passages and books. A single verse, phrase or word can open up like a flower, a passage or idea thought to be mastered and understood can suddenly reveal new, unimagined, depths. Millions of people have studied the Bible for thousands of years, yet more and more books continue to be written about it. There has been in recent times an explosion of *must read* material being produced. I wish I had time to read it all.

So, the biblical story begins, I contend in this book, in Genesis and reaches its culmination in the book of Revelation. It starts in Eden and finishes in the New Jerusalem. It begins with the story of the original creation and finds its fulfillment in the new creation. The whole Bible, after Genesis chapter three, is an eschatological story about the defeat of death and evil and the triumph of God's good will, intention, and purpose.

Central to everything is the crucifixion and resurrection. In order to make the story possible and to bring it to its divinely ordained culmination, Jesus—who was with the Father in the beginning—through whom, by whom, and for whom all things were created, humbled himself and died on the cross. This beautiful planet, unique among the heavenly bodies, was created to be a stage upon which the greatest demonstration of love, wisdom, and power that the universe will ever see would take place. A stage for the sacrificial and vicarious death of Jesus on the cross and his resurrection from the dead. The Old Testament prophets in some measure foresaw this and though they themselves did not understand the total picture, they prophesied it in various ways and laid the theological foundations for recognising it and understanding it when it came to pass.

If we hold, then, that the Bible presents us with this one large story, the book of Revelation is seen in a new way. Wonderfully examined and expounded in hundreds of books, it is usually studied in isolation, a composition separate from the other biblical documents in both Old and New Testaments and therefore difficult to understand. In this book it is seen as an integrated part of the whole, in fact as part of the prophetic corpus. It presents, in this context, the culmination of the divine plan—the creation cleansed and renewed, justice and righteousness fully extended to all humanity and the people of God dwelling once more, as in Eden, in his sanctuary and enjoying his presence. Evil is finally and fully destroyed in all of its manifestations and the new creation destined to continue forever.

Within those parameters, then, this study arrives at two conclusions. Firstly, that the Old Testament prophets and their writings were hugely instrumental in the formation of the Second Temple eschatology, so an appreciation of the Old Testament prophetic literature greatly helps us in understanding the life and ministry of Jesus and the *rationale* of the early church. Secondly, the book of Revelation presents an unfolding of "the Day of the Lord," which forms the common theme in the prophets of God's final and culminating act of righteousness and justice in this age.

Israel's story of divine election lay at the core of their identity as a nation and people, constantly reinforced in the religious practices and rituals that made up their lives. That story, by the time of Jesus, was heavily influenced by the eschatological expectations created by the prophets. The people of Israel expected, looked for, and waited for God's intervention in their history and in their lives once again as he had intervened in the past.

The more we can soak our minds in the Old Testament, then, the more we will understand Jesus and the New Testament. Allusions to the Old Testament in the New are innumerable. Jesus, the evangelists, Paul—all are speaking against an Old Testament background. They are soaked in the Old Testament Scripture, and they are writing—in the beginning certainly—to a people who are similarly soaked in the Old Testament writings and worldview. The events that were happening to them and among them they saw as fulfilling Old Testament expectations. The "last days" had begun, and they were living in them.

That's the story this book has to tell, really. I hope you will enjoy the journey. It's not necessarily an easy book to read in parts, but I believe it's a story that urgently needs telling. The modern church, or a large portion of it, seems to be living in the situation that Jesus predicted when he talked about the "days of Noah and Lot," when people were carrying on their everyday lives, secure in the illusion that everything in the future would always remain the same. Lulled into a kind of historical sleepiness by the relative ease of modern life, we in the West are living, frighteningly, in what James Dobson referred to somewhere as "the illusion of permanence." But it will not always be like this; storm clouds gather, spiritual forces are being marshalled, great and frightening events lie ahead. Great people are needed, and great deeds are waiting to be done. Great courage will be required to lay hold of great opportunities. The times they are a-changing.

GLOSSARY

Canon refers to the list of books considered to be authoritative Scripture by the Jewish or Christian communities. The word "canon" comes from a Greek word meaning "rule," or "measuring stick." It is the standard against which all other revelation is measured.

Eschatology is a branch of theology concerned with what are believed to be the culminating events of history. Some take this in a very narrow sense of meaning "the end times," but it properly refers to the outworking of the accomplishment of all of God's plans and purposes for the creation.

Genre is the term for a style or category of literature, art, or entertainment. The Bible contains several different genres—for example, history, gospel, letters, or prophecy—several different styles or kinds of literature. Identifying the genre of a piece of literature is important because each requires a different approach to its interpretation.

Hermeneutics is the process of biblical interpretation. It involves general rules—such as the need to interpret within context—and rules, or principles that apply to specific genres.

A *meta-narrative* is just a big, controlling story. The Bible in many ways is a story book. It often presents truth to us in the form of stories about the interaction between various people in the plan of God. There is, for instance, the story of Abraham and Lot, of David and Goliath, David and Bathsheba, and so on. To say there is a biblical *meta-narrative* makes the claim that all of these smaller stories are bound together under one big story. The prevailing postmodernism of our times is basically a skepticism towards such meta-narratives, and this has affected the approach of many to the study of the Bible as it has to many other areas of study. So the concept of a biblical meta-narrative is not always accepted among scholars and theologians.

A *motif* is a recurring element in a story, a repeated theme or pattern that forms a larger picture.

Redaction is a form of editing, revising, and updating documents for publication or circulation. Many Bible books appear to have had some level of redaction. For instance, Moses is held by many to be the author of the books of Torah, but they sometimes speak about Moses in the third person, even referring to events after his death. Obviously someone has edited them.

The Second Temple period in Jewish history refers to the time when the Second Temple existed, from about 530 BC to AD 70 when it was destroyed by the Romans. This, of course, includes the historical period covered by the gospels and most of Acts, which is the period I mainly refer to when I talk about it in this book. (Properly, I suppose, it is the *late* Second Temple period.) The first temple, built by Solomon, was destroyed by the Babylonians in 587/6 BC.

The Septuagint is the Greek translation of the Hebrew Bible. It is commonly referred to by the Roman numerals LXX (70). Legend has it that seventy Jewish scholars made the translation over seventy days in Alexandria in the late second century BC.

The Synoptics: The gospels of Matthew, Mark, and Luke are referred to as the *Synoptic Gospels* because they include much of the same material, often in a similar sequence and with similar wording. The content of John's gospel on the other hand is comparatively different. The term *synoptic* comes from the Greek *syn*, meaning "together," and *optic*, meaning "seen."

Except where noted, I have used the NIV translation of the Bible throughout. We turn now to the first section of this book, a study of the Old Testament prophets and their importance to the rest of the biblical story.

Part One

THE PROPHETS

"From the time your forefathers left Egypt until now, day after day, again and again I sent you my servants the prophets. But they did not listen to me or pay attention."

—JEREMIAH 7:25–26

Chapter One

AN INTRODUCTION TO THE PROPHETS

"Something started God's prophets to writing. By the time they had finished, they had produced a body of literature unparalleled in human history. Nothing before or since has equaled the corpus of literature produced by the prophets of Israel."[1]

To many Christians the Old Testament prophetic books effectively remain a mystery. Without extensive study, the genre, form, style, chronology, and history of the prophets are all difficult. Study of these books in Bible colleges is often restricted to third year or even post-graduate level, or left as an optional "elective," which means, in the end, that not many people actually get to do the study. It follows, consequently, that for far too many Christians the books are either "ploughed" through while following a Bible reading plan, effectively ignored, or read devotionally as sources of encouraging personal words from God.

This is a great shame as these books are a major key to understanding the biblical meta-narrative (big story), the biblical story as a whole. In fact it is not too much of an overstatement to say that without an understanding of the prophetic books and of the ministry and message of those who left such

---

1. Robertson, *The Christ of the Prophets*, 1.

an incredible legacy, the New Testament, especially the gospels, cannot be properly understood.

The Old Testament prophets in large measure laid the theological foundations of the late Second Temple period, the historical setting for the ministry of Jesus and the early church. The messianic and eschatological expectations evident in the gospels, with all their associated concepts—the kingdom of God, the return of Jesus, the resurrection, etc.—cannot be properly understood if isolated from the background of the ministry and writings of the prophets. The life and message of Jesus himself cannot be fully appreciated and understood if seen apart from the preparatory work of the prophets. The book of Revelation likewise claims to follow in the tradition of the prophets and, indeed, to bring the prophetic message to its intended conclusion. So the prophetic books are also essential background to understanding the final book of the Bible. That's why this book is presented in three sections focusing on the ministry of the Old Testament prophets, the person and work of Jesus, and the book of Revelation.

So, many Christians have little idea of the importance of the prophets and their message as the context for understanding all that follows them in the unfolding redemptive program of God. There is often, again, only a vague appreciation of how the prophets and their writings fit into the overall biblical picture. I hope that in the following pages we may be able to address these issues in some measure and to reveal something of the immensity of the wisdom, power, and love of God's plan, as outlined by the prophets and unfolded in the rest of the Bible. I hope we can do something towards restoring the prophetic literature of the Bible, and the prophetic ministry so prominent there, to the important place it deserves as a key to the biblical story. The prophets have been God's representatives in the world from ancient times, speaking his words and will into the creation and especially to his elect people.

Some points to start with: This is a book about the prophets and their message and how they relate to the New Testament. Our starting point is the prophetic literature found in the Old Testament. This is not a *survey*, however, of the Old Testament prophetic books, nor is it a critical discussion of those books. There are many very good commentaries, Old Testament surveys, and other Bible study aids which will help in these areas. We begin with the Old Testament prophetic material, but we examine it in the context of the larger biblical story. Only there can we fully appreciate the place the prophets played in God's redemptive program and the true meaning and extent of the messages they brought to Israel and to the other nations.

A number of questions arise as we consider the prophets and their ministry. What was the message (or what were the messages) they brought to Israel? What did that message mean to the people of their own time? Is there any way in which that message, or any part of it, transcends their immediate context, and what does that message mean to us today? Do the words delivered to people in a totally different world three thousand years ago have any kind of meaning that reaches beyond their time to ours today? Is the historically specific message also in any way a historically transcendent message? Is there value for us today in studying these ancient writings and if so, what is it? This book is written to address those questions.

THE BIBLICAL PROPHETS

We will all have some kind of a concept of a prophet in mind, colored perhaps to some extent by a mixture of impressions from the likes of Elijah and John the Baptist—austere and reclusive men dressed in camel-hair coats, eating locusts with wild honey and delivering warnings of impending judgment and doom. The truth is much more varied than that, of course; the prophets were all kinds of often ordinary people called by God to an extraordinary task. Some were "professional" prophets while others were "lay" prophets—farmers, shepherds, priests—and a few women were among their number also. Some wrote books, some wrote histories of the times in which they lived, some left no written record. Some prophesied for a very short time (at least as far as we know of); others had ministries lasting forty years and more. Some prophesied exclusively in Israel and Judah, while others, like Daniel, Ezekiel, and Jonah, carried out their prophetic mandates in and to other nations. They were basically messengers, who heard from God in a number of ways (audibly, or through visions and dreams for example) and conveyed the messages they received to the people of their time. This was sometimes to individuals, sometimes to various groups, and sometimes to national leaders and even entire nations. They also *presented* the divine message in various ways, through prophetic speeches, sometimes in written form and sometimes through symbolic actions.

Prophets (and prophecy) were a lot more common in Israel than is generally realized. They were also widespread throughout the ancient Near East (ANE), the region around Israel. This is shown by both the Old Testament (Num 22–24; 1 Kgs 18:19; Jer 27:8–11) and by other ancient written sources from the surrounding area.

There are some similarities between Israel's prophets and the prophets of the other nations. Certain terminologies, speech forms, means of receiving revelation, and so on, are common to all. However, there are also significant differences. There was, for instance, the Israelite prohibition of divination (Lev 20:27), the strong ethical stand taken by Israel's prophets, and the unique collection of Israel's prophetic literature. The major differences lie in their purpose and the source of their revelation.

Whereas the purpose of most prophets outside of Israel (and some false prophets within) was to act in what they perceived to be their own best interests (sometimes at the behest of their rulers), the purpose of the classical Jewish prophets was to speak for God, to remind the people that they had made a covenant (an agreement) with God (Exod 19:3–8; Deut 5:1–33; 29:1). This had bound them to the Lord as their absolute sovereign and to his laws and regulations as their way of life. If they proved faithless, God would nevertheless remain faithful to his word, including the words of Deuteronomy 28, which spell out both blessings for obedience and judgment for disobedience. When the reminders and consequent warnings fell on deaf ears, the purpose of the prophets then became to deliver the message of God's inevitable and inescapable judgment and, beyond that, of his gracious promises of restoration. The prophets of other nations spoke in the name of their false gods and various spirit sources, whereas Israel's prophets claimed the one true living God as the source of their message.

THE PROPHETIC LITERATURE

The Hebrew Bible divided the books of the Old Testament into three sections—the Torah, the Prophets, and the Writings. The *Torah* contained the five books of the Pentateuch, Genesis through Deuteronomy. The *Prophets* were further divided into two categories: the "Former Prophets" (Joshua, Judges, 1–2 Samuel, 1–2 Kings) and the "Latter Prophets" (Isaiah, Jeremiah, Ezekiel, and the twelve Minor Prophets). The third category, the *Writings*, comprised the remaining books of Psalms, Proverbs, Job, Song of Songs, Ruth, Lamentations, Ecclesiastes, Esther, Daniel, Ezra-Nehemiah, 1–2 Chronicles. It will be easily seen that this arrangement is quite different to that of Christian Bibles, and some of the choices may seem strange to us.

The inclusion of historical narratives (Joshua, Judges, Samuel, and Kings) among the former prophets seems particularly perplexing, a hermeneutical puzzle to us today. David Petersen, in his book *Prophetic Literature*, suggests some answers.[2] During the historical period covered by these books, the prophets played an important—Petersen says a *critical*—role in the program of God for Israel and Judah. The relationship between the roles of the prophet and king will be examined later, but here it should be noted that while granting Israel's request for a king like the other nations, God still

2. Petersen, *Prophetic Literature*, 1–2.

maintained a direct voice in the affairs of the nation through the office of the prophets. Prophetic activity is prominent through the historical records of Samuel and Kings especially. Prophets like Samuel himself, Nathan and Gad (who attended King David), Elijah and Elisha (1 Kgs 17–19:31 and 1 Kgs 21:17–29), Micaiah (who prophesied to the king of Israel, 1 Kgs 22:9), all featured at critical points in the unfolding history. So, through the prophets God maintained a voice in the governance and guidance of the nation.

Secondly, passages such as 1 Chronicles 29:29, "As for the events of King David's reign, from beginning to end, they are written in the records of Samuel the seer, the records of Nathan the prophet, and the records of Gad the seer," reveal that the prophets also functioned as the historians of the time, interpreting history prophetically (from God's perspective, see also 2 Chr 9:29; 12:15; 33:19; etc.). So the prophets provided the written source material for the recorded history of this period which they believed to be a record of God's dealing with his elect people. Petersen says that these two facts show that the presence and role of the prophets are of fundamental importance to understanding Israel's history and thus help to explain the designation "Former Prophets."

Why is the book of Daniel included in the Writings and not among the Prophets? While Jesus himself numbered Daniel among the prophets (Matt 24:15), he is not a prophet in the traditional sense. The book of Daniel is not a collection of prophetic oracles to Israel, Judah, and other nations like the prophetic books proper. It is instead a record of historical events and apocalyptic visions experienced by Daniel while a captive in Babylon. Jesus spoke of Daniel's *function* as a prophet, but historically Daniel was a government official in the Babylonian court. In Daniel's life and writings God is not addressing the people of Israel and Judah directly as in the prophetic books proper. So the book of Daniel is historical narrative and "apocalypse" rather than strictly prophecy.

Our Christian Bibles follow the order found in the Greek translation of the Old Testament (the Septuagint, or LXX) in that the prophetic books appear at the end of the Old Testament. They also include two books displaced from the Prophets in the Jewish organization of the canon: Daniel and Lamentations (the latter of which is linked to Jeremiah in the LXX).

The arrangements of Old Testament books in Christian Bibles is actually very interesting, as they appear in a symmetrical pattern: seventeen historical books are followed by five books of wisdom written in poetic form (Job, Psalms, Proverbs, Ecclesiastes, and Song of Songs), followed in turn by seventeen prophetical books—a pattern of 17–5–17. Then, each of the sections of seventeen books (historical and prophetic) can be subdivided into sections of five and twelve: for the historical books the Pentateuch and the rest, for the prophetic books the five major prophets and the twelve minor prophets. Each section of twelve can then be divided further into nine pre-exilic and three post-exilic books (using conservative dating). So we have something like this:

			Arrangement of Old Testament books in the Christian Bible			
17	Books of history	5	Pentateuch/Torah			
		12	General history	9	Pre-exilic	
				3	Post-exilic	
5	Books of wisdom					
17	Books of prophecy	5	Major prophets			
		12	Minor prophets	9	Pre-exilic	
				3	Post-exilic	

But the study of prophecy in the Old Testament cannot be confined to the seventeen canonical books of prophecy alone. Other Bible books also contain stories about the activities of prophets, and these need to be included in order to grasp the big picture of who the prophets were and what they were sent to do in Israel. There are also a seemingly innumerable number of connections between the message of the prophets and other parts of the Bible both before and after them. So the prophetic ministry and message can be seen to be woven into the tapestry of the larger biblical story.

EARLY PROPHETS

There are a number of people in the Old Testament who are not necessarily designated prophets but who nevertheless fulfill prophetic functions in one way or another. Indeed, the prophetic role is as ancient as the first human beings themselves.

Adam, priest/king in the Edenic sanctuary (of which I will speak later in the book), fulfilled a prophetic function also. Adam walked and talked with God and then spoke God's word into the creation. To him, for instance, was given the task of naming the animals (Gen 2:18–24). This must not be seen as a mere "labelling" of the beasts and birds and fish. We are informed of this task that God set for Adam in the context of God's creation of the woman, and when *she* was presented to Adam he spoke prophetically over her life, "naming" her, giving her identity and purpose, and binding her to himself in his divinely given destiny. "This is now bone of my bones," he said, "and flesh of my flesh; she shall be called woman, for she was taken out of man" (Gen 1:23). Thus the naming of the animals is to be seen, by extension, as part of the creative process, giving identity to the creatures, speaking over them, perhaps even prophetically forming the very nature of the beasts that came before him.

In Jude 1:14 we read that Enoch, described as the "seventh from Adam," prophesied to his contemporaries about the coming of the Lord in judgment, saying, "See, the Lord is coming with thousands upon thousands of his holy ones" (see also *The Book of Enoch* 1:9, and cf. Deut 33:2; Dan 7:10; Matt 25:31). Here, then, is further evidence that the prophetic tradition extends further back into history and even predates the judgment of the flood.

Noah is a kind of new Adam in the post-flood world. He too had a special responsibility toward the creatures of the earth. He too received God's blessing and was told, "be fruitful and increase in number and fill the earth" (Gen 9:1). He too was the "image of God" (Gen 9:6). He too "fell" (Gen 9:20–21). Noah also fulfilled a prophetic function. Like Enoch (and Adam) he walked with God (Gen 6:9) and he heard from God of coming judgment. He was a "preacher of righteousness" in the pre-flood world, condemning that world by his faith and obedience (Heb 11:7).

Abraham was designated a prophet (Gen 20:7). There are probably various aspects to this. He was, for instance, a man who was especially called aside by God, and he would be an intermediary or intercessor between other men and God. He interceded for Abimelek and on another occasion for Sodom when God showed him how he was about to move in judgment on the cities of the plain (Gen 18:17–33; cf. Amos 3:7). Abraham occupies a unique and foundational place in the redemptive plan of God for the fallen creation. Apart from the first eleven introductory chapters, the book of Genesis is devoted to him and his family line. Nearly fourteen of the fifty chapters are devoted to Abraham himself, and this in the book of beginnings. There is obviously something seminal here. Abraham is, in fact, a central character of the whole Bible story, being mentioned in twenty-six of the Bible's books, and it is of some value to us here to trace something of that story through the Bible narrative.

Abraham is both the father of Israel (John 8:39) and the "father of all who believe" (Rom 4:11). Though the promise of salvation for the lost humanity had been hinted at in the garden (Gen 3:15), it is with Abraham that God begins his redemptive program proper. His life marks an important turning point in God's purpose for human beings. God's call came to Abraham to separate himself from all that was familiar to him and to journey to an inheritance in the land of Canaan (Gen 12:1–5). When he set out on that journey Abraham was seventy-five years old (Gen 12:4).

With the call to separate himself to God's purpose for his life, Abraham received an unconditional promise from God (though obviously predicated upon his obedience to the call). The promise had several aspects that reverberate as major themes through the rest of Scripture: Abraham will have *many descendants* and become a *great nation*. These offspring, or *seed*, will inherit the *land* of Canaan (Gen 12:7). *Blessing* will come to them and through them to *all peoples on earth* (Gen 12:2–3). The promise was repeated in the covenant of Genesis 15 (with the added detail of a miraculous heir) and Genesis 17 (where circumcision was added) and established finally by divine oath after Abraham was tested by God (Gen 22:15–18). These repetitions serve to stress the seriousness of what God was establishing in and through Abraham, and a reading of the Old Testament will show that the whole subsequent history of Israel was shaped by God's covenant with his friend Abraham and the promises he made to him. They became the foundation of all that followed.

Isaac's life was directly affected by God's dealing with his father. He was the very embodiment and the miraculous heir of the promise made to Abraham. The promise of land and blessing was repeated to him (Gen 26:1–5, 24)[3] and the reason given was, "because Abraham obeyed me" (v 5) and "for the sake of my servant Abraham" (v 24). Isaac's whole life was shaped by God's promise to Abraham. Also directly impacted was the life of Abraham's grandson Jacob. Isaac prophesied over Jacob the "blessing given to Abraham" (Gen 28:4)[4] and God himself again repeated the Abrahamic promise to him (Gen 28:13; 35:12). So much were the lives and destinies of these two men bound up with God's promises and covenant with Abraham that later references call it "his covenant with Abraham, Isaac, and Jacob" (Exod 2:24, etc.).

Though the land of Canaan was already given to Abraham by God (Gen 12:7), part of God's prophetic declaration over Abraham had included the fact that his descendants would dwell in another land altogether for a period of four hundred years before returning to actually take possession of

---

3. Here, too, we see the first appearance of the promise "I will be with you" that was repeated to so many of God's chosen messengers and found its culmination in Jesus' promise to those who go in his name and authority to fulfill the great commission (Matt 28:20). See Gen 26:3; 31:3; Exod 3:12; Jos 1:5; Judg 6:16; 1 Kgs 11:38; Isa 43:2; See also, Gen 26:24; 28:15; Josh 3:7; Isa 41:10; 43:5; Jer 1:8,19; 15:20; 30:11; 42:11; 46:28; Hag 1:13; 2:4; Acts 18:10.

4. Note that the land is already considered to belong to Abraham and therefore his descendants. God had given it.

Canaan (Gen 15:13-16). This was fulfilled through God's dealing with Jacob's son Joseph and the subsequent descent of the patriarchal families into Egypt. The divine promises and purposes were not forgotten in the foreign land. As Jacob's life was coming to an end, he invoked over Joseph's children the name and purposes of the God of Abraham and Isaac (Gen 48:16-16). And as Joseph's life came to an end, he reminded his brothers that it was God's promise to Abraham that was guiding their destiny. There was a land that was already given to them, of which they would one day take possession (Gen 50:24-25). There in the land of Egypt they quickly increased from tribe to nation size (Exod 1:7). Though away from their promised inheritance, they dwelt nevertheless under the shadow of the promise as God waited for them to increase enough to take the land (Acts 7:17) and for the sin of the land's inhabitants to reach its full measure (Gen 15:16).

At the end of the prophesied four hundred years, we are not told whether or not the Israelites still held on to a faith in the Abrahamic covenant, nor how much of a knowledge of Abraham's God they still retained (though among the elders there was obviously maintained a knowledge of God; see Exodus 3:16; 4:29-31). We are told they "cried out" because of their slavery, but we are not told that the cry for help was necessarily directed to Abraham's God. But God had not forgotten his promise to Abraham, nor his purpose being outworked through Abraham's descendants (Exod 2:24; 3:7-8). He chose Moses and introduced himself as the God who covenanted with Abraham and the other patriarchs (Gen 3:6) and declared that, through Moses, he was now ready to move on to the next phase of his redemptive program and bring the Israelites into the land as he had promised Abraham (Exod 3:7-10). When God later purposed to destroy the people for their disobedience, Moses interceded on their behalf, appealing to God to spare the people on the basis of that promise made to Abraham and the other patriarchs (Exod 32:13; Duet 9:27).

Though pausing at Sinai on their exit from Egypt, where God organized them and sanctified them with his presence, God's oath to Abraham propelled them on from there towards Canaan (Exod 33:1). A covenant had been made between God and the descendants of Abraham (the Mosaic covenant was an extension and confirmation of the Abrahamic covenant, Deut 29:12-15), an organization established, and the tabernacle built where God would live among his people. His plan for them now was to go and take possession of the land he had already given on oath to Abraham centuries before. Israel's entitlement to the land of Canaan always rested on God's promise to Abraham (Deut 1:8; 6:10; 9:5), though they had to go now and physically take possession of it. The exodus itself, God's concern for the people, his provision for them in the wilderness, and the entrance into the promised land—all were on the basis of what God had promised Abraham (Ps 105:37–45; see especially v 42). When Israel had successfully entered the land, Joshua assembled all the people and spoke to them. He reminded them that their possession of the land was the fulfillment of the purpose of God that had begun long ago with Abraham (Jos 24:3–13). God's promise to Abraham would even preserve Israel in times of apostasy, judgment, and dispersion and provide the basis of restoration to the land upon repentance (Lev 26:42).

In David's psalm of thanks, when the ark was brought to Jerusalem, he reminded the nation that God was dealing with them on the basis of his covenant with Abraham (1 Chr 16:16). Even after the breakup of the kingdom, Elijah on Mt. Carmel reminded the people of the northern kingdom of Israel of their spiritual and physical roots by appealing to the "God of Abraham, Isaac, and Jacob . . ." (1 Kgs 18:36). Remarkably, even in their apostasy Israel was protected in some measure because of God's covenant with their father Abraham (2 Kgs 13:23).

Through the prophet Isaiah, God comforted the people of Jerusalem and Judah through this same period by reminding them that they were "descendants of Abraham my friend" (Isa 41:8; cf. 2 Chr 20:7). Abraham was their father (Isa 51:2) and God's redemption began with him (Isa 29:22). After the restoration, when the Israelites were gathered together to confess their sin (Neh 9:1–2), part of what formed the very identity of God to the people, part of their very understanding of who he was, was as the one "who chose Abram . . . brought him out of Ur . . . and named him Abraham" (Neh 9:7; cf. Ps 47:9). The Jews of the New Testament period still considered themselves the descendants of Abraham (Matt 3:9; Luke 3:8; John 8:33, 39; cf. Isa 51:2), his children, and therefore heirs of the promise. In this time also, the eternal state is identified in some way with Abraham (Matt 8:11; Luke 13:28). The covenant sign of circumcision, originally given to Abraham, was still counted in New Testament times as a mark of a real Israelite—even, by some, as necessary for salvation in the church (Acts 15:5, etc.).

God's covenant with Abraham was "for a thousand generations" (1 Chr 16:15; Ps 105:8) and "forever" (2 Chr 20:7). It is an "everlasting covenant" (Ps 105:10). While this can be seen as ultimately fulfilled through Jesus, the true son and heir of Abraham (see Matt 1:1), certain aspects of the covenant—regarding the physical land of Canaan especially—seem to require a more literal fulfillment. Isaiah 11:11–12, which is clearly in the context of the eschatological fulfillment of all things (vv. 6–10), speaks of the regathering (i.e., to Canaan) of God's people (exiles of Israel) "a second time" from the islands of the sea and from the four quarters of the earth. The schism between Ephraim and Judah would be no more, and the hostility between them healed.[5]

While this passage in Isaiah may be referring in the first place to the "new exodus" that takes place through the ministry of Jesus, the fact that such a regathering is taking place in our day is perhaps an indication that we have come to a tremendously significant turning point in God's redemptive program. A physical—though largely unbelieving—nation of Israel, with its capital in Jerusalem, exists in "Canaan" again after nearly 2000 years. Is this an accident of history, a prophetic sign, or something else?

Abraham is mentioned seventy-four times in the New Testament—more than any Old Testament character apart from Moses (seventy-nine times).[6] The gospel came first of all to the Jews as God's covenant people (Rom 1:16. See also Matt 10:5; 15:24; Acts 13:46; 17:2; 18:5–6; Rom 10:1). Jesus was a Jew, a descendant of Abraham, and it is through Jesus that God's promises to Abraham are to be extended to the peoples of the earth (Rom 15:8). In the New Testament it is not surprisingly Abraham's faith that is the most strongly emphasized aspect of his life. In the great chapter on faith, Hebrews 11, twelve verses are devoted to examples from Abraham's life—far more than to anyone else.

To Paul, Abraham's "justification by faith" before being circumcised (Rom 4: 9–12, cf. Gen 15:6) is the basis for his argument that it is faith, not "circumcision," that brings righteousness and makes believers children of Abraham (see Gal 3:6–7). This "justification by faith" for the "Gentiles" (all the peoples of earth) was God's purpose before Abraham and indeed his very intention in calling him (Gal 3:8–9). Paul sees in God's promise to Abraham the first proclamation of the gospel (Gal 3:8). The law was a temporary measure put in place to lead "us" (Jews and Gentiles) to Christ so that all might be justified by faith like Abraham (Gal 3:15–25). Now that faith has come, the law's task and jurisdiction have finished.[7] Very interestingly, Paul sees the ultimate fulfillment of the promise made to Abraham in the giving of the Holy Spirit (Gal 3:14). This was the "end" of God's saving plan. God's people would all be anointed, would all be prophets—they would all know him.

Abraham's story is thus very important in shaping the whole spiritual and physical history of the nation of Israel, right up to New Testament times and even into the present. Indeed God's dealing with Abraham underpins

---

5. So in Acts 1:8 Jesus speaks of the uniting of "Judea and Samaria" in God's New Testament saving plan; see Thompson, *The Acts of the Risen Lord Jesus*, 106, 128.

6. Rea, *Abraham in the New Testament*, 12.

7. James (2:20–24) adds the necessary clarification that Abraham's faith was demonstrated by his obedience, this is especially true in his offering of Isaac.

the whole redemptive story. The divine promises made to Abraham take a new turn with the coming of Jesus. He is the promised seed or offspring of Abraham, he is the real purpose of God. In his light, even Abraham fades into the background (see John 8:56, 58). In the New Testament, God is no longer just the God of Abraham, Isaac, and Jacob, but now "the God and Father of our Lord Jesus Christ" (Eph 1:3).

OTHER PROPHETS TO ISRAEL

Miriam, the sister of Moses and Aaron, is called a prophetess (Exod 15:20). Exactly what prophetic function she fulfilled is unclear but she easily and naturally took the lead in directing the people in praising God for his great deliverance. This is perhaps the first linking in the Bible of prophecy and worship, which we will find in other references also.

In Numbers we have the story of how God put something of his Spirit on seventy of the elders of Israel who then prophesied (Num 11:16–17, 24–30). Of important note here is the implied relationship between prophecy and the Spirit of God and also, in the same verse (Num 11:29), the prophetic insight Moses showed into God's ultimate plan and purpose for his people. "I wish," he said, "that all the Lord's people were prophets and that the Lord would put his Spirit on them!" This cry will resonate far ahead into the new creation itself and find it's fulfillment in the events of the day of Pentecost.

Moses is the prophet *par excellence,* providing, in many ways, the model of the prophetic office (Deut 34:10). He receives messages directly from God which he then delivers to various people as he is instructed. To Pharaoh (Exod 6:20–22), to the Israelites (Exod 19:3; Lev 19:1–2), and to the priests (Lev 21:1). At times he intercedes with God on behalf of the Israelite people (Exod 32:7–14; Num 14:10–25), and he also performs miracles and mighty deeds (Exod 7:8–24; Deut 34:11–12). Moses differs from other prophets in some ways, for instance in the way that he receives revelation (Num 12:6–8; Deut 34:10). This he receives in both oral and written form (Exod 24:4; 31:18; 32:15–16; 34:28). He also differs from other prophets in the *content* of his prophetic messages. Through him God gives not only specific instruction but also legislates the social and religious life of the nation (Exod 20:22–23:33; Lev 1:1–7:37), something which was not repeated until Jesus came. Moses declared that God would raise up another prophet like him (Deut 18:15–18). A series of prophets may be meant but this is also the basis for later messianic expectation and for the New Testament portrayal of Jesus in this prophetic role, this prophecy receiving its complete fulfillment in him (see John 1:21, 25, 45; 5:46; 6:14; 7:40; Acts 3:22–26; 7:37). The heirs of Moses' prophetic office mentioned in Samuel and Kings include Samuel, Gad, Nathan, Micaiah, Elijah, Elisha, and Huldah (see 1 Kgs 13:1, 11; 14:2). Speaking in God's name, they continued the intermediating role begun by Moses and opposed the religious apostasy and syncretism of their particular times (2 Sam 12:7; 1 Kgs 21:9).

Samuel's ministry is also important to Israel's story. He serves as a transitional figure between the judges and prophets (Acts 13:20; 3:24; 1 Sam 7:15). According to 1 Samuel 3:1 he was just a boy when he first heard from God. All Israel recognized Samuel as a prophet and thus recognized that he spoke for the Lord. His is also a transitionary ministry between the rule of the judges (the theocracy) and rule of the kings (the monarchy), serving as God's representative through this time (see Jer 15:1). Samuel was used by God to establish the kingship in Israel (1 Sam 8-10; cf.10:25), so right at the beginning of the monarchy a clear link is established between king and prophet, a link which we will explore later.

Some of the prophets were important political figures (1 Sam 16:13; 1 Kgs 19:15; 22; 2 Kgs 3). They were sometimes sent by God, at great personal risk, to denounce the ungodly behavior of the kings (2 Sam 11-12; 1 Kgs 21) and even became involved in dethroning rulers (1 Sam 15:28; 1 Kgs 14:7-18; 21:19). There are several examples in scripture of prophets as a group or body. For instance, Second Kings mentions the "company of the prophets" as a group who live and work together (2 Kgs 4:1; 6:1; cf. 1 Sam 10:10; 2 Kgs 2:3, 5, 7; 6:1).

Besides Miriam, there are several other women in the Old Testament who are called prophets: Deborah (Judg 4:4), Huldah (2 Kgs 22:14), Isaiah's wife (Isa 8:3), and compare Nehemiah 6:14 where a woman is listed among the false prophets trying to intimidate Nehemiah. Prophecy is thus, in the Old Testament, a "charismatic" (Spirit-appointed and Spirit-anointed) ministry or office carried out by both men and women who were called by God and equipped by God's Spirit (see Num 11:16-17, 24-30; 1 Sam 10:10; Joel 2:28-29).

There were several later prophets in Israel whose activity is noted, but who did not leave books of prophecy written in their names. This is not to say they never engaged in writing themselves or used the services of scribes. Elijah, for instance, wrote a letter to King Jehoram (2 Chr 21:12-15), and others, as we have noted, recorded the history of the times in which they lived. Some of these "non-writing" prophets also played significant roles in the history of Israel.

Nathan was a prophet through the reigns of the kings David and Solomon and played an important (and personally courageous) role in three critical events. Firstly, in the building of the temple (2 Sam 7:1-29; 1 Chr

17:1–27). After initially encouraging David in his desire to build "a house for the Lord," Nathan received a word from God which he conveyed to David, saying in effect, "you are not the one to build the temple, instead God will build a house (a dynasty) for you," and, "one of your sons will build my house."[8] Secondly, when David committed adultery with Bathsheba and subsequently arranged the killing of her husband, the Lord sent Nathan to confront David with his sin (2 Sam 12:1–14). Fortunately, Nathan's parable stirred David's sense of justice and led to contrition and repentance. David was forgiven, but must bear the consequences of his actions within his own family as Nathan, with great courage, spelled out to him. Thirdly, Nathan played an important part in the succession to the throne of David's son Solomon when David was nearing death but had not announced a successor. David's fourth son Adonijah (possibly the oldest surviving son) planned a coup, but when Nathan heard about it he engineered Solomon's succession as David had previously intended (1 Kgs 1:1–53). Nathan wrote a history of the reign of David (1 Chr 29:29) and of at least some part of Solomon's reign also (2 Chr 9:29). He also played a prophetic role in the development of the temple worship (2 Chr 29:25–26). Here again, as also in the life of the prophets Gad and Elisha below, we note the connection between music, worship, and prophecy.

Gad was also a contemporary of Saul and David. He advised David to leave Moab for Judah when being pursued by Saul (1 Sam 22:5). He later bore God's message to David, offering a choice of three punishments for conducting a census of Israel (probably motivated by pride and a reliance on military strength rather than on the Lord); and then, in the midst of the judgment that fell as a consequence, Gad instructed David to build an altar and offer sacrifices (2 Sam 24:1–14; 1 Chr 21:1–22:1). Again, he helped David and Nathan to organize the temple worship (2 Chr 29:25), and he too wrote a history of David's reign (1 Chr 29:29).

David himself is recognized as a prophet in Israel (Acts 2:29–31). He spoke prophetic oracles under the anointing of the Spirit (2 Sam 23:1–7), he restored the presence of God to Israel (2 Sam 6) and led the nation in worship, both in dance (2 Sam 6:14) and, like Miriam, in song (2 Sam 22). He, of course, penned many of the psalms, some of which are prophetic in nature and content.

Elijah was a ninth century BC prophet to the northern kingdom of Israel (1 Kgs 17–19, 21; 2 Kgs 1–2). He is a contemporary of Ahab and Ahaziah, kings of Israel. Elijah's ministry basically involved the clash between the worship of Baal and Yahweh. Six episodes are recorded in his life:

---

8. There are obvious messianic overtones to both of these pronouncements.

his prediction of drought and subsequent flight, the Mt. Carmel contest, his flight to Horeb, the Naboth incident, the oracle about Ahaziah, and his translation before Elisha.

Ahab, the king of the northern nation of Israel, married the Tyrian princess Jezebel (1 Kgs 16:30-33), who began a systematic extermination of Yahweh worship and the propagation of the Baal cult in Israel (1 Kgs 18:4, 13, 19; 19:10, 14). The drought oracle, when Elijah declared that there would be no rain for the next three years (1 Kgs 17:1), was a challenge to Baal's sovereignty over nature. His confrontation with the prophets of Baal on Mt. Carmel brought the challenge out into the open (1 Kgs 18:16-40). The Naboth incident, when Jezebel had Naboth murdered and seized his vineyard (1 Kgs 21:1-19), involved another covenant challenge. In Israel, land owned by a family or clan was a gift or loan from God and was to remain in the family's possession. Jezebel ignored this and seized for herself (or for Ahab) what was God's. Elijah confronted them and pronounced God's judgment upon them. Ahab's son Ahaziah later injured himself and turned to Baal-zebub, god of Ekron or Syria for help and healing, bringing about a confrontation between the power of the kingship and the authority of God's prophet when Elijah confronted him (2 Kgs 1). This violation of the terms of kingship brought God's judgment on Ahaziah, and he died upon his sick bed. Elijah's translation in the whirlwind brought about the dramatic close to his prophetic career.

Elijah stands in the line of ecstatic prophets from the days of Samuel, yet serves in some ways as a forerunner to the eighth-century writing prophets (see 2 Chr 21:11-15). He seems to have been in some position of leadership over the prophetic schools that existed in Israel at that time (see 1 Kgs 18:4, 13; 2 Kgs 2:3-7). As he confronted the idolatry and Baal-worship that filled Israel, he called on the people to return to the exclusive worship of the real (covenant) God, and to the living of their lives according to his righteous standards. In the story of Elijah, the concept of *remnant* is introduced also (1 Kgs 19:14-18). Remnant theology is developed in the classic prophets and is important in the rest of the Bible story; in the midst of judgment and destruction, God protects the remnant of people who remain faithful to him. Based on Malachi 4:5-6, there was a common expectation at the time of Jesus that Elijah's ministry is to be revived at the end of the age (Matt 11:14; 17:10; 27:14; Mark 6:15; Luke 1:17; John 1:21). Jesus indicated that this had reference to John the Baptist (Matt 11:14; 17:12; Luke 7:30-31; cf. Rev 11:3-6).

The New Testament links Moses and Elijah together (Matt 17:3) and in the Old Testament narrative there are a number of similarities between their two ministries. Elijah is sent by God to the apostate king as his representative (see 1 Kgs 17:1), as Moses had been sent to Pharaoh before him. Elijah pronounced judgment against the king of Israel as Moses did against Pharaoh. He was miraculously fed in the desert as Moses and Israel had been before him. The fire of God is prominent in both the ministry of Moses (see Lev 9:24) and that of Elijah on Mt. Carmel. Compare also the way God answers Elijah by fire (1 Kgs 18:38; 2 Kgs 1:10–12) and God's presence and judgment through fire in the Exodus narratives (Exod 3:2; 13:21; 19:18; 24:17; 40:38; Num 11:1; 16:35). Both Elijah and Moses flee for their lives at the threat of royal judgment (Exod 2:15; 1 Kgs 19:2–3). Both are miraculously sustained by God for forty days and nights (Exod 24:18; 34:28; 1 Kgs 19:8), as Jesus would also be sustained in the wilderness temptations (Luke 4:2, cf. Mark 1:12 and Matt 4:11). Joshua and Elisha, who finished the work and ministries of those who preceded them—Moses and Elijah—both demonstrated their fitness for office by a miraculous river crossing (Jos 4:14; 2 Kgs 2:15).[9] The *NIV Study Bible* notes that in the New Testament, John the Baptist ("Elijah," Matt 11:4; 17:12) is followed by Jesus (whose Hebrew name is Joshua, "the Lord saves").[10] These obvious similarities are examples of the interweaving of themes, types, and parallels that fill the pages of the Bible and give support to the idea of a divinely-guided eschatological history. They consequently lend a great deal of credence to the concept of a biblical meta-narrative. More of this in the pages ahead.[11]

Elisha was also a ninth-century prophet of Israel (1 Kgs 19:19–21; 2 Kgs 2:1–8:15; 13:14–21). His ministry extended for more than fifty years, through the reigns of kings Ahab, Ahaziah, Jehoram, Jehu, Jehoahaz, and Jehoash. Eighteen episodes are recorded in his life. He was not as much involved in the battle between the worship of Baals and God as Elijah was. His ministry is rather at the head of the prophetic schools (2 Kgs 2:15; 4:1; 4:38; 4:42–44; 6:1) and involved a display of signs and wonders at individual and national levels. He is more of a "seer" in the tradition of Samuel to whom people turn for help in time of need.

Interestingly, it is in Elisha's ministry that we see again the connection between music, worship, and prophecy. When Elisha is asked to give prophetic guidance to the kings of Israel, Judah and Edom, he calls for a harpist. It is while the harpist is playing that the prophetic anointing (or the spirit of prophecy) comes upon Elisha (2 Kgs 3:9–13). Elisha has gifts of knowledge,

---

9. And the relationship of both with their mentors is described using the same Hebrew root, translated "aid" in Exodus 24:13 and "became his attendant" in 1 Kings 19:21.

10. See notes on 1 Kings 19:16 in Barker, *NIV Study Bible*.

11. How could nearly forty authors, writing across several centuries, create such an interwoven narrative?

foresight and miracles. The "double portion" he requested of Elijah (2 Kgs 2:9) recalls the language and thought of the Jewish inheritance laws (Deut 21:17). Elisha wants to be Elijah's heir (as Joshua was to Moses) and carry on his ministry to Israel, rather than desiring a ministry twice as great as Elijah's, as is popularly misunderstood. Although Elisha's ministry lasted twice as long as Elijah's and the narrative records twice as many miracles through his ministry, nevertheless Elijah is clearly the dominant figure in the Biblical narrative. His miracles are a great deal more dramatic; he dealt with powerful and prominent figures in Israel, where Elisha dealt mostly with more common people; and Elijah is mentioned twenty-nine times in the New Testament, whereas Elisha is mentioned just once.

THE WRITING PROPHETS

The "writing," or "classical," prophets are those prophets who left books written in their names. They ministered in Israel and Judah through the three hundred years that stretched from the mid-eighth to mid-fifth centuries BC. This was the crucial period of three great empires: Assyria, Babylonia, and Persia, each of which played a pivotal role in events within the history of the nations of Israel and Judah. It is the writings of these prophets that forms the core focus of study in this part of this book.

The defining characteristic of a prophet in Israel was not supernatural ability, nor the working of great miracles, but rather it was the faithful communication of God's word. The prophet spoke the words of God and thus spoke authoritatively. It is clear that there were also false prophets in Israel and this was regarded very seriously by God. To speak presumptuously in God's name meant death (Deut 18:19–20). There was a very simple test to establish whether a prophet truly speaks for God or not: "You may say to yourselves, "How can we know when a message has not been spoken by the Lord?" *If what a prophet proclaims in the name of the Lord does not take place or come true, that is a message the Lord has not spoken.* That prophet has spoken presumptuously. Do not be afraid of him" (Deut 18:20–22).[12]

But note the qualification, also: "If a prophet, or one who foretells by dreams, appears among you and announces to you a miraculous sign or wonder, and if the sign or wonder of which he has spoken takes place, and he says, 'Let us follow other gods' (gods you have not known) 'and let us worship them,' *you must not listen to the words of that prophet or dreamer*" (Deut 13:1–5). Prophecy must accord with previous revelation.

---

12. It is interesting to note the element of respect accorded the prophets.

It should be noted that the prophetic message in view here is not mere prediction of the future as would be sought from a soothsayer or oracle, but rather a statement of God's future plans. God "declares" the future, and if God declares something, it must come to pass, so if the thing thus declared does not take place, it is obviously not God who has spoken. However it should be noted also that when a prophetic warning of judgment was issued, the outcome could be altered through the repentance of the offending party, as with the people of Nineveh when Jonah preached to them (this is the desired result of the call to repentance of course). Judgment could also be averted, or mitigated, through prophetic intercession, as with Abraham and Lot.

PROPHETS AND THE FUTURE

The word "prophet" derives from Greek *"prophetes,"* to foresee. However, predicting the future was only a part of their message, as we will see, and that not for its own sake, but rather as something that grew out of their larger message and ministry. Israel's prophets spoke, in the first place, directly to the people of their own day, to the people of Israel and Judah and the nations that interacted with them through the tumultuous events of their own times. We will not understand the message of the prophets if we do not start with this fact. Their primary concern was naturally with their own historical situation. The messages they received from God were addressed to their contemporaries in the first instance. They spoke into their own historical situations, both in the light of God's dealing with the people in the past and in view of God's purposes for them in the future. It was out of this future purpose that the predictive element of their message grew. It was not prediction to prove a point, but rather a declaration of what God would do for his people and for the nations in the light of the present situation and in the light the original purpose he had in calling Abraham. God determined the future and established it by proclamation (Isa 46:10–11).

Various other words were used to describe prophets also, indicating differing aspects of their ministry. The standard name or term for a prophet (Hebrew *nābî'*, 1 Sam 9:9) carried the sense of the divine call to the prophetic task (Isa 6; Jer 1; Ezek 1–2; 1 Kgs 19; Amos 7: 14–16; Exod 3; etc.). They were alternatively described as seers, or visionaries (Amos 7:12), or "diviners" who were able to communicate with God and discover useful information (primarily used of Samuel; see 1 Samuel 9:6). Another term used was "man of God," which was especially used of Elijah and Elisha (see 2 Kgs 6:1–7), and carried the suggestion, says Petersen, of someone holy, powerful, worthy of respect, perhaps even dangerous.[13] Sometimes these terms are used interchangeably.

SUMMARY OF CHAPTER ONE

The prophets played a fundamentally important role as God's representatives to the nation of Israel, as counsellors and censors to the kings, as reformers, and as encouragers of the people of God. An understanding of this divinely designed role is essential if we are to properly understand the story of Israel and the biblical narrative as a whole. There are many prophets mentioned in the Bible apart from those who authored the books that make up the Old Testament prophetic section of our bibles. From Abraham to Moses, Elijah and Elisha, from Samuel to Gad, and Nathan who advised King David, and many who are not so well known, these prophets are all essential elements in the biblical story. Together they serve to demonstrate the prophetic undercurrent to the biblical meta-narrative that reveals a God who is actively involved in the redemption of his lost creation.

The first role and ministry of the prophets was to the people of their own time, as messengers who heard from God and brought his word to the kings and then to the nation. Through the prophets, God maintained an immediate and directive voice in the affairs of the elect people. Some of the prophets served as historians of their times. Some also helped to exemplify and regulate the worship life of the nation. Some were even important political figures. Taken together they demonstrate that God has not been sidelined. He has not been excluded, made redundant or irrelevant, as the human story misinforms us. He maintains his involvement and, as we will see, his control of events unfolding on the earth that still belongs to him. We turn for now to the history of Israel as we continue to lay the foundations for understanding the prophets and their place in the biblical narrative.

---

13. Petersen, *Prophetic Literature*, 6.

Chapter Two

PROPHETS AND THE HISTORY OF ISRAEL

"I will surely bless you, and make your descendants as numerous as the stars in the sky and as the sand on the seashore. Your descendants will take possession of the cities of their enemies, and through your offspring all nations on earth will be blessed . . ." (Gen 22:17–18)

Knowledge of Israel's history is of fundamental importance to understanding the message of the prophets and of the whole Old Testament, as message and history are inextricably tied up together. It is a prophetic history—God speaks and acts in the fallen creation to bring to pass his predetermined plan. The prophets inform us that the God of Israel is the God who acted *within their history*. Israel's religion and history are fundamentally eschatological. The Bible is not a systematic theology, it is a story book, a book of real stories of the experiences of real men and women who encountered God within their everyday lives. They are stories of how God interacted with these people and they with him. This was true both on an individual level and—in the Old Testament especially—it applied also on a corporate or national level. The Old Testament is an eschatological history, and the prophets play a foundational role in the unfolding of the redemptive plan recorded there.

EARLY HISTORY

The events recorded in Genesis form a "prequel" or pre-history to the story of the nation of Israel, which really began with the deliverance from Egypt. This, however, was the outcome of the plans God began to put in place right from the fall itself. Genesis chapters 1–11 trace the godly line of descent from Adam, the father of all who live (Acts 17:26), to Abraham, the father of all who believe (Rom 4:11). It was with Abraham then, as we have seen, that God's plan of redemption began in earnest. Everything that followed of the story of Israel flowed from Abraham's obedience to God's call and from the divine promises made to him. The rest of Genesis tells the story of Abraham's descendants Isaac, Jacob, and the twelve sons of Jacob who finally, with their families, moved down to Egypt together to escape the effects of a famine that was affecting the region. This was also according to God's purposes (Gen 15:13–14, Acts 13:17).

During the 430 years they spent in Egypt, Israel grew in number to possibly over two million people (see Num 1:45–46).[1] To begin with, this was under the protective covering of Jacob's son Joseph who held high political office and wielded great influence in Egypt. But after Joseph died a new Pharaoh began to make slaves of the Israelites, fearing their strength and influence should they rise up and be united against the Egyptians. Even here we can see God's hand at work, allowing this to happen so that the Jews would *want* to leave Egypt. Had they continued in the prosperity, privilege, and comfort they enjoyed in Egypt at first, they might never have been prepared to leave. Their destiny, however, lay not in Egypt but in Canaan, in the land promised by God to Abraham, and there they must go.

It was God's purpose, now he had a *people*, to teach them his *laws* and to bring them into the *land* he had prepared for them. They would be his light in a dark world and through them he would bring salvation to all the nations. Pharaoh oppressed them, they cried out for deliverance, and in response God sent his prophet Moses to bring them up out of Egypt and into the land and destiny that he had for them. God's prophet, speaking God's word, would, in large measure, mold the elect people of God into the prophetic nation of witnesses to his goodness and channels of his blessing that he had called them to be. Moses led them out of Egypt and brought them to Mt. Sinai. This "exodus" was considered the birth of Israel as a nation (Exod 13:8; Lev 11:45; Deut 20:1; Josh 24:17; 1 Sam 8:8; 10:18; 2 Kgs 17:7; Ps 81:10; Jer 16:14; etc. Cf. Exod 32:4; 1 Kgs 12:28). They spent eleven months and

---

1. There is some dispute over these large numbers in the OT. For instance, the logistics of getting this number of people, plus cattle, wagons, etc., through the wilderness is daunting to consider. However, see Deuteronomy 1:10.

five days at Sinai (see Exod 19:1; Num 10:11), where three important things took place that were to shape the future life of the nation: the law was given to them, the priesthood was inaugurated, and the tabernacle was built. Through these, a social order was established, the cultic system (priesthood, sacrifices etc.) was put in place, a covenant was made between God and the people, and God came to dwell among them. It was this covenant, and God's continuing eschatological purpose for Israel implied in it, that was to form the focal point of the message of the classical prophets.

From Mt. Sinai God led the people to Kadesh Barnea on the edge of Canaan. His plan now was for them to move into the divinely destined and favored future he had for them. After spying out the land, however, most of the Israelites decided that the people currently living in the land were too strong for them to overcome and rebelled against Moses (and thus against God), wanting to go back to Egypt. This was a refusal of God's gracious and redemptive purpose for them and a lack of faith in his already demonstrated power to deliver them. God was angered. He pronounced judgment; this first generation of Israelites would go back and wander in the desert for forty years until all who were over twenty years old at this time were dead (Num 14). God would then deal with the new generation.[2] After this period of judgment, Israel—under a new leader, Joshua—*did* cross into Canaan and finally began to take possession of the inheritance God had promised Abraham so long ago.

ISRAEL IN CANAAN

Six centuries earlier God promised that Abraham's seed would become a nation and possess the land and now the promise was fulfilled. If Israel obeyed God, his promised and purposed blessing awaited them (Deut 28:1–14, 30:1–10, cf. Gen 1:28); a people chosen by God would dwell in the presence of God, under the protection of God, enjoying God's peace and prosperity. They would be his people and he would be their God. They would be his light shining in a dark world. They would worship him, and he would watch over them and prosper them. This great potential future did not fully come to pass, however, because the people, in the end, did not meet the conditions. They had made a covenant with God at Sinai, but eventually proved faithless to the terms of the agreement. They did not remain true to God or

---

2. There are some decisions made in life that have unalterable consequences; a certain course of action is decided on, and there is no way back. Such was the decision made here. The outworking of God's purposes in the lives of his people is predicated on their obedience.

obey his laws. They failed, for instance, to completely drive the Canaanites from the land. As a result, they became ensnared by Canaanite Baal worship. The book of Judges outlines sixteen periods of oppression by foreign powers over Israel as punishment by God for their idolatry and designed to turn them back to him. Each episode involved Israel turning away from God, being invaded and "sorely oppressed," and then delivered by a "judge" raised up by God when Israel finally cried out to him for help. The judges were prophetic deliverers, as the Spirit of God came upon them in power to bring about deliverance and to return the people to their eschatological purpose as a nation. Israel had no overall ruler during this time, and the Bible says, "every man did what was right in his own eyes" (Judg 21:25). It was a period when Israel was ruled by God directly through the judges and the prophets he raised up.

Five hundred years of rule by kings then began (1–2 Sam; 1 Kgs 1–11; 1 Chr; 2 Chr 1–9). Israel asked God through the prophet Samuel for a king who would rule them and protect them from their enemies so they could be like the other nations (1 Sam 8:1–9). God agreed to their request, though he warned them that they would receive heavy burdens in taxation and conscription to the king's army (1 Sam 8:9–22). During the reigns of Saul, David, and Solomon (who each reigned for around forty years), Israel was united and its boundaries extended. The reigns of David and Solomon especially constituted the golden age of Jewish history. Israel grew in strength and extended its regional influence as its people lived securely and prospered under the blessing of God as these kings led them in the ways of God. During this time there were several prophets who served the kings as advisors and counsellors and brought the word of the Lord to them at critical times.

The kings taxed the people heavily, however, as was foretold, and Solomon conscripted them as laborers in his building projects. This caused resentment to build up which came to a head when he died. In the latter part of Solomon's reign, also, he was influenced by the many foreign wives he had taken and began to worship other gods (1 Kgs 11:4–8). The Lord told him (presumably through an unnamed prophet—cf. 1 Kgs 11:26–39; 2 Chr 11:2–4) that after his death most of his kingdom would be torn away and given to someone other than his son.

Upon Solomon's death events transpired just as God had said they would. Jeroboam, a servant of Solomon, led the ten northern tribes in rebellion against Solomon's son Rehoboam, and thus the kingdom was split in two (1 Kgs 12; 2 Chr 10). The southern kingdom of two tribes (Judah and Benjamin) reverted to the name "Judah" and continued to be ruled by David's descendants. The northern kingdom maintained the name Israel and was ruled over by a succession of different houses or dynasties. It was in this period that the classical prophets ministered.

The story of the northern kingdom from here on is all bad. It continued as a nation for just over two centuries (c. 930–722 BC), during which time nineteen kings reigned from nine ruling families. Eight kings were either assassinated or committed suicide. Not one of the nineteen was considered good by God, because each followed either the worship of the golden calves they had set up as a substitute for the true God,[3] or they followed the more evil cult of Baal. Through prophets like Elijah and Elisha, God warned Israel to repent but they would not. Eventually, God's grace and patience were exhausted and his wrath fell on Israel. Assyria marched down, and in 722 BC the capital, Samaria, was captured and Israel ceased to be a nation. Many of the people were taken captive into Assyria and in their place foreign peoples were imported. This is the origin, in part, of the "Samaritans" of the gospel period.

The history of Judah, the southern kingdom, ran together with the history of Israel but lasted nearly a century and a half longer. Judah also had a sad history of idolatry and wickedness, especially under one of its kings, Manasseh (2 Kgs 21:1–8). Time and again God warned them through the prophets to turn back to him, to the keeping of the covenant they had made with him, but they would not. Because of this, God said he would bring disaster on Jerusalem and Judah, forsaking them and handing them over to their enemies. Eight of Judah's twenty kings, however, are said to have been good in God's sight and there were times of real revival in the worship of the true God under their leadership and the influence of the prophets. But eventually Judah's sin came to fullness, and God this time brought the Babylonians against them. Many of the people of Judah were taken captive to Babylon in 606 BC. A second invasion (597 BC) was followed by a third, with the destruction of Jerusalem and the majority of captives taken away in 586 BC. Judah ceased to be a nation, and for seventy years the land had rest, as foretold by the prophet Jeremiah (Jer 25:1–14). This is known as "the captivity," or "exile."

RESTORATION AND RETURN

The same prophet who had foretold the seventy year judgment of Judah had also prophesied that when it was accomplished God would bring the people back into their own land (Jer 24:4–7). In the year 536 BC, King

---

3. And to discourage the people of the northern kingdom from going to Jerusalem to worship (1 Kgs 12:26–30).

Cyrus, of the Media-Persian empire that had conquered Babylon, allowed the Jews to return to Jerusalem (2 Chr 36:22-23; Ezra 1:1-4). He was possibly influenced in this by the prophet Daniel, who held a high office in his government (Dan 6:1-3; 9:1-19). This had also been foretold by Isaiah (Isa 44:28; 45:1-7).[4] The captivity had been accomplished in three main stages, and now the return took place in three stages also. The first came with the decree of Cyrus, when 50,000 exiles and slaves returned to Jerusalem under the leaders Shesh-bazzar and Joshua. About eighty years later, Ezra made the 900 mile journey back with more exiles (457 BC), and a third return was led by Nehemiah some thirteen years following that. The city walls were repaired, and, at the urging of the post-exilic prophets, the temple was rebuilt and the sacrifices and priesthood reinstated. This then was the situation at the end of the Old Testament.

It can be seen that the prophets played a vital role throughout the history of Israel. They brought the word of God to the people and their rulers at strategic times and at major turning points in the outworking of God's redemptive program for his elect people.

The period between Malachi and Matthew covers some 400 years. Only a remnant of the Jews in Babylon chose to return to Judah. Most of the people preferred to stay in Babylonia and Assyria, where they were now established, treated well, and many were prospering. So, at the end of Malachi we have the Jewish remnant back in Judea for about 140 years; a small, dependent Jewish state has been established there, Jerusalem and the temple rebuilt, and the law and the rituals restored as far as possible. There was, however, no ark in the temple, and so no manifest presence of God with the people. Israel was still ruled over by foreign powers, and the territory they held was small.[5] There is little or no scriptural record of a prophetic voice

---

4. Though many dispute the date of this "prophecy."

5. Israel's history through the period between the Old and New Testaments runs in four main periods:

1) The Persian period (538-333 BC): King Cyrus of Persia conquered the Babylonian Empire and allowed the exiled Jews to return to Jerusalem and allowed a form of independent Jewish rule. The temple was rebuilt, the walls repaired, but Israel was still under Persian rule during this time.

2) The Greek period (332-165 BC): Alexander the Great with his Greek and Macedonian army invaded and destroyed the Persian Empire, thereby gaining control over Judea. This is the beginning of the Hellenistic (Greek) influence in this part of the world that is so evident in the gospels. After the death of Alexander, his empire was divided into three or four parts, and Israel was caught between the competing Greek rulers, sometimes subject to one, sometimes to another.

3) The Hasmonean period (164-64 BC): A Jewish tribe, or family, the "Maccabees," revolted against the Hellenistic rule, provoked by the excesses of one of the rulers, Antiochus. From 142 BC there was once again an independent Jewish state in Judea,

in Israel during the inter-testament period, but see Luke 2:25–38 and its implications.

THE PROPHETS AND THE KINGS

As noted, the role of the classic prophets developed in Israel in conjunction with the rise of the kingship. When God allowed the establishment of a monarchy in Israel, he did so on the basis that the kings were to rule according to the principles he had Samuel set down for them. They were, especially, to rule in accordance with his word (1 Sam 10:25; Deut 17:16–18). The king was to familiarize himself with the law, to make his own copy, to read it constantly, and to follow its decrees. He was, in other words, to remember he was the servant of the Lord and that the people he ruled over were in a covenant relationship with God. But the kings were not always faithful to these principles, and God sent the prophets to them to watch over their behavior and so over Israel's fate. The history of Israel and Judah through this time also shows the huge influence of the kings in determining the behavior of the people in the two nations.[6]

	Regulations of kingship in Israel: Deuteronomy 17:14–20
1	The king must be the man the Lord chooses.
2	The king must be an Israelite, not a foreigner.
3	The king must not acquire great numbers of horses for himself.
4	The king must not take many wives, or his heart will be led astray.
5	The king must not accumulate large amounts of silver or gold.
6	The king must write for himself a copy of the law.
7	The king must keep this copy of the law with him and read it all the days of his life • so he may learn to fear the Lord. • so he may follow it carefully. • so he will not consider himself better than his brothers.

The kings of Israel ruled over God's people, under God's covenant, in God's land, and they were not independent of God's oversight. They ruled, but

---

lasting about eighty years.

4) The Roman period (63 BC–AD 313). Judea became a Roman province. The Jews were granted some measure of autonomy, but in reality Judea was ruled from Rome. This is the prevailing situation at the opening of the New Testament.

6. This is both a major strength and a major weakness—as God foresaw—of the one-person leadership model.

they ruled under God, and the prophets were the mouthpieces of God. The prophetic office, Dumbrell says, "is set up to contain whatever threat the kingship may pose to the covenant." Its function is to recall for Israel the fact and implications of the Sinai covenant. "The prophet acts as God's prime minister, sent to regulate the political structures of Israel by God's word," he says.[7] This illustrates, in part at least, the role of the prophets in the leadership of God's people, in both the Old and New Testaments, bringing a prophetic voice to keep God's people true to God's word and purpose.

As noted above, the prophets sometimes wielded real political influence in the life of the two nations. They officiated at the installation of kings (1 Kgs 1:32–35), served as military advisors to the kings, and operated as divine counsellors (1 Kgs 22:6–28; 2 Kgs 6:9–12; Isa 37:2–3; Jer 27:12–15). At first the prophets delivered their message directly to the kings and their courts (1 Kgs 18:16–45; 20:13–28; 21:1–29). But increasing resistance to the prophetic message from the kings led to the prophets addressing the people themselves and presenting their messages in written form. God remembered his oaths, they wrote, and would keep his word. Though the people departed from the terms of the covenant to which they were responsible, God would not. What he had said, he would do, both in terms of blessing and, if necessary, in terms of judgment.[8]

SUMMARY OF CHAPTER TWO

Prophets have continually played an important role in the unfolding story of Israel's history. Time and again God sent messengers, counsellors, and deliverers to guide the nation in its eschatological destiny. God allowed Israel to have a king as they desired, but he also established the office of prophet to regulate the effect of the kingship on the direction of the nation. The classical prophets were raised up by God at a particular time in the history of Israel. As the religious and moral lives of the kings and the people began to degenerate, the prophets spoke out about what was happening and urged a return to covenant faithfulness. When this did not eventuate, they began to prophesy judgment.

---

7. Dumbrell, *The Search for Order*, 62.

8. Daniel recognized the failure of Israel's kings to listen to the prophets. In his prayer of repentance he confessed, "We have not listened to your servants the prophets, who spoke in your name to our kings, our princes and our fathers, and to all the people of the land" (Dan 9:6).

As a consequence of the continued refusal to return to the terms of the covenant on the part of the people and their rulers—and as the more direct result of Solomon's disobedience to God and burdensome rule over the people—the nation split in two and eventually both nations were destroyed by foreign invaders. The remaining people were carried away into captivity and exile. A generation later, a remnant of the people returned to the land, rebuilt the temple, re-established the priestly/sacrificial system, and established a small dependent state in and around Jerusalem. The prophets ministered through, and spoke into, these tumultuous historical events. They played a key role in explaining to Israel what was taking place, speaking to the people and their leaders from God's perspective and in his name.

God had a purpose. That purpose had been interrupted by human weakness in Eden and was again interrupted by human weakness in Canaan. But God is greater than human weakness; he had a plan, and that plan would not ultimately be defeated. The prophets continued to guide and urge the people towards their God-ordained destiny. They continued to declare the will of God for the present and for the future. In the next chapter we look at how to interpret the message of the Old Testament prophets and what relevance their message may have for us today.

Chapter Three

UNDERSTANDING THE PROPHETS

"He must remain in heaven until the time comes for God to restore everything as he promised long ago through his holy prophets..."
(Acts 3:21)

SEVENTEEN OF THE OLD Testament books in our Christian Bibles come under the heading of prophecy. Five of these books (Isaiah, Jeremiah, Lamentations, Ezekiel, and Daniel) are referred to as "Major Prophets," and the last twelve books of the Old Testament are referred to as "Minor Prophets." The terms major and minor refer mainly to the lengths of the books and not to their intrinsic nature or value. The writing prophets are referred to as the *classical prophets* because their writings became the standard for interpreting Israel's faith by those who came after, both Jews and Christians.

The existence of the prophets and prophecy in the biblical history clearly shows that God works within the world of human experience and within human history. He involves himself in the lives and experiences of individuals and nations. He is not some kind of Deistic divinity who has wound the world up like an old clock and then withdrawn to watch disinterestedly as the spring unwinds, as individual lives flash by and nations come and go in an unending stream across the course of history. God cares. God is involved. He is a personal God; he has a plan, and he intervenes in the world to facilitate the outworking of that plan. That his plan is ultimately good, very good, is the testimony of the prophets and their writings. The prophets were not sent in the first place to merely pronounce judgment but to call the people of Israel and Judah to turn back to the proper worship of the true God and thus enjoy his covenant blessings. Even after judgment became inevitable because of the refusal of the people to heed the warnings, the prophetic message was capped with promises of later restoration to grace and favor within God's presence.

The authors often tell us little about themselves beyond who they spoke to and what they spoke, and there are problems in precisely dating some of the prophets because in many instances there is a lack of chronological references directly associated with their oracles. Among the Minor Prophets, some contain no datable evidence at all, while others contain no specific dates for their oracles, and there are more than one possible date for others. Nor is the dating of some of the Major Prophets straightforward. The date of Isaiah (traditionally put at c. 701 BC) is complicated by the view of many modern scholars that the book was written by two or three "Isaiahs" in different historical contexts both prior to and following the exile. The book of Jeremiah has existed since ancient times in two editions—one much longer than the other. The traditional date of Daniel (c. 530 BC) is disputed by those who hold that long-range predictive prophecy is not possible.

The books contain not only the words *of* the prophets, but sometimes also words *about* the prophets. Who were these latter words written by? If editing or redaction has indeed taken place, the question then arises as to the source(s) of that redactive material. Clearly there were written sources (1 Chr 29:29; 2 Chr 26:22) and probably also oral sources. Jeremiah used Baruch as a scribe (Jer 36:5) and editing or additions could perhaps be attributed to those who were either disciples of the prophets like this, or perhaps to later redactors who were prophets in their own right.

Prophecy communicated the words of God to the individuals and groups of people under his care. God spoke to these individuals and peoples directly through the prophets and their messages. This communication often began with phrases such as, "this is what the Lord says" (Jer 10:18, etc.) and, "this is the word that came to Jeremiah from the Lord" (Jer 11:1). These phrases expressed the claim of the prophets that they were God's mouthpieces, speaking in God's name and so with his authority (see Hos 1:1, 3:1; Joel 1:1; Jon 1:1; Mic 1:1; etc.). The focus of the prophetic communication, then, was not on the prophet and his thoughts but on the divine message. God spoke through the prophet.

INTERPRETING THE PROPHETS

The first goal of all interpretation is to discover, as far as possible, the meaning of the text as intended by the original writer and the way it was understood by the original audience or readers.[1] What did the text mean to them in their time and their situation? The next question that naturally then arises is, "how does that meaning apply to us today?" These are the twin tasks of exegesis and hermeneutics, of correct interpretation.

There are a number of factors that make this task far from easy. There are language difficulties, cultural differences, and great historical distance to name a few. It is as if we are the audience of a stage play in a foreign country in which nearly everything is strange to us. In this illustration, the stage set represents to us the historical background and setting, with which we are not familiar. The interaction of the actors on the stage represents the text—the words are not spoken to us, the language is unknown to us, and the interaction does not directly involve us. We are outside looking in. We have to work hard in each of these areas to discover what it all means and whether it has any application in our familiar world. Fortunately, in the case of the Bible, some of this work has already been done for us. We have a number of good translations of the text for instance and there are many good word studies, surveys, dictionaries, introductions, commentaries, and other reference books which can and should be consulted. We need to know as much about the historical background of the prophets and their message as possible. They were real human beings speaking at real moments in history to their own particular audiences.

In seeking to interpret the prophets, the nature of the prophetic genre must be taken into account. All the prophetic books proper are collections of stories from the prophet's lives, together with prophetic speeches and a large number of prophetic oracles. An oracle is a particular, self-contained, command, message, or revelation from God. The two main categories of oracles used by the prophets are "oracles of judgment," that is, the announcement of judgment and the reason for it (e.g., Isa 30:1–14), and "oracles of salvation," promising the eventual blessing of God (e.g., Jer 28:2–4; Isa 40:1–5). These collections are not necessarily arranged in chronological order. So the prophetic books record warnings and announcements of divine judgment for sinful individuals and nations and then, beyond that, proclamations of salvation from a merciful God whose grace is bigger than sin and whose plan cannot be thwarted by human weakness.

---

1. This basic axiom of traditional hermeneutics is now challenged by post-modern interpreters—a debate for another book.

We need also to consider the literary style of the prophetic books. Although some of the books contain narrative sections, a great deal of the prophetic material was written as poetry. In most ancient cultures, poetry was a highly prized mode of expression (like popular songs today). Because it contains rhythm, certain balances and structure, it is easier to memorize than prose—an important consideration in societies where not everyone could read and write. All the prophetic books contain a large amount of poetry, and some are written exclusively in poetry. The prophets also used a kind of poetic prose that contained these same characteristics. Hebrew poetry used a number of common structures, especially "parallelism," where the second line (or following lines) either reinforced or contrasted the first line, or in some other way added to it. Besides these special structures, poetry in all cultures uses special language—imagery, similes, metaphors, hyperbole, personification, and other word pictures. These are very important in interpreting both poetry and prophecy and need to be identified and interpreted first.

Some of the prophetic books feature writings in another genre referred to by Bible interpreters as apocalypse, or apocalyptic writing. Examples of this kind of literature can be found in Daniel (7–12), Isaiah (24–27), Ezekiel (38–39), Joel (2:28–3:21), Zechariah (1–6 and 9–14), and in the book of Revelation in the New Testament. Apocalyptic literature is less direct than prophecy, using symbolic language and visions to describe spiritual realities behind events taking place in our world and its content is often presented in the form of dreams and visions. It makes extensive use of symbolism (including symbolic numbers) and hidden meanings. While prophecy mostly draws its images and symbols from the realm of reality, apocalyptic literature often draws from the realm of fantasy. There are many-headed dragons, fire-breathing horses with the heads of lions and tails like snakes, locusts with human faces, and other interesting images besides. While in prophecy God acts and speaks directly within the lives of individuals and groups, in apocalyptic literature God intervenes supernaturally from *outside* human experience and history. Events in apocalyptic literature tend to happen on a cosmic scale and involve final solutions. Stars fall from the sky, the moon turns to blood, and earthquakes shake the planet. Apocalyptic literature reveals God's sovereignty over the universe and over human history, which may seem at times to be chaotic, random, and out of control. Because God is sovereign and because he is good, he will ultimately put right all that is wrong and bring to pass his pre-determined end(s), though the very heavens be shaken in the process. When I talk about "the end of the world" in this book, I am talking about this divinely ordained destiny and fulfillment of creation rather than just about a passing away of the present physical order in a cosmic conflagration.

Many theologians interpret apocalypse historically, as coded language written to encourage people in situations of persecution or severe trial. This means that it has direct application only to the particular historical situation that produced it, though principles contained within the story may apply more widely. Alternative approaches to its interpretation will be dealt with in the final section of this book when we look at the book of Revelation. It obviously requires a special hermeneutical approach to interpreting its visions and symbols and to ascertaining its meaning, and the task can be difficult. But as long as the interpretation and meaning are sought largely from within the Bible itself, some understanding can usually be arrived at.

THE PROPHETIC MESSAGE

One of the characteristic features of the prophets' message was their insistence on righteousness, justice, and genuine love. These are the proper expressions of Israel's relationship with God (Amos 5:21-24; Isa 58:1-10; Mic 6:8). They are also expressions of the heart of God, and the prophets are often defenders and advocates of the weak, the powerless, the poor, and the outcast (Isa 1:16-17; Zech 7:8-10). Another major theme of the prophets was their criticism of Israel's constant tendency towards idolatry (Jer 7:9; Hos 13:1-2). This breaking of the first and second commandments was a besetting sin of both Israel and Judah, and something God spoke to them about again and again.[2]

The major basis of the prophetic message was the Sinai covenant between God and Israel. It has been said that the classic prophets were "covenant enforcers," messengers of God calling on Israel and Judah to remember and to be faithful to this agreement they had made with God.[3] Speaking against the background of the covenant, the prophets spoke in God's name to people who were neglecting the promises they had made to God and living lives in contradiction to his will as revealed in the terms of the covenant. Hence the common word-picture used in the prophets of marital infidelity, where God is pictured as the husband betrayed by an unfaithful wife. The subsequent announcement of judgment for breaches of the covenant was meant to produce contrition and repentance in the hearts of the people or, failing this, to demonstrate God's faithfulness to the terms of the covenant.

---

2. This was dealt with through the Exile. Israel saw that God's word was sure and certain. He was the God who controlled the destinies of individuals and nations.

3. Fee and Stuart, *How to Read the Bible*, 166.

But the prophetic message went beyond addressing this broken covenant relationship between Israel and God to include messages from God to the surrounding cities and nations also. They too were objects of God's concern and their wickedness also would result in judgment (Isa 13–23; Jer 46–51; Ezek 26–32; Amos 1–2). They too were recipients of the promises of future salvation as God had promised Abraham (e.g., Isa 19:23–25, cf. Gen 12:3).

After the pronouncement of judgment, Israel's eventual restoration became the other major theme of the prophets. They predicted a return from exile to life back in the land of abundance and prosperity (Jer 3:18) under the leadership of a just Davidic king (Amos 9:13–15; Isa 11:1–10; Hos 3:5). God's love for his people was stronger than their weakness and faithlessness and the prophets developed a style of preaching judgment followed by salvation, of denunciation followed by promise. Thus we see in the prophetic message a recurring pattern of *warnings* concerning the consequences of continued sin, the proclamation of *judgment* when sin continued, and, beyond the judgment, the promise of future *restoration*.

The question then arises as to how this ancient material, spoken to another people in another time, speaks into our lives and applies to us today. We can see for a start that there are some issues and general principles that obviously apply directly in both the ancient setting and in our situation also. For example, the prophets spoke against injustice; immorality; idolatry; hypocrisy; greed; and empty, formalistic worship. These issues, attitudes, and practices are always wrong and they are also taken up and reinforced in the New Testament. The nature of God is another constant—he is always good, always holy, and always faithful to his word and to his purposes.

Then there are principles and issues that apply more indirectly. If something is either condemned or commended in the ancient text, we can ask ourselves if there is some correspondence or analogy to anything in our situation. In what ways, for instance, might idolatry be manifested among us today (see Col 3:5)?[4] In what ways might we too be guilty of "breaking covenant" or of spiritual adultery?

We also have the *example* of how God dealt with people involved in various practices, both good and bad. Because he is unchanging he will presumably deal with us in the same way if we involve ourselves in the same

---

4. The prophets spoke out very strongly against idolatry. The worship of anything other than the true God distorts the relationship between God and his "image" and makes the very concept of "God" smaller. "To whom will you compare me, or who is my equal?" God asks (Isa 40:25; cf. 46:5). This then distorts everything else and makes everything smaller—God's purpose, plan, and human beings themselves. We become like that which we worship.

sort of practices. This is a biblically intended application of the Old Testament stories (1 Cor 10:1–12), and we are supposed to draw lessons for our own lives from these biblical examples.

In many ways then, this ancient material can be seen to be applicable beyond the immediate historical situation in which it arose. A particular difficulty arises, however, with the prophetic promises of salvation, or God's future blessing, made to Israel and Judah. Which of these is historically specific and which, if any, have a wider application? I hope to be able, in this book, to provide a framework for interpreting this particular hermeneutical issue.

PREDICTIVE PROPHECY

As part of the prophetic cycle of sin, judgment, and restoration, the prophets began to speak of the ultimate judgment of Israel's expulsion from the land. All of the blessings promised to Israel were blessings *within the land of Canaan* (see Deut 28:1–14). The blessing in fact *was* residence in the promised land, where God would dwell with them and they would be his people. Canaan was, in effect, a reconstitution of Eden—God's people once again brought into God's sanctuary and enjoying God's provision and presence.[5] If Israel obeyed the commands of God and remained faithful to the covenant, then great blessing lay before them. But as did Adam and Eve, they proved themselves unfaithful, and instead of enjoying the covenant blessings, the curses of Deuteronomy 28 came upon them, leading ultimately to expulsion from the land (as Adam and Eve were expelled from the garden) and exile in the foreign land of Babylon.

But the prophets also began to speak, beyond the exilic judgment, of the ultimate "restoration," the end of exile and a return to God's favor, to the land, and to his presence. It was this future restoration, and the promises that attached to it, that formed the basis of the predictive element of the writing prophets. The fulfillment of these promises of restoration began to take place when the Jewish captives in Babylon were allowed to return to Canaan. However, much that had been promised remained unfulfilled when the remnant did return to the land. Israel was still ruled over by a foreign nation; there was no new covenant, no outpouring of the Spirit, no Davidic king, no presence of God. In some measure the exile continued; the promised restoration was not complete (cf. Neh 9:36–37). The real return

---

5. The New Jerusalem is the final and eternal manifestation of this foundational purpose of God. See chapter sixteen.

from exile was to take place much later, through the ministry, death, and resurrection of Jesus, when all these missing blessings began to be fulfilled.

It was Jesus himself, David's son, who—as we will see in the pages ahead—was the key to all the promised blessings and restoration promises. He was to be the new temple; he was the presence of God returning to Israel, leading them to inherit God's true riches (Eph 1:3), and beginning to reign himself (the true Israel) over the nations in fulfillment of the prophecies. He *did* deal with the enemies of Israel—not, as was popularly imagined, with the pagan nations surrounding and ruling over Israel, but with the real enemies of Israel and of all humanity: sin, death, and evil in its origin in the demonic realm.

We can see from this that there were to be two layers of meaning for the predictive prophecies: a partial fulfillment taking place within the direct historic situation of the prophets and a later, more complete, fulfillment through the life and ministry of Jesus. From the perspective of the prophets and their audience, however, the gap between the two events could not be seen. It seemed, from their perspective, as if the realization of all the predicted promises would take place at one time. Like sections of a telescope, the promises folded into one another chronologically. From their point of view, it was like looking at a mountain range from a distance, which seems at first to be two-dimensional, a flat scene against the horizon. However, as we draw closer the perspective changes; the individual mountains can be seen and all the valleys and spaces in between them come into view.

Fee and Stuart suggest another picture again; it is like someone looking at two flat discs, a smaller one in front with a larger one behind it. From the side it can be seen that there is a space between them but from the front the smaller one is superimposed on the larger one so they appear to be one.[6] The smaller disc in front would represent the predicted events that were fulfilled with the historical return of the Jewish remnant to Canaan after the captivity in Babylon and the second, larger disc representing those that were fulfilled in the life and ministry of Jesus and the early church.

There is a further complication, however. Some of the prophecies fulfilled in the ministry, death, and resurrection of Jesus seem to await an even greater fulfillment in the events surrounding his second coming. The prophesied resurrection took place—but only of Jesus, the first fruit. The general resurrection is still to come. The Son of David began to reign, but not yet openly for all to see. Jesus healed all who came to him, but sickness continues in the world. Theologians call this an "already/not yet" eschatology. The kingdom has already come on earth but not yet in complete power.

---

6. Fee and Stuart, *How to Read the Bible*, 182.

The age to come has begun already but the present sinful age continues in parallel with it. There remains a time yet to come—a final prophetic day—when these prophecies will be realized in all their fullness. The many predictive prophecies relating to worldwide or even cosmic conflagration, whether literal or figurative, have clearly not yet taken place. Joel's prophecy, for instance, of the outpouring of God's Spirit was fulfilled on the day of Pentecost, according to Peter (Joel 2:28–32; Acts 2: 16–21). However, the aspects of Joel's prophecy relating to judgment on a cosmic scale—"blood and fire and billows of smoke, the sun turned to darkness and the moon to blood," etc.—were not completely fulfilled at that time.[7] There remains, it seems, a further prophetic day of fulfillment. Thus, instead of two layers of prophetic realization, we have three layers, in some cases, before God's eschatological plans and purposes are fully brought to completion. The first, again, in the immediate historical situation of the prophets themselves, a second in the life and ministry of Jesus, and then a third, yet to be realized, final day of fulfillment.[8]

All of the predictive prophecies are centered on God's plans and promises of restoration. God declares the end from the beginning and we can see, then, the central and essential part played by the classic prophets in the development of biblical theology and eschatology. God called the writing prophets to describe and decree not only the judgment of the exile in Babylon, not only the return of Israel from exile in Babylon, but, more importantly, the larger return of all humanity from the exile in the world outside of Eden (see Rev 17–18), back into God's presence forever (Rev 21–22)—the fulfillment of God's complete plan for the creation. There had been human failure in Eden and Canaan, but God's purpose, plan, and power were bigger than both and would in the end triumph over human weakness.

SUMMARY OF CHAPTER THREE

The prophets bore a message from God that had an immediate application to the people of their own historical situation. But important parts of that message were not confined to that historical situation only. A great deal of application can be found in our time, and lessons drawn for our instruction. There are promises and predictions that speak of God's future intentions, also. That predictive element of prophecy arose from God's determination to

---

7. Though, note the violent wind and "fire" that accompanied the outpouring of the Spirit at Pentecost.

8. This is the nature of prophecy. The fulfillment might seem plain, but is often multifaceted when seen in hindsight. It has more than one level of meaning and application.

follow judgment with restoration, punishment with promise, in fulfillment of his creative purpose. God declared what he was going to do to restore Israel and redeem the creation. These promises and declarations of future restoration and blessing were to take place on a number of levels and at different times, but the prophets, unable to see this, sometimes "telescoped" them together so they appeared to be one event.

The prophetic message in its full import is then transhistorical—it reaches far beyond the confines of the few centuries that gave it birth and speaks into the larger purposes of God that span all of human history and find their fulfillment in Jesus and in an expected "day of the Lord."[9] The prophetic message in all its fullness can only really be understood in that history-spanning context. To the eschatological content of that message we now turn.

---

9. See next chapter.

Chapter Four

ESCHATOLOGICAL THEMES IN THE PROPHETS

"This then is how you should pray: Our Father in heaven, hallowed be your name, your kingdom come, your will be done on earth as it is in heaven . . ." (Matt 6:9–10)

"Eschatology" is derived from the Greek word *eschatos* meaning "last" and refers in theology to the study of the "last things." In its fullest meaning it refers not just to "end time events," but to the outworking of God's *purpose* and *direction* for human history and human destiny. God had an end in mind from the beginning; he is Alpha and he is Omega. This *end*, or end purpose, permeates the whole Bible story. It flows through the narrative, poetry, prophecy, history, and theology of the biblical literature to unfold the divine wisdom, the divine power and love, the great *mystery* of God's pre-ordained plan for the creation. This again is what I mean by "the end of the world" in the title of this book—that is, the realization of God's plan and purpose in all of its fullness, the creation arriving at its pre-ordained end.

Regarding eschatology then, the prophetic literature reveals firstly that God does not just *know* the future and then *predict* it, but rather he *controls* the future, he *forms* the future by divine fiat, he declares the future into being (Isa 46:10–11; 48:3–5). Matthew often uses the phrase, "this took place to fulfill what the Lord had said through the prophet," or other similar phrases, and then quotes from one of the prophetic books. In other words, the outcome is the result of what was spoken prophetically before (Matt 1:22; 2:5–6; 2:15; etc.). What God speaks must come to pass, woven into being by the power of his spoken word (Gen 1; Heb 11:3; Rom 4:17). Secondly, the prophets reveal that God has a purpose for the creation and especially for human beings; and because he is good, his purpose is good also. That goodness involves justice and righteousness, the putting right of every wrong, the fulfillment of every divine promise of blessing and favor, and the total eradication of evil in all of its manifestations and consequences. Thirdly, we see in the prophets that God is moving all of human history—moving both world events and individual destinies—towards the fulfillment of that good purpose. History is not cyclical, open-ended, or endless, but it has an end, a fulfillment, a consummation. Fourthly, that *end* will be marked by the confluence and climax of all the great biblical themes in a great "day of the Lord." It was the writing prophets who declared and clarified those themes.

Our postmodern society is skeptical of any kind of meta-narrative, any "big story," that gives hope and direction to the future. The concentration is on the present; the future is feared as uncertain in its mindless randomness. The prophets speak directly to that fear and uncertainty, offering a story with a climax, a "happy ending," a decisive, divine intervention into the physical reality of this world. This is an important part of the relevance of biblical eschatology for today's world.

The message of the prophets, as we have seen, followed a pattern—the covenant is broken, therefore judgment is coming; but beyond judgment there is a future restoration. This they said would happen through the coming of the messiah, the outpouring of the Spirit, a new creation, and other associated promises. Many of the events thus predicted by the prophets were fulfilled within that time period, many more were fulfilled at the time of Jesus and the early church. But, some undeniably address a climactic end of human history. The prophets declare that history is marching inexorably towards God's predetermined end. All of these ideas and concepts form the eschatological themes of the prophetic literature, which, many and varied though they may seem, may all be essentially gathered together under two overarching, interconnected motifs: the "kingdom of God," and the "day of the Lord."

THE KINGDOM OF GOD

"They [first-century Judaism] believed that Yahweh would become King . . . the exile would end . . . evil would be defeated . . . Yahweh

. . . would return to Zion . . . Central to this whole expression of Jewish hope . . . as part of the controlling element of the story, is of course the whole prophetic corpus."[1]

In Matthew's gospel both John the Baptist and Jesus open their public ministries with the proclamation that "the kingdom of heaven is near" (Matt 3:1; 4:17). Matthew prefers the kingdom of *heaven* to the kingdom of *God,* but the terms are interchangeable (see Mark 1:14–15). This provides us with the interpretive perspective to understand what is taking place in the gospels—i.e., the kingdom of God is "drawing near"; the King has come—and anchors the ministry of Jesus firmly within the Old Testament story. Matthew opens his gospel with the declaration that Jesus is a son of Abraham, with all the overtones that that carries in terms of God's redemptive purposes (cf. Gal 3:16), and a son of David—an heir to David's throne. He came to that which was his own, and he came to rule.

John and Jesus do not introduce a new concept in their proclamation of the kingdom of God. The kingdom is not an exclusively New Testament concept as it is so often treated by Christian Bible interpreters and teachers. There is no comprehensive explanation or description of the concept of the kingdom of God in the gospels because none was needed. Jesus was speaking—as was John before him—to a largely Jewish audience for whom the kingdom of God was a well-understood concept intrinsic to their view of the world, a central part of the story of Israel. To sever the kingdom of God from its Old Testament roots is to give up any possibility of understanding it correctly. N. T. Wright describes the kingdom as, "simply a Jewish way of talking about Israel's God becoming king." And when God became king, he goes on to say, "the whole world, the world of space and time, would at last be put to rights."[2]

The kingdom of God is first of all a Jewish concept with two main aspects. It was understood, firstly, that God was sovereign in the present world already (Ps 103:19; Dan 4:17; etc.). But to the Jews the kingdom of God also spoke of the time when God would actualize his government within their experience, the time when Israel's God would begin to reign on earth through a son of David in a restored Israel. That would bring about the conclusion of Israel's story. So the kingdom of God is "shorthand" for the consummation of the Old Testament Jewish story. All the promises given to Abraham, those given through Moses and those given to David, would be fulfilled when God began to rule and the kingdom came. Promises of

---

1. Wright, "The Servant and Jesus," www.ntwrightpage.com/Wright_Servant_Jesus.htm.

2. Wright, *Jesus and the Victory of God,* 202–3.

election, of land, of wise and just Davidic leadership, of the glory of God's presence, of peace and prosperity, of Israel's rule over the nations—all would be fulfilled when God began to rule, when his kingdom came on earth.

This is what the disciples meant when they came to Jesus after his resurrection and said to him, "are you at this time going to restore the kingdom to Israel?" (Acts 1:6). Jesus had been talking to them about the kingdom of God (Acts 1:3) and they naturally thought that because he had proved his power and authority by triumphing over death itself and was now returned to them, he was obviously the messiah and this was obviously the time to bring in the messianic kingdom.

The kingdom of God was to happen within space and time. It was not to be some "spiritual" reality only, or some hidden thing that no one could see or understand. It was not a nebulous concept that no one could quite grasp the meaning of and that did not, anyway, make much of a difference to their everyday lives as it is sometimes understood today. God's kingdom would come on earth. God would reign in the real world. Everyone's lives would be affected irrevocably and forever. A number of interconnecting elements, though perhaps held in different measure by different groups, emerge from the prophets to make up the overall concept of "the kingdom of God." They include the following:

The Age to Come

Jewish eschatology by the time of the Second Temple period recognized two *ages*, the present (evil) age and the "age to come." The present age is characterized by sin, sickness, death, demonic activity, and the rule of evil men. The age to come, then, when the kingdom came on earth, would be characterized by the opposite distinctives of healing, forgiveness, righteousness, justice, peace, and the rule of God over the nations with Israel at the head (Matt 12:32; Mark 10:30; Acts 1:6; 1 Cor 10:11; Gal 1:4; Eph 1:21).

God Returning to Zion

This is one of the great Jewish expectations of the Second Temple period. Both the tabernacle and Solomon's temple had been filled with the glory of God (Exod 40:3–36; 1 Kgs 8:1–11; 2 Chr 7:1–3). God's presence within the tabernacle/temple is what distinguished his people from all the other nations on the earth (Exod 33:15–16). However, because of Israel's persistent sin, God determined to thrust them from his presence in Canaan (Jer 7:15; cf. Gen 3:23–24; Jer 52:3). Ezekiel then describes the Lord's presence leaving the temple (Ezek 9:3; 10:4,18–19; 11:22–23), and then the temple—God's house, the place of God's presence in the midst of his people—was itself destroyed by the Babylonian invaders (Jer 52:12–23).

Ezekiel also prophesied that the presence of the Lord would later return to Zion and would again fill the new temple (Ezek 43:1–5; 44:4). Other prophets agreed (Hag 2:6–9; Zech 1:16–17, 8:3; Isa 52:8, 59:20; Mal 3:1). But when the exiles returned to Jerusalem and rebuilt the temple, there was no ark, no mercy seat; and the glory, God's presence, did not return (see Ezra 6:13–18. Cf. Exod 40:33–38; 2 Chr 5:4–14). So the promise of God's return to Zion formed part of the expectation of what would happen when the kingdom of God came on earth (Zech 8:3).

Messiah

It is evident that by the time of the New Testament the various promises and sometimes difficult-to-interpret declarations of the prophets had produced the expectation of the end-time appearance of a number of different personalities—from Elijah (Mal 4:5), to a prophet like Moses (Duet 18:15), and of course the messiah (see John 1:19–21).

The messiah was a figure emerging in the pages of the Old Testament, especially in the psalms and prophets, who would act to restore Israel. Again, a number of ideas surrounded the concept. The basic meaning of messiah was "anointed one" and those anointed in the Old Testament were people called by God to specific tasks. Prophets were anointed, the priests were anointed, and kings chosen by God were anointed. The basic purpose of such anointing was to authorize them to act on God's behalf. So the anointed one/messiah was to be God's agent of redemption for the nation. In the New Testament, of course, the word is translated "Christ," and a count of how many times the word is used in the New Testament will show just how pervasive this concept was in the late Second Temple period.[3]

Another crucial element in the prophetic understanding of the messiah was the theme of royalty, particularly of a restored Davidic kingship. The golden age of David and Solomon together with God's promises to David form the background to much of the messianic expectation. God promised David that after he died, he (God) would raise up one of David's offspring to succeed him who would have an everlasting house, kingdom,

---

3. Unfortunately, the title "Christ" has come to operate almost as a surname for Jesus in the current church. It would perhaps be better translated "messiah" again so that it retains the Old Testament background meaning, as N. T. Wright does in his New Testament translation, *Kingdom New Testament*.

and throne—who would have royal authority (2 Sam 7:1–16). Isaiah prophesied of a son raised up from the house of David sitting on a throne of justice and righteousness forever (Isa 9:6–7; 16:5), Jeremiah of a "branch," or descendant, of David to be a king who would do what was just and right (Jer 23:5; cf. 30:9; 33:17, 21). Ezekiel, too, takes up the thought of an everlasting Davidic kingship (Ezek 34:23–24; 37:24–25). Hosea says that after many days of living without a king, in the last days, Israel would again seek God and a return to a Davidic kingship (Hos 3:4–5). Zechariah's prophesied king, who brings righteousness and salvation, comes riding into Jerusalem on a donkey, as did David's son Solomon (Zech 9:9; 1 Ki 1:38). The messiah would be a descendant of David.

A New Exodus

The exodus was the foundational event of Israel's history, as God stretched out his hand in power to bring the people out of Egypt. He brought them to Sinai and then from there into the land of promise. In the exodus event, the nature and power, the wisdom and love of God were revealed. In the exodus, too, the nature of Israel as the chosen people of God was revealed for all to see. They were different from every other nation, made special by God's election.

However, after Israel and Judah proved faithless to the covenant that God had made with them at Sinai, he removed them from the land and scattered them among the nations again. The prophets who predicted this also foresaw a time when God would bring about a second exodus, gathering the people this time from *all* the nations and bringing them back to the land. "In that day," prophesied Isaiah, "the Lord will reach out his hand a second time to reclaim the remnant that is left of his people from Assyria, from Lower Egypt, from Upper Egypt, from Cush, from Elam, from Babylonia, from Hamath, and *from the islands of the sea*. He will raise a banner for the nations and gather the exiles of Israel; he will assemble the scattered people of Judah *from the four quarters of the earth*" (Isa 11:11–12. See Isa 43:5–7; 49:9, 12, 18; etc.).

The context clearly associates this second exodus (see Isa 11:16) with the appearance of the messiah (Isa 11:10) and with the day of the Lord. Jeremiah said that this new exodus would become more important to Israel's identity than the first (Jer 16:14–15; 23:7–8). Ezekiel associates it with a time of judgment and purging of Israel (Ezek 20) when God would give them a new heart and put a new spirit in them (Ezek 36:26–27) and bring them back to the land in prosperity and blessing (Ezek 36:28–32). This, too, was part of the coming kingdom.

A New Covenant

Jeremiah associates the new exodus with the making of a new covenant between God and his people (Jer 31). The concept of covenant is foundational to the prophetic literature. The Abrahamic and Davidic covenants shape the prophetic understanding of Israel's story from both the historical and eschatological perspectives, and the Mosaic covenant forms the very basis of the ministry of the writing prophets.

Because of the demonstrated inability of both Israel and Judah to keep the covenant standards, God promised that in the coming time of restoration he would make a new covenant with them (Jer 31:31). It would be different from the old covenant. The first was external, written on tablets of stone; the new would be internal: *"I will put my law in their minds and write it on their hearts"* (Jer 31:35). The new covenant would bring a personal knowledge of God for all, with forgiveness and cleansing (Jer 31:34). It would be permanent and would involve a work of grace in which God would impart a "fear of God" (Jer 32:40). Both Isaiah and Ezekiel attached the new covenant idea to the messianic expectation of a restored Davidic kingship (Isa 55:3; Ezek 37:24–27). Although Ezekiel doesn't use the term "new covenant" in the passage in Ezek 36:24–38, he sets the same scene as Jeremiah—a time of national restoration, of general cleansing—the internal dimension of what God promised to do and of the covenant formula, "you will be my people and I will be your God."

The Outpouring of the Spirit

A major characteristic of the arrival of the kingdom of God was to be a general outpouring of the Spirit (see Isa 32:15; 44:3; Ezek 39:29). Perhaps the best known prophecy, because it was referenced by Peter on the day of Pentecost, was from Joel; "Afterward, I will pour out my Spirit on all people. Your sons and daughters will prophesy, your old men will dream dreams, your young men will see visions. Even on my servants, both men and women, I will pour out my Spirit in those days and they will prophesy" (Joel 2:28–29; Acts 2:16–21).

There are many implications to this. The prophets were the truly Spirit-led and Spirit-inspired ministers of the Old Testament. They were called by the Spirit to their prophetic offices and ministries (see Exod 3;

Isa 6; Jer 1; Ezek 1; Amos 7:15). The prophets were the ones who knew the Lord who spoke to them through dreams and visions. They were the ones who proclaimed the word of the Lord and operated in the power of the Spirit. Joel says that with the outpouring of the Spirit the people of God, in the kingdom of God, would be a *prophetic community*. They would *all* be prophets in fulfillment of Moses' prayer of Numbers 11:29. All would be included, young and old, men and women. They would all know the Lord as he spoke to them in dreams and visions. They would all proclaim the word of the Lord when the Spirit was poured out on them, and there would be supernatural results for all.

Justice

It is difficult to overstate the all-pervasive importance of this concept in the prophets. Justice is one of the major common themes of the prophetic literature. It has its basis in the nature of God himself; "Righteousness and justice are the foundation of your throne . . ." said the psalmist (Ps 89:14). This verse might not be found in the prophets, but it perfectly reflects the prophetic stance.[4] God is holy and righteous, he is faithful and true, merciful and loving, and all of that requires that he be just. This is the way he acts in the world and this is what he finds delight in: "let him who boasts boast about this: that he understands and knows me, that I am the Lord, who exercises kindness, justice and righteousness on earth, for in these I delight" (Jer 9:24).

God is often described in the prophets as a judge (Isa 2:4; 3:13; 33:22; cf. Gen 18:25), who judges righteously (Jer 11:20). He claims for himself the right to judge (Ezek 7:3, 8, 27; 18:30; etc.), and in the act of judging he is made known (Ezek 35:11) and exalted (Isa 5:16). He will judge *all* the nations (Joel 3:12; Mic 4:3). Justice was also required of those who would be the people of God; they would be like him in this respect. "He has showed you, O man, what is good. And what does the Lord require of you? *To act justly* and to love mercy, and to walk humbly with your God" (Mic 6:8). God's people are to act with justice in all their dealings with each other and with all others.

God's regard for the poor, weak, and disadvantaged is a principle of justice, and references to his concern for social justice in the prophets are pervasive. Isaiah urges Israel to be righteous (i.e., to stop doing wrong) and to do right—which is seen as seeking justice for the oppressed, the

---

4. See Isa 5:16; 9:7; 16:5; 28:17; 32:1; 32:16; 33:5; 51:5; 56:1; 59:9; 59:14; Jer 9:24; Hos 2:9; Amos 5:7; 6:12; etc.

fatherless, and the widow (Isa 1:17). He pronounces woe on those who mistreat the poor and the oppressed, the widows and the fatherless. Jeremiah warns Israel's kings that they are required of God to deal justly with the poor and needy (Jer 22:1–5). Ezekiel berates the princes of Israel for their mistreatment of the alien, fatherless, and widow (Ezek 22:7). Zechariah declares that true justice equates in large part to treating the alien, fatherless, and poor with compassion (Zech 7:10). Many other references in the prophets make it clear that the deliberate, compassionate treatment of the poor and helpless is extremely important to God. Justice is especially required of rulers and leaders because of the effect their decisions have on those they rule over (Jer 22:1–5; cf. Dan 4:27, etc.). The anointed leader who was to come would rule in justice and righteousness (Isa 9:7; 11:1–4; 16:5; 42:1; Jer 23:5; 33:15).[5] Both righteousness and justice are foundational principles of the divine rule. They are inseparable. Righteousness requires justice—the putting right of all wrongs, the balancing of all inequities, the answering of every cry for help.

Justice will be the eschatological result of the return of the messiah when the whole world—even the whole creation—will be put right in the day of the Lord (Isa 66:15–16; cf. 2 Thess 1:6–10). The kingdom of God, then, would be an expression of his justice. God's eschatological people would actively seek to right the injustices of the world and to better the lot of the poor, the needy, and the oppressed of the world (see Acts 10:31; Gal 2:10).

Forgiveness and Healing

The prophetic literature is full of pronouncements of judgment and woe, yet it was the prophets who also revealed a God of mercy and grace, of forgiveness and healing. The first call of the prophets is a call to repentance. If God's unfaithful people will repent, he will forgive and heal the land. Even when repentance is declined and judgment becomes inevitable there was the gracious promise of future restoration. Judgment is infused with mercy.[6] Of course for mercy to be able to flow, for forgiveness to be completed, real

5. All the laws of Israel are designed to facilitate justice (Exod 21–23). This is the basis of the "eye for an eye" law of retaliation for serious injury (Exod 21:22–25), the principle of justice upon which the western judicial system still operates. The penalty reflects the crime, not too little and not too much. The first biblical example of the principle of justice is found in Genesis chapter 3, immediately upon the rebellion of the first humans against the rule of God. Justice is applied individually and irrevocably.

6. The message of mercy and forgiveness is, of course, projected against a backdrop of a God of righteousness and justice.

contrition and repentance are necessary. Outward conformity and a formal, empty worship are not enough. Obedience is better than sacrifice. Nevertheless, forgiveness is an integral part of the prophetic message, which says in effect, "God is angry because of your unfaithfulness and is determined to judge—but if you repent, he will forgive."

God is righteous and just, so destruction was coming because of their refusal to repent; but he is gracious and compassionate, and after judgment he would heal. "Come, let us return to the Lord. He has torn us to pieces but he will heal us; he has injured us but he will bind up our wounds" (Hos 6:1).

The complete restoration to God's favor and grace that the prophets envisaged would require complete forgiveness and healing. Isaiah saw God's servant who would bear the iniquities of God's people and through his sacrifice bring healing (Isa 53:4–5). Zechariah saw a cleansing fountain: "On that day a fountain will be opened to the house of David and the inhabitants of Jerusalem, *to cleanse them from sin and impurity*" (Zech 13:1). Malachi saw a day of healing for the people of God, which necessitated complete forgiveness (Mal 4:2). Final forgiveness was to be an integral part of the new covenant (Isa 43:25; Jer 31:34; Ezek 36:25). The sins of Israel and Judah would be completely removed (Jer 50:20; Isa 40:2). Healing and forgiveness would bring glory to God and issue in peace and prosperity for his people (Jer 33:6–8). The inauguration of the kingdom would bring about a time of healing.

Victory over Israel's Enemies

For the Jews of the Exile onward, evil found one of its strongest expressions in the fact that Israel lived under the government of pagan nations and was consequently unable to fully live by the covenant guidelines given to them by God. This evil found its manifestation in the desire of Israel's enemies to defeat and destroy God's people. "Israel is a scattered flock that lions have chased away. The first to devour him was the king of Assyria; the last to crush his bones was Nebuchadnezzar king of Babylon" (Jer 50:17).

The messiah would defeat Israel's enemies and restore the divine order of God's rule to the world. He would reign on David's throne and restore justice and peace to the world (Isa 9:6–7; 11:2–4). His kingdom would be established on earth. Israel's enemies would be defeated and punished as they deserved (Isa 10:5, 12, 30:31; Jer 50:18; Isa 14:3–5; 48:14).[7]

---

7. The defeat of evil was also seen in apocalyptic terms. The whole world, even the whole creation, would be judged (Isa 24) then renewed (Isa 65:17–25). This apocalyptic scenario found its full expression in Daniel, where the pagan nations are seen as beasts

Resurrection

The idea of resurrection is first used by Hosea as a metaphor to describe the restoration of the nation after its judgment and exile (Hos 6:1–3) and later used more fully by Ezekiel (Ezek 37:1–14). Hosea also hints at physical resurrection and the defeat of death (Hos 13:14). Isaiah clearly introduces the idea of a physical resurrection for God's people (Isa 26:19). Death, he says, will be "swallowed up" (Isa 25:8), a term borrowed by Paul when he writes to the Corinthians about the resurrection (1 Cor 15:54). And in Daniel the concept is fully developed into a general resurrection leading to everlasting life for the righteous and everlasting shame for others (Dan 12:2). When the kingdom came, there would be resurrection.

The End of Exile

This is the summation of many of the kingdom of God themes above. The prophecies of judgment and exile had happened just as the prophets said they would, God was true to his word. So there was every reason to expect the fulfillment also of the promises of restoration. However, even when the remnant of Jews returned to Canaan and Jerusalem after the exile in Babylon many of these prophetic promises regarding the restoration remained unfulfilled as we have seen. This obviously meant that despite the return of a remnant to the land, the promised full restoration had not yet come. This was clearly part of post-exilic thinking among the Jews. "But see," Nehemiah prayed, "we are slaves today, slaves in the land you gave our forefathers so they could eat its fruit and the other good things it produces. Because of our sins, its abundant harvest goes to the kings you have placed over us. They rule over our bodies and our cattle as they please. We are in great distress" (Neh 9:36–37, cf. Ezra 9:8).

We need to remember that for Israel, religion was never a "spiritual" thing only. It was not just a personal, private, inner concern and practice as it is with much of Christianity today, something that didn't necessarily impact the real world around them. When God acted on Israel's behalf, he acted *within their history*. The fact that he had not fully restored the nation was of great consequence to the Jewish worldview. Obviously, the exile had not yet completely come to an end.[8] When it did finally end, God would rule over the nations through Israel. The kingdom of God would be established on earth.

(Dan 7) that will be overcome finally by the "son of man" (cf. Matt 26:64).

8. A concept owed to N. T. Wright, *NTPG*, 268–71.

The Inclusion of the Gentiles

God had always intended that his blessing would fill the earth (Gen 1:28; 9:1). That blessing would later flow through Abraham and his descendants to embrace all the peoples of the earth (Gen 12:3). The prophets took this up, Isaiah saying that in the last days all of the nations would come to the mountain of the Lord (Isa 2:2). The messiah would gather the nations (Isa 12:4) and his name and renown would be told among the nations (Isa 12:4). Aliens would join Israel and unite with the house of Jacob (Isa 14:1; 19:19–25). God's temple would be a house of prayer *for all nations* (Isa 56:6–7). Significantly, both Israel and messiah were to be "a light for the Gentiles" (Isa 42:6; 49:6), bringing salvation to the ends of the earth because it is "too small a thing" for the messiah to restore Israel only. God himself will beckon to the Gentiles (Isa 49:22).

Jeremiah was appointed a prophet *to the nations* (Jer 1:5), and so through him God addresses Judah and "all the other nations" (Jer 36:10; 46:1). Jeremiah proclaims that God is "king of the nations" (Jer 10:7), and to him the nations will come (Jer 16:19). He prophesies of a time when all nations will gather to Jerusalem to honor the Lord (Jer 3:17).

Micah prophesies of a time when *many nations* will say, "come and let us go up to the mountain of the Lord . . . he will teach us his ways so that we may walk in his paths" (Mic 4:2). Zephaniah declares that the nations on every shore will worship the Lord, "everyone in its own land" (Zeph 2:11). Zechariah says that many nations will be joined with the Lord "in that day" and will become his people (Zech 2:11; 8:22). Malachi closes the Old Testament revelation with the words, *"My name will be great among the nations, from the rising to the setting of the sun"* (Mal 1:11). When the kingdom came on earth it would bring all nations under God's rule.

The "kingdom of God," then, was a phrase encompassing a whole group of Old Testament Jewish ideas and concepts. All of these themes came together to form the varied eschatological expectations among the Jews of the Second Temple period. They provide the essential background to understanding the coming of the messiah, the king of Israel, who would deal with the evil of foreign overlords, renew the covenant, lead a new exodus, and bring the exile to an end. All of this they understood as the coming of the kingdom of God. This was, in effect, vindication for Israel and the conclusion of Israel's story—the end of all of God's promises and intentions for the elect nation.

THE DAY OF THE LORD

The "Day of the Lord" is the second significant and pervasive eschatological motif, or major theme, of the Old Testament prophetic literature. As it was developed in the prophets it came to refer to a time when God would intervene in human history in an overwhelming and climactic way to bring to conclusion his purpose for the creation. The day of the Lord in the prophets generally involves both judgment and blessing, destruction and salvation. It is such a prominent theme in the Minor Prophets especially, that some commentators see it as the underlying motif that helps to bind this collection of books together.[9]

We have seen previously that Jewish eschatology divided time into two ages, the *present age*, which is evil and temporary, and the *age to come*, which was to be the time of God's blessing. Between these two was to be the Day of the Lord, the birth pangs of the new age, a day of judgment and shaking (see Isa 2; 12; 13:6–13; 24; Amos 5:18; Zeph 1:7; Joel 2; and cf. Matt 24; 1 Thess 5:2–11; 2 Pet 3:10; etc.).

The Day of the Lord is the common designation in the prophets given to that time when all of the promises, warnings, and prophecies given to Israel *and to the nations* would finally be concluded. The old order would pass away and the age to come would begin. "Every valley shall be raised up, every mountain and hill made low; the rough ground shall become level, the rugged places a plain. The glory of the Lord will be revealed, and all mankind together will see it" (Isa 40:4–5). Thus in the prophets it is the Day of the Lord that brings focus, or an "end," to the whole biblical eschatology. The biblical history is not a meandering, pointless, random, and unrelated chain of events; it has a beginning, it has an end, it has a fulfillment and consummation in the Day of the Lord.

The actual phrase, "Day of the Lord" only occurs in Isaiah 13:6, 9; Ezekiel 13:5; Joel 1:15; 2:1, 11, 31; 3:14; Amos 5:18, 20; Obadiah 15; Zephaniah 1:7, 14; and Malachi 3:23. But the number of variations on this phrase that also convey the idea of God's climactic intervention shows that the concept is much broader. References to the "day of God's *anger*," or "day of God's *wrath*," and similar expressions, occur in Isaiah 2:12; 34:8; 61:2; Jeremiah 46:10; Ezekiel 7:19; 30:3; Zephaniah 1:18; 2:2–3; and Zechariah 14:1. Other designations include "the day of the Lord's sacrifice" (Zeph 1:8), "the great day of the Lord" (Zeph 1:14), "day of trouble and distress," "day of destruction and desolation," "day of darkness and gloom," "day of clouds and thick darkness," "day of trumpet and battle cry" (Zeph 1:15–16). Then there are

---

9. See Barker, *Dictionary of the Old Testament*, 138–39.

terms such as "that day" (over 200 times in the Old Testament, e.g., Isa 17:7; 30:23; Hos 2:18; Mic 2:4; 5:10; Zech 9:16; 14:4, 6, 9), "those days" (Joel 3:1), "that time" (Jer 31:1; Zeph 3:19, 20), or simply "the day" (Ezek 7:10) or "the time" (Isa 49:8). "The last days" can probably be added to the list also (Isa 2:2; Hos 3:5; Mic 4:1).

Old Testament passages referring to the Day of the Lord—as with a lot of Old Testament prophecy—often speak of both a near and a distant fulfillment. There is a Day of the Lord for Israel, a Day of the Lord for Judah, a Day of the Lord for Babylon (Isa 13:6–9) and other nations, and then a final eschatological Day of the Lord for all the earth. The prophets again telescoped these events so that they appeared close to one another, so some Old Testament references to the Day of the Lord describe historical judgments that have already been fulfilled in some sense (Isa 13:6–22; Ezek 30:2–19). Others refer to divine judgments that will take place at the end of the age (Joel 2:30–32; Zech 14:1–21; Mal 4:1–3).

The Day of the Lord in the prophets is not a literal single day, but a series of events involving darkness and light, judgment and salvation, wrath and restoration. It is a time of terror for those opposed to God, a time of redemption for the godly. It is a time of justice when all wrongs will be put right. Amos, the first of the prophets (chronologically) to announce the Day of the Lord, cautioned that it would not just be a time of triumph for Israel, as popularly anticipated, but also (firstly) a day of judgment—a two-edged sword. "Woe to you who long for the Day of the Lord!" he wrote, "Why do you long for the Day of the Lord? That day will be darkness, not light" (Amos 5:18).

In the canonical organization of Scripture, the first example of the Day of the Lord—"For the day of the Lord . . . shall be upon every one that is proud and lofty, and upon every one that is lifted up; and he shall be brought low . . ." (Isa 2:12)—comes in the context of an oracle that predicted that in the last or future days a time would come when "all nations" would flow to the house of the Lord (Isa 2:2). There would be an end of all war (Isa 2:4), and the proud would be humbled (Isa 2:11–17) or try to hide from the judgment of God (Isa 2:19–21). This use clearly indicates a picture of *final judgment and salvation* (cf. Isa 13:10–13).

Petersen summarizes it as a day of worship (Hos 9:5; Zeph 1:7) but also of doom (Amos 5:18–20), of destruction for Israel and other nations (Mic 2:4; Hab 3:16; Zeph 1:9; Mal 4:1; Obad 15) and a time of cosmic disorder (Joel 2:31). There is the expectation on that day, he says, of a new political ruler (Hag 2:23), and it would be a very unusual day (Zech 14:6–7).[10]

---

10. Petersen, *Prophetic Literature*, 211.

Malachi describes it as "a great and terrible day" (Mal 4:5), and tells us that before it comes, "Elijah" will appear in some way.

THE DAY IN THE NEW TESTAMENT

> *The day of the Lord resonates across the canon and is picked up in the NT in the context of the work of Jesus Christ and the inauguration of the church. It continues to employ powerful and evocative images of cosmic upheaval and divine judgment to emphasize the overwhelming importance of this day.*[11]

The gospels refer to a "day of judgment" (Matt 10:15; 12:36; Luke 21:34, 35) and Jesus himself describes a time of coming judgment and salvation (using terms from the Old Testament prophets, especially Daniel and Joel) that resembles the Day of the Lord described by the prophets (Matt 24, Mark 13, Luke 21). He uses the terms "at that time" (Matt 24:30) and "that day" (Matt 24:36). He introduces the idea that the coming time of disaster is a warning that the end of the age is near, and soon the Son of Man will return and gather his chosen ones (Mark 13:24–27).

The phrase also occurs in 1 Corinthians 5:5; 2 Corinthians 1:14; 1 Thessalonians 5:2; 2 Thessalonians 2:2; and 2 Peter 3:10—the New Testament writers too expected a future Day of the Lord. But, as with the Old Testament, there are a number of variants—e.g., "Day of our Lord Jesus Christ" (1 Cor 1:8), "Day of Christ Jesus" (Phil 1:6; 1:10; 2:6) and "Day of God" (2 Pet 3:12; Rev 16:14). Other related phrases include "the last days" (2 Tim 3:1; Jas 5:3; 2 Pet 3:3), "the coming of our Lord Jesus Christ" (2 Thess 2:1), "the end of the age" (Matt 24:3; cf. Matt 13:39, 40, 49), "the end" (Matt 24:14), "the coming wrath" (1 Thess 1:10), "the day of God's wrath" (Rom 2:5; Rev 6:16, 17; 11:18), or sometimes just "wrath" and variations (Col 3:6; 1 Thess 1:10; Rev 14:10, 19; 15:1, 7; 16:1, 19; 19:15). Sometimes the writers just use phrases like "those days" (Matt 24:19, 22, 29), "that time," or "that day" (Matt 24:23, 30, 36). Revelation describes the day when God will finally defeat the forces of evil as "the Day of God Almighty" (Rev 16:14). Death will be defeated (Rev 20:14–15) and God will create a new heaven and earth (Rev 21:1–7).

The New Testament writers, however, reinterpreted the Day of the Lord, as they did with all Old Testament prophecy, to center it in the life and ministry of Jesus. In Acts the Day of the Lord is picked up when Joel is quoted by Peter in Acts 2:17–21. Barker says again, "Peter's sermon in Acts

---

11. Barker, *Dictionary of the Old Testament*, 142.

2 . . . explicitly links the events of Pentecost with the prophecy of the day of Lord in Joel 2:28–32. This connects the beginning of the church to the prophetic concept of the Day of the Lord." But he goes on to say that other mentions of the Day of the Lord have eschatological overtones. "The full weight of the Day of the Lord is still anticipated, but through Jesus the NT writers see its fulfillment coming to pass (Rom 2:5, 16; 1 Cor 1:8; Phil 1:6; 1 Thess 5:2–8; 2 Thess 1:10; 2:2; 2 Pet 3:10, 12)."[12]

In the New Testament the Day of the Lord began with the "Christ event"—the incarnation, ministry, death, resurrection, and ascension of Jesus—together with the outpouring of the Spirit on the day of Pentecost. In a very real sense, Israel's judgment fell on Jesus. In N. T. Wright's terminology, Jesus became Israel and bore God's wrath on Israel's behalf. Those who accepted and believed in him he then led into God's promised restoration and blessing in the new creation.

Yet there remains for the New Testament writers a future Day of the Lord also, which they saw in the events surrounding the promised return of Jesus. The apostle Paul refers to "the Day of our Lord Jesus Christ" in this sense and connects it to the second coming (1 Cor 1:7–8; 5:5; Phil 1:6–11; 2:16; 1 Thess 5:2). Paul equates the divine *justice* that will take place then to a concept of everything being "put right," i.e., the unrepentant punished and the righteous justified or rewarded (2 Thess 1:5–10). In writing to the Thessalonians, he clearly identifies the Day of the Lord with the return of Jesus and the gathering together of the elect. He says that day is a future event that will be preceded by "the rebellion" and the appearing of a "man of lawlessness" (2 Thess 2:1–15).

So the "Day of the Lord" is an eschatological term referring, in both the Old and New Testaments, to the final consummation of God's plans and purposes for Israel, for all the nations, and indeed for the whole creation. A series of climactic events rather than a literal day, it will be accompanied by social calamities and physical cataclysms (Matt 24; Luke 21:7–33) and by an open manifestation of God's presence and power. It will include the final judgment (Rev 20:11–15), final vindication for God's people, and it will culminate in the new heaven and the new earth (Isa 65:17; 66:22; Rev 21:1).

SUMMARY OF CHAPTER FOUR

These, then, are the two great themes of the prophetic eschatology: the coming of the kingdom and the Day of the Lord. They have their roots in the promises made to Abraham and to David and in the nature of God himself

---

12. Ibid.

as sovereign, righteous, and just. They form the foundation for understanding all that is to follow in the New Testament. The king was coming, and he would deal with all that plagued Israel still. He would establish the rule of God on earth, and he would bring in the Gentiles. The great overwhelming day of justice and salvation was coming also, when all that was wrong would be put right, and the new age would begin. God would once again act within history to turn the world the right way up, to sweep aside all that was wrong, to deal with evil forever—in all its manifestations and consequences—and to establish righteousness in the earth. The glory of God would cover the earth.

The prophets and their audience saw these two events telescoped into one, of course, and in some ways they were right. The fulfillment of both events—of all the prophetic predictions in the end—center in the person and work of Jesus. "The testimony of Jesus is the spirit of prophecy" (Rev 19:10). But two events there are: Jesus is enthroned, his kingdom is being established on earth as it is in heaven; but injustice and unrighteousness continue awaiting his return in power. The next two sections of this book will deal with these two prophetic expectations—the coming of the messiah king to establish his kingdom on earth as recorded in the gospels, and the events of the Day of the Lord as outlined in the book of Revelation. Finally in this section, however, we need to consider the greatest prophet of all.

Chapter Five

THE GREATEST PROPHET OF ALL

"Jesus regarded himself, and was regarded by his contemporaries, as a prophet . . . Jesus regarded himself as, intended to act as, and was perceived to be acting as, an eschatological prophet, announcing the Kingdom of God . . ."[1]

IT IS POSSIBLE TO approach the study of the Old Testament prophets (as with any biblical book) in various ways. We can study each of them, for instance, "in their own right," that is, individually and in isolation from the rest of the biblical narrative. There is benefit and value in this approach in helping to analyze and understand the text, but we must not think that having done that we have then understood the full meaning of what is written. The prophets must also be studied within the context of their place in the biblical canon if we are to understand them properly, and within the canonical context their message cannot be fully understood apart from the life and ministry of Jesus. He was the end and fulfillment of many of the prophetic themes and the agent for the fulfillment of all others, so any attempt to interpret the prophets without taking this into account must result in an incomplete understanding. Luke says of Jesus when he was with the two disciples on the road to Emmaus, "beginning with Moses and all the

---

1. Wright, "The Servant and Jesus," www.ntwrightpage.com/Wright_Servant_Jesus.htm.

Prophets, he explained to them what was said in all the Scriptures *concerning himself...*" (Luke 24:27).

At his baptism Jesus was anointed as Israel's messianic king, David's son—God's choice to rule over Israel and bring God's kingdom on earth. He was anointed as high priest, to offer up a once-and-for-all sacrifice to purify Israel forever (cf. Heb 4:13–5:10). He was anointed also as a prophet, *the* prophet, to Israel—God's greatest divine messenger to the nation (Luke 4:18–21).

So, whatever else he was, Jesus was not less than a prophet, in the line of the Old Testament prophets, fulfilling and bringing to completion the very story of Israel that the Old Testament had laid out. It must be remembered by Christians that the promises of God through the prophets had been made to Israel. Jesus came as *Israel's* messiah, the new covenant was made with *Israel*, the outpouring of the Spirit was promised to, and fulfilled upon, *Israel*. It is only as the completion of the story of Israel that the "Gentiles" are called to be part of the people of God. They are "grafted in" in the words of Paul (though we have seen that this is what God had intended from the beginning. The human mandate has always been to fill the earth with the blessed image of God). Jesus himself saw his life and ministry as being continuous with, as bringing to completion and fulfillment, the message and work of the prophets of the Old Testament. "Do not think that I have come to abolish the Law or the Prophets," he said, *"I have not come to abolish them but to fulfill them"* (Matt 5:17). On another occasion he said, *"Everything must be fulfilled* that is written about me in the Law of Moses, the Prophets and the Psalms" (Luke 24:44). And another time, "this has all taken place *that the writings of the prophets might be fulfilled*" (Matt 26:56).

JESUS IN HIS HISTORIC SETTING

How would Jesus have been perceived by the people of his time? How would the people of his day have seen him as he travelled through their towns and villages? What would they have made of the things they saw Jesus doing, the things they heard him saying, and of the stories they heard *about* Jesus? He was a first-century Jew and related in speech and action to the people of his time, so for them to think of him as somehow divine, as God incarnate, would have been as far beyond the possibility of their thinking as it would be beyond ours were it not for the New Testament revelation and centuries of debate and discourse within the church. We cannot read our understanding, based on further revelation, back into their time. We misunderstand the gospels if we read every mention of "the son of God" as a statement of

Jesus' divinity or of his place as the second person of the Trinity.[2] The fact is that most of the people he interacted with saw him, certainly at first, as a prophet.[3] Someone proclaiming a message from God, talking about the coming of God's kingdom, pronouncing—like the prophets of old—both judgment and restoration, and performing mighty deeds, would naturally have been seen as belonging in this category.

When he questioned his disciples about how he was popularly understood, they answered, "Some say John the Baptist; others say Elijah; and still others, Jeremiah or one of the prophets..." (Matt 16:13–14). At Jesus' entry to Jerusalem he was proclaimed a prophet (Matt 21:11). The chief priests and Pharisees were afraid to arrest him, we are told, because the people held him to be a prophet (Matt 21:46). King Herod was concerned when he heard that Jesus was popularly perceived as a prophet (Mark 6:14–15). When Jesus raised a young man from the dead at Nain, the reaction of the people was to proclaim him a "great prophet" (Luke 7:16). The two disciples whom Jesus questioned on the road to Emmaus understood him to have been a prophet (Luke 24:19). The woman Jesus spoke with at the well in Samaria perceived him to be a prophet (John 4:19). When Jesus miraculously fed the great crowd on the shores of the Sea of Galilee they began to say he was "the prophet" spoken of by Moses (John 6:14, cf. Duet 18:15). An incident in the house of Simon the Pharisee shows that he was widely perceived as a prophet and his behavior was judged on that basis (Luke 7:39). The chief priests and Pharisees in Jerusalem recognized he was understood to be a prophet (John 7:45–52). When Jesus was teaching in the temple courts at the Feast of Tabernacles, some of the people again began to proclaim him the prophet Moses had spoken about (John 7:40). To the blind man healed by Jesus he was obviously a prophet (John 9:17). It is evident from the Gospel record, then, that Jesus was widely held to be functioning in the prophetic office. He acted like a prophet, he spoke like a prophet, and this was the category into which the people of his time largely placed him. The more widespread recognition that he was more than a prophet came later.

---

2. We also note in the gospels that any hint of something more than merely human about Jesus caused considerable consternation to the people of his time (see Luke 2:9; Matt 27:54; Mark 5:15–17; Luke 8:37). This was true even with his immediate disciples (Matt 17:6; Mark 4:41; Matt 14:26; etc.). The common words in the gospels for peoples' reactions to the supernatural in Jesus are fear and terror (see Matt 14:26; 17:6; Mark 4:41; 5:15).

3. Among his Jewish contemporaries, that is. He also inevitably interacted at times with the Roman occupiers, and from them he elicited a mixture of responses, from respect and belief (Matt 8:5–13) to brutality (Matt 27:27–31), superstition (Matt 27:19), and treachery (Luke 23:22–25).

Significantly, Jesus identified himself as a prophet, saying on one occasion, "only in his hometown, among his relatives and in his own house *is a prophet without honor*" (Mark 6:4; Matt 13:57). On another occasion he is quoted by Luke as saying, "I must keep going today and tomorrow and the next day—*for surely no prophet can die outside Jerusalem!*" (Luke 13:33). Jesus claimed to be anointed of God for a special task and ministry (Luke 4:18), and as we have seen in earlier chapters, it was the prophets who possessed the Spirit for ministry. He was anointed as a messenger/prophet to Israel at his baptism (Matt 3:16; Mark 1:10–11; cf. Matt 17:1–5).

His ministry bore all the marks of the Old Testament prophets. Like them, he claimed to receive messages from God and he communicated those messages to the people of God. He preached against the religious formalism of his time, predicting the judgment of God against the nation if they remained unrepentant. He was concerned for social justice, the poor, the needy, and the outcasts. He performed miracles and predicted future events. Like the Old Testament prophets he sometimes acted out aspects of his message—turning the water to wine, cursing the fig tree, journeying to Jerusalem, cleansing the temple, etc. He spoke about the coming of the kingdom of God and God's future judgment and blessing for Israel and the nations in the Day of the Lord. He pronounced woes against those who served God hypocritically (Matt 23:13–36).

The gospels, indeed, portray Jesus as a formidable prophetic figure—a powerful and exciting man whose life and teaching, manner, words, and deeds challenged the world and people of his time. He is (correctly) presented in theological writings today as a "man of his time," completely contextualized in the culture and society of his day. But we must remember also that he was executed—after only a very short time of public ministry—for being seen as an extreme *threat* to that culture and society.

In his public speaking and preaching he was authoritative, strong, astonishing, challenging, powerful, daring. Luke informs us on one occasion that "no-one dared ask him any more questions" (Luke 20:40). He often spoke in hyperbole and superlatives of men with logs in their eyes, of swallowing camels, of plucking out your own eyes, of mountains being cast into the sea. He was scathing in his denunciation of hypocrisy and cant—"Blind guides! Whitewashed tombs! Brood of vipers! Children of your father the Devil!" And when he faced cruelty and irreverence he could react with powerful indignation—violently overturning the tables of moneylenders and driving them from the temple with whips, publically denouncing, on another occasion, the cruelty of synagogue leaders who complained of Sabbath healings. Of Judas, who betrayed him, he said it would have been better for him if he had never been born (Matt 14:21).

He was not swayed by men and had no regard for who they were (Luke 12:14). He sometimes stirred violent passions in people—he was either the devil incarnate (Matt 9:34; 12:24; Mark 3:22) or the Son of God (Matt 14:33; 27:54; John 11:27). He was not afraid of any opposition from any quarter. Many Christians, says N. T. Wright, have been sloppy in their thinking and talking about Jesus. "We have often muted Jesus' stark challenge," he says, "then wonder why our personal spiritualities have become less than exciting and life-changing."[4] Such a man was Jesus—a powerful, outstanding personality, powerful in speech and action and insistent in pursuit of justice and true moral goodness. A true prophet in every way.

He was more than a prophet of course. The New Testament claims, for instance, that all of the functions and authority of the three anointed offices of Old Testament Israel met in Jesus (see Heb 4:14; John 12:12–15). But it is certain that while some of his contemporaries saw him as more than a prophet, and while some perceived him as a false prophet, the widespread perception of Jesus of Nazareth was that he was a prophet in the vein of the Old Testament prophets before him.

JESUS AND THE OLD TESTAMENT PROPHETS

Jesus is similar to the Old Testament prophets in some ways but differs from them in others. Like them, Jesus had a public ministry to Israel, calling on the nation to repent and fulfill the purpose and plan of God. But unlike the Old Testament prophets, who used introductory phrases such as "this is what the Lord says . . . ," thus claiming God's authority for their message and ministry, Jesus spoke in his own authority, using phrases like, "I tell you the truth . . . ," or, "I say to you . . ."

Jesus goes far beyond *speaking* the word of God, he claims to *be* the word of God. Like the Old Testament prophets, Jesus came to Israel with a message from God, but unlike them he himself *was* the message. They claimed to bring the word of truth, he claimed to *be* the truth. "In the past," the writer of Hebrews confirms, "God spoke to our ancestors through the prophets at many times and in various ways, but in these last days he has spoken to us by his Son, whom he appointed heir of all things, and through whom also he made the universe" (Heb 1:1–3). The Old Testament prophets called Israel back to the faithful keeping of the covenant, the words and laws of Moses. At the center of Jesus' message, on the other hand, was a call to a personal commitment not to the Mosaic covenant, not to a keeping of Torah, but to himself.

---

4. Wright, *The Challenge of Jesus*, 10–11.

JESUS AS THE PROPHET

There was, clearly, among the Jews of the Second Temple period, an expectation that a great prophet, as important as Moses himself, would be soon raised up by God to help transform their nation and to speak the authoritative word of God to Israel again (John 1:21, 25; 6:14; 7:40) as Moses himself had predicted (Duet 18:15; cf. Acts 3:22; 7:37). Jesus claimed that Moses had been speaking this about him (John 5:46), and he also laid claim to this office when he spoke as he did on the mountainside, "you have heard that it was said to the people long ago (i.e., by Moses), "Do not murder." ... But *I tell you* that anyone who is angry with his brother will be subject to judgment" (Matt 5:21-22, etc.). What Jesus was doing here was revolutionary in his time and cultural setting, and his claims must have been shocking to those who heard them. He was claiming that *his* words now superseded the words of the covenant delivered to Israel by Moses. Israel was the elect nation of God, the people he called to himself and to whom he gave the commands written on tablets through Moses on the mountain. On another mountain Jesus now begins to reconstruct the people of God around his own person and his own words. Another great prophet had arisen in Israel.

JESUS' USE OF OLD TESTAMENT PROPHECY

The gospel writers make it clear that Jesus had a strong sense of divine destiny (Luke 2:49; 4:18-21, 43; John 12:27) and saw his life and ministry as a fulfillment of the Old Testament story and prophecies (Luke 24:25-27; Mark 14:49; John 5:39). The "I am" claims of John 6:35, etc., are direct references to Old Testament promises and events. Acts of Jesus such as the entry to Jerusalem (Luke 19:28-40) and the installation of the new covenant (Luke 22:14-20) are deliberate fulfillments of Old Testament prophecy (Zech 9:9; Jer 31:3-34). Jesus understood himself, too, in terms of Daniel's "son of man," to whom the kingdom would be given (Dan 7:13-14; cf. Matt 8:20, etc.) and his disciples as the *saints* to whom judgment would one day be given (Dan 7:22; cf. Matt 19:28; Luke 22:28-30). Jesus describes his coming arrest in the words of Zechariah 13:7 (see Mark 14:27), and his later return in the words of Daniel 7:13 (see Mark 13:26; 14:62).

He made frequent use of the Old Testament Scriptures, quoting them, alluding to them, using them to support his teaching and actions, and using them to make comparisons between his ministry and that of Old Testament characters. Many of these references to the Old Testament are to passages in the prophetic books. Near the beginning of his ministry, for instance, Jesus cites Isaiah 61:1–2 as fulfilled in him, in his person and ministry. "The Spirit of the Sovereign Lord is on me, because the Lord has anointed me to preach good news to the poor. He has sent me to bind up the brokenhearted, to proclaim freedom for the captives and release from darkness for the prisoners" (Luke 4:18–19). A great deal of Jesus' teaching was, in fact, about himself. He came not to teach theology or ethics, but to introduce *himself* to Israel. He pointed to himself as the answer to Israel's quest for a right relationship with God.[5]

In his own prophetic pronouncements Jesus made extensive use of the Old Testament prophets. He rebukes Israel's leaders in words from Isaiah (Mark 7:6–7; cf. Isa 29:13) and his disciples in quotes from the prophets also, "having eyes do you not see and ears do you not hear . . ." (Mark 8:18; cf. Jer 5:21; Ezek 12:2). He explains the lack of understanding and belief of those who listen to him in Isaiah's terms (Mark 4:12; cf. Isa 6:9–10). In his warnings to the cities that have rejected him, Jesus alludes to Isaiah's oracle against Babylon (Matt 11:23; cf. Isa 14:13, 15). He warned Jerusalem in words from Jeremiah, "behold your house is forsaken and desolate" (Matt 23:38; cf. Jer 22:5). He used Daniel's "abomination of desolation" as a signal for the impending judgment of Jerusalem (Mark 13:14; cf. Dan 11:31; 12:11). In Luke 23:30 he quotes Hosea 10:8 about a time when people will call on the mountains and hills to fall on them. He warns his disciples of the judgment of Gehenna (Mark 9:48) in the words of Isaiah 66:24. The early Christian understanding of Malachi 3:1, "See, I will send my messenger, who will prepare the way before me . . ." as being fulfilled in John the Baptist comes from Jesus (Matt 11:10).

His rebuke to those who are misusing the temple (Mark 11:17) is couched in the words of both Isaiah and Jeremiah: "Is it not written, 'my house will be called a house of prayer for all nations? But you have made it a den of robbers'" (Isa 56:7; Jer 7:11). In his trial before the high priest, Jesus again echoes the words of Daniel (Mark 14:62; Dan 7:13). He prophesies the cosmic signs that will accompany his coming in glory in the words of Isaiah (13:10; 34:4; cf. Matt 24:29) and the manner of his coming in the words of Daniel (7:13; cf. Matt 24:30). He predicts his arrest as a criminal in the words of Isaiah (Isa 53:12; cf. Luke 22:37) and his abandonment by the disciples at that time in the words of Zechariah (Zech 13:7; Matt 26:31).

Jesus' use of the prophetic material to describe his purpose and ministry was extensive. These are a few examples of direct references, if we add to these all of the *allusions* he made to the prophets and also the prophetic

---

5. Note especially the Jesus of John's gospel where the "I am" sayings (referencing the prophets) and the "signs" John uses reveal a Jesus who is the source of the "abundant life" that God had promised to the nation through the prophets.

actions he engaged in, we see that he closely identified himself with the prophets and the prophetic literature of the Old Testament. His understanding of himself and his mission was clearly anchored in the Old Testament prophetic story.

JESUS, PROPHET TO ISRAEL

Jesus, it must always be borne in mind, was a prophet to the nation of Israel. He was speaking into *Israel's* story, bringing completion to what God had been doing ever since calling Abraham out of Ur and Israel out of Egypt. He was announcing the arrival of the kingdom of God, the fulfillment of all Jewish hopes, covenant promises, and eschatology—of all that the prophets had proclaimed and predicted. Israel's story was now being fulfilled in him.

Secondly, as part of this, Jesus was a prophet, once again—as with the prophets of old—bearing "an urgent, eschatological and indeed apocalyptic message for Israel,"[6] *"repent, for the kingdom of God is at hand . . ."* The kingdom of God was coming upon them, change was needed or judgment would follow. Much is written about the coming of the kingdom in the ministry of Jesus, but the first word of his proclamation, a command from the Son of God, was important also. The kingdom is a just kingdom. That kingdom was being inaugurated, not—as Israel thought—through Moses or through Torah, but through him, through Jesus. He was the king, and through him God was beginning to rule. Failure to respond to him, to accept his message and his right to rule, would again bring awful consequences on the nation (Matt 24:1–2). It was this generation of Israelites, and not another, who must choose once more to heed the message of God's prophet or bear the consequences (Matt 23:33–39; 24:34; Luke 11:50–51). The choice could not be delayed, could not be passed off. God was moving now; the king had come, and he called all to follow him.

Many people did choose to follow him—thousands of them—in Jerusalem, Judea and Samaria, and in Jewish enclaves in the surrounding provinces and nations. All of the early followers of Jesus were Jews who believed that Jesus was the messiah and that through him God's promises and purposes, as declared through the prophets, were finally being fulfilled. But the "Jewish nation" as a whole, led by the temple authorities and entrenched interests, chose not to receive him (John 1:11). Some of those, again, chose to follow a different version of Israel's story, the way of open rebellion against Rome, the military option. In consequence, the Roman armies levelled Jerusalem and tore the much-admired temple stone from stone. A million

---

6. Wright, *Jesus and the Victory of God*, 150.

Jews were killed, and according to the historian Josephus thousands more were sent to the mines of Egypt and the coliseums of the empire and the rest were scattered among the surrounding nations. For two thousand years there was not to be a Jewish nation in Canaan again. The Arch of Titus, built in celebration of the terrible event, still stands in Rome today.

JESUS AND THE DAY OF THE LORD

As the prophets had done before him, Jesus also prophesied of a future time of great distress marking the end of this age and the beginning of the new age (Matt 24:1–44; Luke 21:5–36). He used words such as "in those days" (Matt 24:19, 22), "at that time" (Matt 24:23, 30), "that day" (Matt 24:36), and "the end" (Luke 21:9). These, as we have seen, are shorthand references to the prophetic day of judgment and restoration. The events described would be worldwide in scale (Matt 24:7–14), and Jesus uses the apocalyptic language of cosmic cataclysm taken from Isaiah's description of the Day of the Lord (Matt 24:29; cf. Isa 13:10; 34:4) and echoing Joel's description of that same day (Joel 2:31; cf. Luke 21:25–28; Dan 7:13). The events described would usher in the end of the age, the return of the Son of Man (Matt 24:14, 27–30, 42–44), and the final salvation of the elect (Matt 24:31).

Also, like the Old Testament prophets, Jesus telescoped the events of the near and far future so they appeared to be one. Some of the prophesied events took place when the Romans destroyed Jerusalem in AD 70 (e.g., Matt 24:2; Luke 21:20–24). Other events clearly await a future fulfillment: "Immediately after the distress of those days," he said, "the sun will be darkened, and the moon will not give its light; the stars will fall from the sky, and the heavenly bodies will be shaken." And "at that time the sign of the Son of Man will appear in the sky, and all the nations of the earth will mourn. They will see the Son of Man coming on the clouds of the sky, with power and great glory. And he will send his angels with a loud trumpet call, and they will gather his elect from the four winds, from one end of the heavens to the other" (Matt 24:29–31; cf. Matt 26:64 and Isa 27:13). Jesus several times spoke of "the last day" as a time of judgment and salvation (John 6:39, 40, 44, 54; 12:48). He also spoke of "the day of judgment" (Matt 10:15; 11:22, 24), or sometimes, as noted above, he just used "the day" (Matt 25:13; Luke 17:30) or "that time" (Matt 13:30; 24:10, 23, 30; 25:1; Mark 13:21, 26, 33; Luke 21:27) as referring to this time also.

Jesus, too, must be understood in context if we are to fully appreciate who he was and what he was accomplishing, and the prophets provide something of that context. He was not *just* a prophet, but he certainly came in the prophetic tradition, and his work and message were one with the message and work of the other prophets. He was both continuing that work and message and bringing it to completion. He was *a* prophet, he was *the* prophet, and he was the one the prophets spoke about.

SUMMARY OF CHAPTER FIVE

Jesus was perceived by the people of his time to be a prophet ministering in the same way as the prophets before him. Often misunderstood and diminished by contemporary theologians and preachers, he was a powerful and formidable prophetic figure the like of whom had not been seen in Israel for centuries. Whatever else he was, he was not less than a prophet, operating—in preaching and practice—in the tradition of previous prophets to Israel. Claiming himself to be the prophet whose coming was foretold by Moses, he announced that the kingdom of God had come now, in him, and that it was time for Israel to come back to a right relationship with God through him. In him, now, was to be found all of the blessings promised to Abraham and the prophets. If Israel did not turn to him, however, judgment would follow. Beyond that, he too prophesied of a coming Day of the Lord in which would take place the final judgment, accompanied by cataclysmic events and culminating in the final salvation of God's people and the renewal of the creation.

Jesus, then, was a prophet in the line of the great Old Testament prophets. Unlike them, however, he was much more than a prophet. In and through Jesus, God undid the results of the human rebellion. In Jesus, God came to that which was his own, to take it back, cleanse it, and renew it. To the life and ministry of Jesus the Messiah we now turn.

Part Two

JESUS

"In the past God spoke to our forefathers through the prophets at many times and in various ways, but in these last days he has spoken to us by his Son, whom he appointed heir of all things, and through whom he made the universe. The Son is the radiance of God's glory and the exact representation of his being, sustaining all things by his powerful word. After he had provided purification for sins, he sat down at the right hand of the Majesty in heaven."

—Hebrews 1:1–3

*"In love a throne will be established;
in faithfulness a man will sit on it—
one from the house of David—
one who in judging seeks justice
and speeds the cause of righteousness."*

—Isaiah 16:5

Chapter Six

KING JESUS

"Pilate had a notice prepared and fastened to the cross. It read: JESUS OF NAZARETH, THE KING OF THE JEWS . . ." (John 19:19)

THE PROPHETS AND THEIR writings laid the foundations for the eschatology of the Second Temple period, including the messianic expectations that are so evident in the gospels. The prophets, however, presented a multifaceted picture that was not always easy to decipher. The gospels reveal a situation where there seemed to be a broad consensus concerning the larger eschatological picture but substantial differences as to the details. It *is* clear, however, that part of that larger picture for Israel as a whole was the expectation of a messiah figure, an "anointed one," who would act on God's behalf to bring in God's kingdom and bring Israel into the fullness of the destiny that God had promised them and called them to (see Acts 1:6). The messiah was God's agent of redemption for the nation. The "age to come" would begin with him, and through the messiah, through Israel, God would extend his rule over the nations forever.

"Messiah," or its Greek equivalent "Christ," appears hundreds of times throughout the New Testament, the vast majority of times in reference to Jesus. The authors of the New Testament were convinced that Jesus was the expected messiah, in fulfillment of the Old Testament prophecies and expectations. So it is that the gospels, rather than beginning a new story, actually present the culmination and fulfillment of Israel's (Old Testament) story. As noted in the preface, in some ways we could say that the gospels (and Acts) actually belong more to the Old Testament than they do to the New Testament, bringing Israel's story to completion in Jesus and in the "new Israel" (or *fulfilled* Israel) that was brought to birth through his life, death, and resurrection. Israel's story has no culmination without the gospels and Acts, no *end* without Jesus and the New Testament church.[1]

The New Testament opens with Matthew, who is especially concerned to show that Jesus fulfills the Old Testament story. He opens his account of Jesus' life (and thus the New Testament) with the claim that Jesus is the messiah. Matthew's genealogy traces Jesus' ancestry (through Joseph) back to David. His account of Jesus' miraculous conception claims that this is what was predicted by Isaiah. In the account of the visit of the Magi, the child Jesus is called "the one who has been born king of the Jews" (Matt 2:2). At Jesus' baptism the Spirit comes upon him, and the Father speaks a blessing over him—he is God's anointed one. Jesus' disciples accept him as the messiah (Matt 16:16). Jesus rides into Jerusalem to the acclamation of crowds of people welcoming him as "the son of David" (Matt 21:1–10). Jesus is crucified as "the king of the Jews" (Matt 27:37). Again and again, Matthew uses phrases such as "all this took place to fulfill what the Lord had said through the prophet" (Matt 1:22), and, "this is what the prophet has written" (Matt 2:5), or, "this has all taken place that the writings of the prophets might be fulfilled" (Matt 25:56. See also 2:15, 17, 23; 3:3; 4:14; 8:17; 12:17; 13:14, 35; 21:4; 24:15; 26:54; 27:9; etc.). Matthew's Jesus is the Jewish messiah, come in fulfillment of the Old Testament prophecies. The king has come, Matthew tells us; the kingdom is here, now, in Jesus.

The other gospel writers agree. Mark tells us in his opening verse that the good news is about Jesus *the messiah*. He has Peter confessing to Jesus that he believed Jesus was the expected messiah (Mark 8:29), and, significantly, he has Jesus himself giving the same confession to the high priest (14:61–62) and also revealing to Pilate that he is indeed Israel's king (15:2). Luke's account of the angelic promise to Mary was that her son would be the messiah (Luke 1:32–33), and he has Jesus explaining to the disciples that he was the messiah spoken about by Moses and the prophets (Luke 24:25–27). John tells us that he has written his account of the life of Jesus just so that we might believe that Jesus was the messiah (John 20:31). He also informs us that the common people, albeit with mixed motives, accepted Jesus as messiah and intended to make him king by force (John 6:15).

---

1. The Epistles, then, are commentary on the completion of Israel's story and its application to the rest of the world. The book of Revelation in turn brings the story of Israel and the Gentile nations to its final conclusion as will be seen in later chapters.

Peter's message to the Jews of Jerusalem when the Spirit was poured out in fulfillment of the prophetic promises was that this proved that Jesus was the Messiah (Acts 2:16–17, 31–33, 36). The early apostolic message to their Jewish audience was the good news that the messiah had come in the person of Jesus (Acts 5:41–45). Saul's early success in preaching was attributed to his ability to prove from the Old Testament Scriptures that Jesus was the messiah (Acts 9:22. Cf. 17:3; 18:5; 18:28). These are a handful from among the many references to Jesus as the messiah, or Christ, throughout the Gospels and Acts and the more than five hundred references throughout the whole New Testament. So, the New Testament message began with the proclamation that Jesus was the expected Jewish messiah. Throughout Paul's writings and the other New Testament books, the common designations for Jesus are "Jesus Christ," "Christ Jesus," or simply "Christ," the Greek equivalent of messiah. The New Testament authors considered themselves to be living within the unfolding of the events foretold by the Old Testament prophets, to be living through the fulfillment of Israel's story. The messiah had come, and he was Jesus.

THE KINGDOM OF JESUS

The Jewish expectations surveyed above, then, form the essential background to understanding the cry of both John the Baptist and Jesus when they each opened their public ministries with the proclamation, "repent, for the kingdom of heaven is at hand" (Matt 3:2; 4:17). "Messiah" meant God's anointed, he who had authority to act on God's behalf and he who was David's son—heir to Israel's throne. In Jesus the king had come, and he set about his task of bringing in the kingdom on earth as it was in heaven.

In the Synoptic Gospels the kingdom of God formed the core of Jesus' message. Of the approximately one hundred and forty times the kingdom of God is mentioned in the New Testament, over a hundred of those are found in the first three gospels. Fifty-four of these, in turn, appear in Matthew, forty-one in Luke, and nineteen in Mark.[2]

Jesus fulfilled the Old Testament kingdom expectations but he did it in unexpected ways. He *did* usher in the age to come, but, unforeseen by anyone, it was to come in two phases. During the first stage the present evil age continues in parallel with the age to come. This is the time for the gathering in of the Gentiles, which will end when he returns and the glories of the coming age will be fully revealed.

---

2. Spivey, Smith, and Black, *Anatomy of the New Testament*, 203.

Jesus did indeed deal with evil, but not just among the nations opposed to Israel—he dealt with it at its very source in the hearts of men and women and in the demonic realm. Sin, the devil, and evil were the real enemies, and Jesus confronted and defeated them all (Acts 10:38; Heb 2:14; 2 Pet 5:8; 1 John 3:8). The prophets had spoken of a new covenant (Jer 31:31-34; Ezek 11:18-20) and Jesus accomplished this, but he did it through the sacrifice of his own life on the cross (Luke 22:20; 1 Cor 11:23-26; Heb 9:11-28; 12:24 etc.). Jesus announced the kingdom, *his* kingdom, and instructed his disciples to set about establishing it throughout the world.

When he rode into Jerusalem and entered the temple, Jesus was himself God returning to Zion in fulfillment of the prophetic promises. The Jews had looked for a new temple filled again with the Shekinah, but God had a bigger plan, "*the earth will be filled* with the knowledge of the glory of the Lord, as the waters cover the sea" (Hab 2:14). As God had revealed to the prophet Ezekiel when he appeared to him in Babylon (Ezek 1-3), his glory would no longer be confined to the temple in Jerusalem (see Isa 6:3; 40:5; Dan 2:35; Zech 14:9; and cf. Matt 12:6; 21:12; 24:1-2; Luke 2:8-11; John 2:19-22; Rev 21:22). God's temple now would be made up of "living stones," of those all over the earth who chose to follow Jesus. In these and many other ways, Jesus' kingdom was different from what was expected.

THE KING AND THE CROSS

There is another major principle of Christianity that, perhaps more than anything else, illustrates the unexpected nature of the kingdom Jesus was bringing in. John writes, "Carrying his own cross, he went out to the place of the Skull . . . *There they crucified him* . . ." (John 19:17-19).

There is something at the heart of the gospel—at the very center of the Kingdom message—that is illustrated, captured, made evident, and demonstrated by what took place on the cross. Jesus triumphed *through the cross* (Col 2:15). The king entered into his kingdom *by way of the cross* (Phil 2:8-11). Everything in creation, in both the natural and spiritual realms, was reconciled to God—put back into the right order—through the cross (Col 1:19-20). Forgiveness came to human beings through the cross (Col 1:14). The power of evil was broken through the cross (Col 2:15).

Though not understood by many, the prophets had predicted that the victory of the messiah would come about through suffering. "Concerning this salvation," Peter wrote, "the prophets, who spoke of the grace that was to come to you, searched intently and with the greatest care, trying to find out the time and circumstances to which the Spirit of Christ in them was pointing *when he predicted the sufferings of the messiah* and the glories that would follow" (1 Pet 1:10–11).

Jesus reinforced this to the disciples after his death and resurrection. "How foolish you are," he said to them, "and how slow of heart to believe all that the prophets have spoken! *Did not the Christ have to suffer these things and then enter his glory?*" (Luke 24:25–26).

The cross lies at the heart of the "good news" and of the kingdom of God. It is only those who are willing to take up the cross who can follow Jesus (Matt 16:24), only those who are willing to lose their lives who will find them (Matt 16:25). The Lamb himself is counted worthy and is at the center of the throne, because he was slain (Rev 5:6, 11). It was through suffering that he overcame where Adam gave way to temptation and pleasure (Heb 5:7–8). There is a principle right at the heart of the gospel that is woven into the nature of the kingdom and of creation itself. Jesus described it as he faced the hour of his death, "the hour has come for the Son of Man to be glorified. I tell you the truth, unless a kernel of wheat falls to the ground and dies, it remains only a single seed. *But if it dies, it produces many seeds.* The man who loves his life will lose it, while the man who hates his life in this world will keep it for eternal life" (John 12:23–26).

Here Jesus describes the principle of life-through-death that he himself lived by and by which he calls the subjects of his kingdom to live. The kingdom is advanced through sacrifice and suffering—that's the inescapable, unavoidable pattern. The prophets themselves were often called to share in his suffering (see Heb 11:32–38). The church is called to share in his suffering (Phil 3:10). Suffering is part of the destiny of the church (1 Thess 3:3). *"We must go through many hardships to enter the kingdom of God"* (Acts 14:22). We cannot of course *add* to Jesus' vicarious and redemptive suffering, but we can *share in it*, and in fact we are called to do precisely that.

The people of God have always triumphed through sacrifice and suffering. Abraham waited twenty-five years for the fulfillment of the promise, then offered up his son who *was* that fulfillment. Joseph came to his inheritance through great trial. Job triumphed through adversity. Israel itself was born out of a time of great suffering. The prophets were an example of patience in the face of suffering (Jas 5:10). All of the faith heroes of Hebrews 11 triumphed through suffering. Most of the New Testament apostles gave their lives for their faith in Jesus. The early Christians recognized that this was a privilege accorded to them by God (Acts 5:41), a part of the prophetic function of God's anointed people. Christians are not exempted from suffering; they are called to it. This is the consistent testimony of the New Testament. Victory is given to those who overcome, and overcoming is not possible without some form of trial or opposition that needs to be risen above and conquered. Only through adversity is triumph possible. Conflict is the womb of spiritual growth and victory.

Christian historian N. T. Wright explains it wonderfully: "The early church understood their vocation as Jesus' followers to include, as a central and load-bearing element, their own suffering, misunderstanding and likely death . . . the suffering of Jesus' followers is actually, like Jesus' own suffering, not just the inevitable accompaniment to the accomplishing of the divine purpose, but actually itself part of the means by which that purpose is to be fulfilled."[3]

Sacrifice and suffering exist on several different levels, beginning with plain self-denial—the willing foregoing of what anyone else would consider natural, permissible, "normal," even sometimes advisable, in the service of God. This is the sacrificial Christian life. Fasting, for example, is a Christian discipline illustrating this principle. Or, in another example, the missionary leaves all that is familiar—family, friends, his/her own country, people, and culture—to extend the kingdom in another culture and among another people. Another man or woman leaves a well-paid job with excellent prospects to work "full time" in Christian ministry or in some service to others. Ordinary Christians give generously and sacrificially to help those less fortunate than themselves. The mere living of a consistent and effective Christian life requires a great deal of discipline, self-denial, self-sacrifice, and the conquering of constant temptation. This is sacrifice by choice. At another level are the things suffered by many from others just for being Christians—misunderstanding, prejudice, opposition, rejection, discrimination. In some places and at some times there is open persecution. At the high end of the spectrum, the living of a Christian life, or the keeping of a Christian testimony, leads to martyrdom, the laying down of life physically for the cause of the kingdom and for the king. To this life of sacrifice are we all destined as Christians. No longer our own, we are bought with a price, and we follow the example of Jesus who laid down his life for us.

The biblical authors point out that suffering—from the "trials of life" encountered in differing measure by all human beings, to those special trials that come about as a result of being a Christian—is in some measure actually redemptive: "for a little while you may have had to suffer grief in all kinds of trials. These have come so that the proven genuineness of your faith—of greater worth than gold, which perishes even though refined by fire—may result in praise, glory and honor when Jesus Christ is revealed" (1 Pet 1:6–7; cf. Jas 1:2–4; 1 Pet 3:14).

---

3. Wright, *How God Became King*, 198–99.

The early Christians understood this. After a flogging at the hands of the Jewish Sanhedrin we are told, "the apostles left the Sanhedrin, *rejoicing because they had been counted worthy of suffering disgrace for the Name*" (Acts 5:41).

This principle is illustrated in the Christian ordinances. The rite of water baptism is the identification of the believer with Jesus in his death and resurrection. The old life of self-centered indulgence is left behind and a new life of self-denial centered in Christ is embraced. The "table" is an invitation to take part in the great salvation story (1 Cor 10:16), to participate in the sacrifice and suffering of the one who won his crown through the cross. The Christian communion rite actually embraces the whole biblical story, centered, itself, around a number of other "meals." It is necessary in the first place because of the self-indulgent meal shared by the first man and woman (Gen 3), which brought suffering upon the human race in the beginning (Rom 5:12). It embraces the Passover meal, which celebrated the birth of Israel out of great suffering and at the cost of the sacrificial lamb (Exod 1–12). It looks forward to the final victory for the church at the "marriage supper of the Lamb," which is the celebration of those who have overcome and are joined forever to Jesus (Rev 19:9). It too will come about after a time of great suffering in the world (Matt 24:21).

Self-denial, perseverance, patience, and endurance; contending (and, when necessary, suffering) for the faith; triumphing over adversity, danger, and temptation; overcoming all that comes against us; the cross life, the life laid down for Christ and the kingdom—these are the biblical hallmarks of the constant, effectual Christian. This is following the example of him who entered into his kingdom through the cross. *"Anyone who does not take his cross and follow me is not worthy of me,"* Jesus said (Matt 10:38). That which is so clearly and powerfully for us an instrument of Jesus' death is the instrument of our own death also. The cross is the path for those who would follow Jesus, the way to victory, the pattern for the overcoming Christian life. It is the shape of the door through which the kingdom is entered and will admit no "baggage"; all must be laid aside before entering. Through the cross the Christian enters the new creation where it is the will of God that is done on earth as it is in heaven, and that will sometimes leads through the valley.

But Paul—himself called to suffer much for the Lord he served (Acts 9:16)—wrote, "I consider that our present sufferings are not worth comparing with the glory that will be revealed in us" (Rom 8:18). Our "light and momentary troubles," he tells us, "are achieving for us an eternal reward that far outweighs" what we are called to endure now (2 Cor 4:17), and he urges us to have an eternal perspective on our lives. "We fix our eyes," he tells us in the next verse, "not on what is seen, but on what is unseen. For what is seen is temporary, but what is unseen is eternal" (2 Cor 4:18).

Messiah king has come, the writers of the New Testament tell us—he is Jesus. He won his kingdom through the cross, and we too who choose to enter his kingdom are called and destined to that same cross-life on behalf of the King. This is the very nature of the life of the kingdom.

SUMMARY OF CHAPTER SIX

All of the authors of the New Testament were convinced that Jesus was the expected messiah who had come in fulfillment of the Old Testament prophecies. Jesus was "the son of David" to whom the throne of Israel belonged. He was the king who came to establish his kingdom on earth. This is the culmination and the conclusion of Israel's story, Messiah had come in the person of Jesus. The king had come; the kingdom was here, now, in him. He fulfilled all of the kingdom expectations that the Jews had derived from the teachings and predictions of the prophets, but he fulfilled them, often, in unexpected and unlooked for ways.

A major aspect of this unexpected nature of the kingdom was that it is brought in through the suffering of the messiah and consequently through the suffering of those who follow him. This reality reverberates throughout the New Testament and throughout church history. It is those who overcome who receive the victory and the reward.

We will return to this in another chapter ahead, but here we should note that this is a truth that needs reasserting in some parts of the church in our time, where the thought of suffering for the gospel is perceived as being out of God's "blessing." The triumphalism of much of the modern church needs to be balanced again against the truth that the rebellious world by its very nature is antagonistic to the rule of Jesus and therefore to the Christian church. "If they have persecuted me," Jesus said, "they will persecute you also" (John 15:20). If the church really carries out its prophetic function to critique and confront the powers of this fallen world then sharing in the sufferings of Jesus becomes inevitable.

Chapter Seven

KINGDOM STORIES

"Jesus spoke all these things to the crowd in parables; he did not say anything to them without using a parable." (Matt 13:34)

It is evident from this and other scriptures that a tremendous amount of Jesus' public teaching took place in the form of parables, certainly in his early ministry (see also Mark 4:11, 33). He was not unique in his use of parables in the biblical literature; they were used, for instance, by the wise in Israel (Prov 1:6) and by the prophets: "I spoke to the prophets, gave them many visions *and told parables through them*" (Hos 12:11; cf. Ezek 17:2-3; 20:49; 24:3). Yet Jesus used them to an unprecedented and unparalleled extent in his teaching ministry. About thirty-five percent of his teaching as recorded in the Synoptic Gospels is in the form of parables.[1] One major commentator lists forty-nine parables plus another twenty-seven possible parables (depending on the definition used) in the Synoptics.[2] Working on the principle of John 21:25 we could assume that the parables we have in the gospels are just a selection of those used by Jesus. A great number of books have been written about these parables, yet they remain among the most misunderstood parts of the New Testament literature. "The parables,"

---

1. Snodgrass, *Stories With Intent*, 22.
2. Stein, *Introduction to the Parables*, 22-26.

Snodgrass says, "are among the most abused and mistreated stories ever told—twisted, shortened, subverted, realigned, and psychologized."[3]

Often they are presented as clever illustrations that Jesus used in his teaching—"earthly stories with heavenly meanings." The young preacher is urged to study them as models of how to illustrate his or her sermon with examples drawn from everyday life. Jesus is the master illustrator, filling his teaching with pictures cleverly drawn from the common world of the people of his time—farming, home life, banking, law courts, and so on. Of course, illustrating Christian teaching from the common stuff of everyday life is helpful, but we must not think that we have then understood and plumbed the depths of the meaning of the parables or anything like it.

The fact that the New Testament preachers who followed Jesus did not learn from Jesus and use parables in their preaching should make us stop and think. What were the parables about? Why do they feature so prominently in the ministry of Jesus yet not in the ministry of those who immediately followed him? Why is the teaching of Paul, for instance, not equally full of parables? Why did Jesus alone so often use this cryptic form of teaching?

One reason, clearly, that Jesus used them is that parables, like songs, are much easier to remember than straightforward instructional-style teachings. We would imagine that the individual parables would be repeated by Jesus on numerous occasions (with some variations—cf. Matt 25:14–30 and Luke 19:11–27) and would have become familiar to his audience and repeated by them to others. The Good Samaritan, the Lost Sheep, the Sower, the Pearl of Great Price—all are familiar to readers of the New Testament because the parables are easily retained in the memory. Similarly, telling a story is always an effective form of teaching that captures the imagination and holds the attention of the audience. A great deal of the scriptural presentation of truth is given to us in story form. In the stories of Adam and Eve, of Noah and the ark, of Daniel in the lion's den, and a myriad other stories, we see how God works in the world and how he acts in people's lives. We are ourselves participants in the larger story, and we are invited to draw our own conclusions from these biblical narratives and alter our behavior as a consequence.

In a well-told story, too, the listener can perceive a possible new reality, can imagine a new world where things are different from what they are in the world we inhabit. Like our movies of today, a story enables the storyteller to create another world that can fire the imagination, stir emotions, stimulate thinking, and prompt action. Every new and great movement starts with a new story, a new way of looking at reality, and Jesus was the

---

3. Snodgrass, *Stories with Intent*, 6.

master storyteller, creating in his parables a whole new version of Israel's story that at turns astonished, mystified, thrilled, and challenged those who heard him. It was a new story rooted in his own person and presence, in the eschatological purpose that his coming had begun to bring, finally, to a fulfillment. In the hearts of some of his listeners the new story took root and began to grow. In the hearts of others it created opposition that led eventually, for Jesus, to the cross.

N. T. Wright says that the reason Jesus told so many parables was that his vision of the kingdom that he was bringing in was so different from that of his first followers. It was shocking, he says, to the point of being incomprehensible, and the parables were the only way he could get it through to them.[4] The parables, taken together, spell out the nature of Jesus' kingdom.

Thirdly, we must always remember when talking about Jesus that we are dealing with the greatest mind, the most powerful and pure intellect, in all of human history. An unfallen intellect, unfettered by any restriction, doubt, prejudice, or self-interest. And this unbelievably powerful human being was on the greatest *mission* of all of human history, dealing with the eternal destinies of the whole human race, at the known cost of his own life. He was dealing with cosmic realities. He was putting in place a new creation. He had come to reclaim, redeem, and renew the creation that belonged to him but had been stolen away. Critically, he was bringing to completion the eschatological story of Israel. But he was also giving an unexpected twist to that story, reinterpreting it in a way no one had foreseen. He was reconstituting Israel around himself, superseding the law of Moses with his own teaching, remodeling the twelve tribes with his own twelve disciples, replacing the temple and its entrenched leadership with himself. He was claiming for *himself*, in sometimes cryptic words and sometimes unusual prophetic actions, the throne of David and therefore the government of Israel. He claimed to be greater than Abraham, greater than Solomon, greater even than the temple. He claimed to be greater than anyone who had come before him. In fact, he claimed to be somehow one with Israel's God and therefore the author and finisher of Israel's destiny. We must not "damn him with faint praise" in regard to the parables, as is so often done in other areas of his life and ministry (such as calling him a "great teacher"), by labelling them "clever illustrations" or "wonderful stories." It is true that the shorter parables are often clear enough illustrations and definitions of the kingdom that Jesus had come to establish. But far from being mere illustrations for his preaching, the major parables are cryptic stories dealing with eschatological issues, cosmic issues, new-creation issues. "I will open

---

4. Wright, *How God Became King*.

my mouth in parables," it is said of Jesus, *"I will utter things hidden since the creation of the world"* (Matt 13:35; cf. Ps 78:2). We need to take these kingdom stories very seriously.

Witness the first of the New Testament's parables, the parable of the Sower (Matt 13:3-23), which Jesus said was the key to understanding all the parables (Mark 4:13). This agricultural allegory is explained by Jesus in terms of the kingdom message and its opposition from satanic forces, from superficial piety, from the mystery of human suffering, and from materialism. It is the story of the kingdom's eventual triumph over such opposition through those who receive it with understanding. No small matters here, no mere clever illustration. This is the great battle of the kingdom of God against satanic, humanistic, and materialistic forces. Here is a call to all Israel to heed his words, to understand that Israel's story, as told by the prophets, was being fulfilled now in him. Or witness again the parable of the Wheat and Weeds (Matt 13:24-30). In his explanation Jesus speaks of its meaning as covering the whole world, all human beings, the kingdoms of darkness and light, angels, the devil, the end of the age, and of eternal reward and judgment (Matt 13:36-43)[5]—again the great cosmic struggle explained in a simple agricultural allegory. These are the great issues Jesus was dealing with, and these are the great issues he was talking about in many of the parables.

The parables of the Faithful and Wise Servant, the Wise and Foolish Virgins, the Bags of Gold and the Lazy Servant, and the parable of the Sheep and Goats (Matt 24:45-25:46) are all dealing with the events surrounding the return of Jesus at the end of the age, with the Day of the Lord and with eternal judgment and reward. The parable of the Fishing Net is about the final judgment and its awful possible consequences at the end of the age (Matt 13:47-50). Again, no "clever illustrations" here. These are great issues; these are eschatological issues of eternal consequence. Some of the parables are also deliberately seditious stories ("stories with intent," Snodgrass calls them, "prophetic instruments")[6] designed to undermine the existing order (based on misinterpretation of Torah, temple, and cultic system[7]), and to replace that order with a new one centered in Jesus himself.

So, in the parables Jesus is sowing the seeds of the kingdom message (*"the kingdom of heaven is like leaven . . . like a mustard seed . . . like treasure*

---

5. Snodgrass, *Stories with Intent*, 206. "This parable deals with the mystery of the kingdom, [it is] present but in an unexpected way . . . how can the kingdom be present if evil is still present?"

6. Ibid., 8.

7. By the "cultic system" we mean the whole system of the temple, priesthood, offerings, and sacrifices of Israel's religious life.

hidden in a field . . .") and advancing the new story of Israel in the face of opposition from the guardians of the old. Those with understanding and receptive hearts received and embraced the message, but the antagonistic, through these same stories, were entrenched in their opposition. "Those who have understanding will be given more, those who do not have it will lose everything they thought they had."

And many of the people who heard him responded to him; they came to him, great crowds of people (Matt 4:25; 15:30; 19:2; Luke 8:42; 14:25; etc.). They were astonished by the power and authority of his preaching, touched by his ready acceptance of even the worst of them, irresistibly drawn by his demonstrations of power over sickness and disease, delighted by his success in refuting and confusing his unpopular critics. They proclaimed him a great prophet. They welcomed him into Jerusalem as the Son of David. They wanted to make him king by force. Those crowds, those words, those intentions and actions—as far as they were understood—generated the opposition from the entrenched interests and the self-righteous that led eventually to his death, as he knew they would. Jesus was speaking and acting against the shortcomings of the present order just as the other prophets had done before him. The cryptic nature of the parables enabled Jesus to speak scathingly (and publically) against those in power who opposed him (see Mark 12:12). They understood his intention, but the nature of a parable—a story with a variety of possible meanings—meant Jesus could get away with it for a time. But the Synoptic Gospels make it plain that the parables were, eventually, in some measure, responsible for the determination of his opponents to put him to death. When the chief priests and Pharisees heard Jesus' parables, Matthew tells us, they knew he was talking about them and looked for a way to arrest him (Matt 21:45–46; cf. Matt 26:1–4; Mark 12:4; Luke 20:19). These are powerful stories.

There were a number of other things also that contributed to the opposition that led to his arrest and death. There was his open denunciation of the hypocrisy of some of the religious and political authorities (Luke 11:42–53),[8] the prophetic cleansing of the temple (Luke 19:45–48), and the general agitation that his teaching caused (Luke 23:4–5, 14). There was his attitude towards the Sabbath (Mark 3:1–6; Luke 6:1–11; 13:14). For John, it was the raising of Lazarus that provided the final straw—such a powerful and undeniable "sign" that the authorities feared everyone would turn to him (John 11:45–53; 12:9–11). It was this sign, John tells us, that led to the messianic welcome he received on his entrance to Jerusalem (John 12:12–

---

8. Although they didn't all oppose him, see John 7:50 and Mark 15:43 with John 19:38–39.

18). Again the Judean authorities feared everyone was turning to him (John 12:19). There was also his "blasphemy" (in the eyes of those who opposed him) in claiming to be one with God (John 19:7). It is apparent from all of this that Jesus was seen to be a troublemaker who threatened the religious and political stability of the nation. The parables he told against the opposing authorities added fuel to the fire. He was dangerous, and his stories were dangerous. He was an agitator, and his stories were seditious.

JESUS' PARABLES AND THEIR MEANING

The parables of Jesus vary in length and form. Some of them are straightforward similes that explain various characteristics of the kingdom of God: "the kingdom of heaven is like a mustard seed . . . , like yeast that a woman took and mixed into a large amount of flour . . . , like treasure hidden in a field . . . , like a merchant looking for fine pearls . . . , like a net that was let down into the lake . . . , like a king who wanted to settle accounts with his servants . . . , like a landowner who went out early in the morning to hire men to work in his vineyard . . . , like a king who prepared a wedding banquet for his son . . ." (Matt 13:31–50; 18:23–35, 20:1–16; 22:2–14). These again are the seeds of the kingdom from which, when planted in a receptive heart, an understanding of the nature of the kingdom will grow.[9] Taken together, these parables produce a much clearer picture of what the kingdom of God that Jesus was bringing in actually looked like.

The meaning of some of the parables are explained to us by Jesus himself. "Suppose one of you has a hundred sheep and loses one of them. Does he not leave the ninety-nine in the open country and go after the lost sheep until he finds it? And when he finds it, he joyfully puts it on his shoulders and goes home. Then he calls his friends and neighbors together and says, 'Rejoice with me; I have found my lost sheep.' *I tell you that in the same way there will be more rejoicing in heaven over one sinner who repents than over ninety-nine righteous persons who do not need to repent*" (Luke 15:4–7; 12:16–21; etc.).

The meaning and intent of some of the parables is straightforward. At the conclusion of the parable of the Good Samaritan the point being made is self-evident to those listening, and Jesus simply remarks, "you go and do

---

9. We must remember, of course, that the meaning of the simile is to be derived from the whole parable and not just the introductory picture. Thus, the kingdom of heaven is not like a mustard seed, but like a mustard seed that grew into a tree that gave shelter to the birds of the air. Small beginnings but a huge outcome is the point of the simile. We must interpret the others in similar fashion.

likewise." Again, for those who have ears to hear, *this is what the kingdom looks like.*

Often the meaning of a parable is readily drawn from the context that called it forth. See, for example, Luke 14:15, "when one of those at the table with him heard this, he said to Jesus, 'Blessed is the man who will eat at the feast in the kingdom of God.'" This provides the occasion for the parable of the great banquet that follows in verses 16–24. Or, see Luke 18:1, "then Jesus told his disciples a parable to show them that they should always pray and not give up," and the parable of the Persistent Widow that follows in verses 2–8.

Again, there is Luke 18:9 and the parable in verses 10–14. Or further, Luke 19:11, "to some who were confident of their own righteousness and looked down on everybody else, Jesus told this parable . . ." and the parable of the Pharisee and Tax Collector that followed in verses 12–27. Then there is Luke 21:5–28 and the parable in verses 29–30. The context in each case helps us determine the meaning.

But some of the major parables are indeed seditious stories with not-so-hidden meanings designed to undermine the false interpretation of Israel's story that was being propagated by some of the religious and political authorities of Jesus' time.

The Parable of the Father and His Two Sons

One of the clearest examples of this is the parable found in Luke 15:11–32, normally referred to as the parable of the "prodigal son." It is the story of a father and his two sons and normally preachers and exegetes focus on the first son, the younger one who asks his father for his inheritance, takes it and goes off to waste it all on wild living. When the money is gone and he falls on hard times, he comes to his senses, realizes his mistake, and determines to go home and ask for his father's forgiveness. When he does this, he is received with great joy. That's how the parable is normally interpreted, it is the parable of the "Lost Son." Much is made of the cultural impropriety of the son asking for his inheritance, of his remorse and contrition, of the father's great love, and so on. The story is embellished with descriptions of the father waiting each day on the rooftop of the house, peering into the distance in hope and expectation of his lost son's return. It is clothed in modern garb, in the "here and now." It is "everyman's story" of a lost and repentant sinner coming back to a right relationship with father God. It is an evangelistic story; a response is called for from the congregation, "who will come to your senses today and come back to the Father . . . ?"

Now this "everyman's" story is a real story, of course. Many have lived it, many are still living it. They have taken all the good things the father has provided for them—gifts, talents, skills, abilities, provision—and are wasting them all on "wild living." Or they are just using them to make their own way in the world, living self-centered, self-focused, self-absorbed lives, leaving the father (God) out of the picture. And this part of the parable could, conceivably, be used as an illustration of that story if it is clear it is being used as an *illustration* only. But that would be to completely remove it from its context and use it in the way that any real-life story could be used, because that is nothing like the meaning of the parable. The context is found earlier in the chapter: "Now the tax collectors and 'sinners' were all gathering around to hear him. But the Pharisees and the teachers of the law muttered, *"This man welcomes sinners and eats with them"*" (Luke 15:1–2). It was in response to this charge, and the attitude behind it, that Jesus spoke this parable (and the two before it).

Besides the younger son there are two other people in the story, the father and the other son, the eldest and heir, and the parable is really about their different attitudes and responses to the return of the younger brother. The father responds with compassion, a ready forgiveness, with mercy, and love, which releases great joy and celebration in the household. The older brother responds with a lack of compassion, with complete self-centeredness (the opposite of compassion). He thinks only of himself, and his attitude shuts him out of—and would have put a stop to—the joy and celebration that were taking place because of his brother's return. He instead falls into envy, into bitterness, self-pity, intolerance, and judgmental anger.

The father tried to talk sense to him, saying, "all the benefits of the house are yours to enjoy whenever you want . . ." But the older son, swallowed up by self-interest and jealousy, taking no heed, scornfully dismisses his own brother as "this son of yours." The father, trying to elicit some compassion from him, responds by calling the younger man "this brother of yours . . . ," but he has no success.

The *attitude* of the older brother is what this parable is all about—an attitude that kept *him* from participation in the joy and blessing that was filling the house and, worse still (and more to the point in the parable), would have kept his own brother away from the forgiveness and acceptance offered and from the joy of a restored relationship with the father.

That's what Jesus was getting at here, aiming the story directly at the Pharisees and teachers of the law who criticized his welcoming of the "sinners" who gathered around him. Jesus was attracting crowds (Luke 14:25), and among the crowds were people whose lives were not all they should be—people like the younger son, people who were lost but recognized something in Jesus and came to him. Jesus responded to them like the father in the parable. The Pharisees and teachers of the law, on the other hand, responded to them like the older brother, with scorn and condemnation. And that was the whole point of what Jesus was saying: "Who is worse, the younger brother who sinned but came to his senses, or the older brother whose lack of compassion would have kept his brother from the father's love?" "Who is worse, these sinners who recognize their need and come to me, or you who would keep them from me, and so from the Father's love?"

Beyond this, the parable was clearly aimed at Israel itself. God's plan, beginning with Abraham, had been intended to undo the effects of the fall for all creation. The blessing was to be *through* the Jews (John 4:22) but not just *for* the Jews; it was intended for all the nations. "I will make you into a great nation and I will bless you; I will make your name great, and you will be a blessing . . . *all peoples on earth* will be blessed through you" (Gen 12:2–3; 18:18; 22:18). Abraham was to be the father of *many* nations (Gen 17:4). He who was to come out of Judah would be owed the obedience of *the nations* (Gen 49:10; Isa 11:10). The coming servant would bring justice to *the nations* (Isa 42:1; 51:4–5). David's descendant would summon the nations (Isa 55:5). Israel was to be a light to the nations, a city on a hill (Deut 4:6; Isa 2:2), declaring God's glory among the nations (1 Chr 16:24, 31; Isa 12:4) and gathering "brothers" from among the nations (Isa 66:20). The temple was to be a house of prayer *for the nations* (Isa 56:7). Jesus sent his disciples to all the nations to call them to become part of the reconstituted Israel (Matt 28:19) and declared that he has no intention of returning and bringing the creative/redemptive program to a close until that work is completed (Matt 24:12).

So this parable is a prophetic rebuke to Israel. Instead of being a light to the Gentiles, they had shut the nations out. Instead of offering a way for the nations to come to God, they had said "you cannot come here." Instead of offering the father's warm welcome they had offered the older brother's selfish disdain and rejection to those who would come. Israel *was* the older brother in the parable. God had bestowed many wonderful blessings on the nation. All the treasures of the father's house belonged to them; God's word, his promises, his presence, prosperity, peace, the covenants, the temple with its priesthood and sacrificial system, the law, the Sabbath . . . But instead of using these things to attract the nations, Israel had used them to shut the nations out, to keep them away. "We are too holy for you . . . you can't come here."

"My house," Jesus quoted later, "will be called a house of prayer for all nations . . . but you have made it a den of robbers" (Mark 11:17). Israel had stolen the blessing for themselves; they had kept it from the nations. We are not told how the Pharisees and teachers of the law reacted, but they could hardly have missed the point that they were being rebuked.[10]

The Parable of the Tenants

In this parable (Matt 21:33-46) Jesus recounts the story of Israel from beginning to end in regard to its historic opposition to God's purposes. He places himself in the line of messengers that God has sent to the nation throughout its history and predicts that Israel's leaders, having rejected the prophets sent by God, will eventually reject him also, putting him to death. Again they are accounted thieves and robbers of God's inheritance in Israel. His listeners are readily able to tell him how justice should be applied to the situation, and Jesus agrees—Israel will be judged and the kingdom given to the Gentiles. This time the priests and Pharisees were in no doubt that he was speaking against them and sought for ways to arrest him. These, again, are powerful stories.

The Parable of the Wedding Banquet

This is perhaps the most transparent of the parables of Jesus regarding criticism of Israel's entrenched interests, and the application is patently obvious. The parable in Matthew 22:1-10 (Luke 14:16-24 records another version) is so obviously spoken against Israel's leaders as to need little comment (cf. Matt 21:45-46, "when the chief priests and the Pharisees heard Jesus' parables, they knew he was talking about them"). This, again, is a powerful, prophetic denunciation of Israel's rejection of God's messengers (the prophets) and of God's purposes for them. It again threatens judgment on the nation that may be an allusion to the destruction of Jerusalem by the Romans.

Master and Servants

In regard to the parable of the man who gave his servants money to use while he went away, found in Luke 19:12-27 (called the parable of the Talents in Matthew 25:14-30), N. T. Wright finds its meaning (in the light of what follows—Jesus' entrance into Jerusalem and the cleansing of the temple) as Israel's God coming back to his people *in the person of Jesus arriving*

---

10. The parable is written for us also; we are meant then to apply the lesson to ourselves as well. We are commanded to go and be witnesses to the nations. What if we too stay at home and keep the blessing for ourselves?

in Jerusalem. He finds his servants misusing what he has given them. The temple, God's house, has been turned into a symbol of Israel's failure to do what he left them to do. Only one result is possible, and the temple cleansing is an acted-out parable of its coming destruction. Again, this is a tremendously seditious prophecy in the sight of the temple authorities. Jesus told several stories about masters and servants, Wright says, *to illustrate what he himself was doing*.[11] These are powerful stories.

SUMMARY OF CHAPTER SEVEN

The parables are a diverse group of stories that help in understanding the nature of the new kingdom that Jesus was bringing in. Some of them were simple similes that illuminated various aspects of that kingdom, some were straightforward examples for the would-be participants in the kingdom to follow, but many were deliberately aimed at changing the current and popular misinterpretation of Israel's story. They were designed to undermine the misunderstandings being lived and taught by the "blind guides" and to create a new story, centered in radical and whole-hearted attendance upon Jesus and his words. They are to this day a unique body of illustrative teachings that demonstrate the immense intellectual capacity and ability of the one who created them and the intense and targeted focus of his ministry.

Collectively, the parables are a powerful, prophetic reinterpretation of Israel's story, in many cases undermining the authority and controlling interests of those who had twisted that story into something that was virtually the opposite of what God had always intended. The kingdom of God was coming on earth, and it was radically different from what was currently being espoused and practiced in Israel. And it was insistent in its demands for change. The old and the new were on a collision course. The old wine skins could not contain the new wine of Jesus' kingdom. New, fresh skins were needed. The kingdom was bigger than historical Israel; it was to fill the whole earth, and every man, woman, and child must be invited to share in it and thus inherit the eschatological promises of God. The parables were collectively so powerful that the speaker must be silenced. Jesus must die.

We too must be very careful that the story we are telling is really the kingdom story told by King Jesus. The parables are still seditious stories if interpreted and taught correctly. They are designed to undermine the existing order and its entrenched interests. They offer an eschatological interpretation of history, focusing on a coming "end," and so emphasize the temporary and preparatory nature of the present world order, an emphasis missing

---

11. Wright, *How God Became King*, 97–100.

from large parts of the church today. They spell out a life-style radically focused on King Jesus and his kingdom coming on earth and the necessity of living out the kingdom precepts. They challenge our concepts of how to live in the world, calling into question the self-focus, the lack of compassion and mercy, and the injustice that are so often prevalent. For too long robbed of their power by misinterpretation, these kingdom stories need to be correctly and courageously retold and applied by the prophetic community of today. If we do that, then we too might be considered as dangerous radicals by the entrenched interests of our own time. But it is surely time for the church to confront the false story being told by those entrenched interests. It is time for the prophetic church to clearly begin again, by word and deed, to tell the real story of the King and his kingdom coming on the earth.

Chapter Eight

JESUS AND HIS ACTS OF POWER

"God anointed Jesus of Nazareth with the Holy Spirit and power, and . . . he went around doing good and healing all who were under the power of the devil, because God was with him . . ." (Acts 10:38)

IT IS OBVIOUS FROM the gospel accounts that as well as being a powerful speaker Jesus was also widely credited with performing many "mighty deeds," or powerful acts, for which there was no natural explanation. This is acknowledged even by those, like King Herod, who were wary of him (Luke 9:7–9). Most of these mighty deeds were works of physical healing, but there were also works of power over the realm of nature (e.g., turning water to wine), over demonic spirits, acts of supernatural provision, and even the resuscitation of some who had died. The disciples on the road to Emmaus spoke of Jesus as a prophet "mighty in word *and deed*" (Luke 24:19). So much were these *healing* miracles, especially, a part of the life and ministry of Jesus that Matthew describes that ministry more than once as being one of "preaching, teaching, and healing" (Matt 4:23; 9:35).

So, Jesus was widely acknowledged as a worker of miracles in line with other prophets whom God had sent before him. The great miracle-workers of the Old Testament had been the prophets Moses, Elijah, and Elisha, and some of the miracles of Jesus bear resemblance to miracles performed by these three. For example, Moses fed crowds in the wilderness—as Jesus did also.[1] Elijah brought a widow's son back to life, as did Jesus. Elisha healed a leper and Jesus healed ten lepers.

Jesus pointed to the miracles he was doing as evidence that he was indeed sent by God and worked in God's name (John 10:25), and he called on people to believe in him on account of those demonstrations of power (Matt 11:5; John 10:37–38, 14:11, cf. Acts 2:22). The Pharisee Nicodemus supported Jesus in this when he spoke of the miraculous signs that Jesus was doing (John 3:2) and acknowledged it meant that "God was with him." Peter, in his address to the household of Cornelius, again said that Jesus healed all who were under the power of the devil "because God was with him" (Acts 10:38). A great prophet and miracle worker had again arisen in Israel.

MIRACLES AND MEANING

The miracles of Jesus, when taken by themselves as isolated events, reveal various aspects of the nature and character of Jesus such as his compassion and his extraordinary power. They also cast some illumination on the worldview of the early church which produced the accounts of these miracles. There is some value in studying them in this way. To be properly understood, however, the miracles of Jesus must be examined on two further levels: firstly, in the full context of his person and mission, how and why did Jesus perform his "mighty deeds?" John the Baptist performed no miracles,[2] yet Jesus said of him that "there has not risen anyone greater than John" (Matt 11:11). Why then were the miracles such a prominent part of Jesus' ministry?

Part of the answer to this, of course, is that the miraculous power demonstrated in the ministry of Jesus was a natural outcome of who he was, a natural expression of his kingship and authority over the creation. He was the creator come among his creation; all things were made by him, through him, and for him (Col 1:16). He "came to that which was his own" (John 1:11), and he set about extending and demonstrating his kingdom authority over the creation, over the realm of nature, over Israel, the temple, the Sabbath, the law, over sickness and disease, over sin, over the demonic

---

1. Jesus tied the two together; see John 6:1–58. In fact what Moses did (or God did through Moses, as Jesus pointed out) was a "picture" of Jesus. Another example of the amazing interweaving of types and antitypes, predictions and fulfillments, pictures, themes, and motifs that run through the Bible—evidence again of inspiration and meta-narrative.

2. That we know of—an argument from silence.

realm, over death. The creation was not as it should be and he began to put that right.³

Another part of the answer as to why the miracles played such a part in Jesus' ministry lay, as we noted above, in his nature and character. His throne, say the prophets, is established in righteousness and justice. He is merciful and good. When he met with injustice, when he encountered the results and consequences of sin in sickness and death, he was moved to act (Matt 14:14; 20:34. Cf. Matt 9:36; 15:32; Mark 1:41). On several occasions the gospel writers make mention of the compassion that motivated him to acts of power (Matt 9:35–36; 14:14; 15:32; 20:34; Mark 1:41; 8:2).

Commentator Michael Brown sees in Jesus Israel's (Old Testament) "divine healer" come in the flesh, bringing the divinely promised and intended "shalom," or abundant life. In him the kingdom of God had broken into human history and the glory of the Son is revealed in his mighty healing deeds. A new day had dawned, an eschatological jubilee in which Jesus offered, through the power of the Spirit, freedom from both sin and sickness.⁴ Other commentators agree, "Jesus has inaugurated," says one, "a new era that provides the reality anticipated in the Old Testament."⁵ Another sees the mighty works as expressions of Jesus' authority to bring in the kingdom of God. What we see Jesus doing in the gospels, he says, is a new creational / new exodus restoration of the image of God.⁶ N. T. Wright too sees the healing miracles as part of the inauguration of the "sovereign and healing rule of Israel's covenant God." Most, if not all of them can be seen, he says, as restoring to membership in Israel those who were excluded as ritually unclean by sickness or whatever else, as well as bestowing the gift of wholeness (*shalom*).⁷ The "acts of power," then, in the ministry of Jesus must be seen as evidence and consequence of the eschatological breaking in of the kingdom of God, of God moving once more within human history to work what had long been promised and divinely intended. In Jesus, a just and compassionate God had come to his people to lead them into a new day of wholeness, restoration, and blessing.

The greatest display of the supernatural in the Old Testament was in association with the ministry of the prophet Moses as he delivered Israel out of Egypt and led them into the inheritance that God had promised to

---

3. The process continues through the Holy Spirit inspired church; cf. Acts 1:1.

4. Brown, *Israel's Divine Healer*, 208–47.

5. Ladd, *Theology of the New Testament*, 266.

6. Watts, "Jesus and His Mighty Deeds" (lecture, Harvest Bible College, Melbourne, July 10, 2003).

7. Wright, *Jesus and the Victory of God*, 191.

Abraham. The miracles in this instance were displays of God's power over those who held Israel in bondage (Egypt and its gods) and they were evidence that God was with Moses (Exod 4:1-9). Jesus was the prophet like Moses, a new Moses leading a new exodus, leading people out from under the bondage of this world and its gods and into the eternal inheritance God purposed for them. He was leading people out of the kingdom of darkness and into the kingdom of God. The miracles in his ministry too, were displays of power over all that holds people in bondage and evidence that God was at work through his life and ministry (John 10:25-38).

LITERARY CONTEXT

The second level on which the miracles can be examined is within their literary framework or context, and this too is important if we are to understand their full import. All of the gospel writers act as thoughtful and careful editors, selecting limited material from the various sources at their disposal—whether from memory, from eyewitness accounts, or from written or oral material which existed in various forms. Each of the writers informs us that a wealth of such accounts of the works and words of Jesus was available to them. Why then did they include and exclude what they did? Why for instance, do the "blind, the deaf, and the lame"—mentioned so often in the prophets (Isa 29:18, 35:5; Jer 31:8; etc.)—figure so much in the healing accounts? Jesus healed all who came to him, did he never encounter other forms of sickness and disease? While this applies to all of the gospels, including the Synoptics, it applies even more so to John, who, though admitting to being aware of a huge amount of information regarding the acts of Jesus (John 21:25), chooses to include just eight miracles in his gospel, which he labels as "signs." It is also clear from John's own account that he had a clear purpose in mind in doing this (John 20:30-31).

In the rest of this chapter we turn to examine one of John's miracles in its literary context in order to show just how important and helpful this can be in drawing out the full meaning of the miracles and the very deliberate way Jesus always acted, even in regard to the many acts of power he is credited with. For this we consider what is perhaps Jesus' greatest miracle, the raising of the dead Lazarus after he was four days in the tomb.

This miracle is the last of seven "signs" that John includes in the account he writes of the life of Jesus. John's gospel is a complex, masterful revelation of Jesus—of his person, of his nature, and of his mission. This miracle and its consequences form the hub around which the narrative and plot of the gospel turns.

Many commentators give an outline of John that contains essentially two main parts;[8] 1:19 through to the end of chapter 12, and chapters 13 through 20. C. H. Dodd gave these two parts the titles "the book of signs" (because the signs, or miracles, are contained in this section) and "the book of the Passion," which begins with the last supper and covers the crucifixion, resurrection, and post-resurrection appearances of Jesus.[9] Each book then ends with a summary statement (12:37–50; 20:30–31). The first concerns the public ministry of Jesus, the second focuses on a private ministry to his disciples.

Our purpose lies, initially, with the first part of the gospel where seven miraculous events appear. Six of these are referred to as signs, either directly (2:11; 4:54; 6:14; 12:18), or by implication (6:2; 9:16). The fifth miracle, Jesus walking on water (6:16–21), is not referred to as a sign but is clearly, in context, included among the others (and cf. 6:26).[10] Though Jesus did many more signs (see 2:23; 3:2; 6:2; 11:47; 20:30–31; 21:25), here we have seven of special significance to John's purpose. The raising of Lazarus is the last and greatest.

Besides the raising of Lazarus, the gospel writers mention two other cases of raising the dead in the ministry of Jesus; the son of a widow at Nain (Luke 7:11–15) and the daughter of Jairus (Matt 9:18–19; Mark 5:22–24; Luke 8:41–42, 49–56). These two miracles are not included by John. Beyond the gospels there are only the two accounts of Peter and Paul raising someone from death (Acts 9:36–43; 20:7–12). These few cases would seem to show that resuscitation was exceptional even in the ministry of Jesus and the first apostles.[11]

Resuscitation is really very rare in the bible. Death is the inescapable end of human life as a consequence of sin. There is little point in bringing back to life those who have died unless there is to be a change in their very nature so that sin and death are no longer the inevitable result of their being alive once more (cf. Heb 9:27). Otherwise they merely face the same fate once again. What is needed is a *resurrection* to an entirely new kind of life.

That the Jews of the first century believed in such a resurrection is evident from biblical examples like Martha's response to Jesus when he declared that her brother would rise again, "I know he will rise again in the resurrection at the last day" (John 11:24). N. T. Wright traces the

8. Between a prologue (1:1–18) and an epilogue/appendix (chap. 21).

9. Dodd, *Interpretation of the Fourth Gospel*, 297, 289. Others prefer "the book of signs," and "the book of Glory"; see Brown, *The Gospel according to John*, cxxxviii–cxxxix.

10. The miraculous catch of fish in chapter 21 occurs after 20:30–31. Nothing is said of it being a sign like the others.

11. Even taking Matthew 10:8 into account.

development of the concept of a resurrection of the righteous in the Old Testament to passages in the prophets such as Isaiah 53:7–12; Daniel 12:2–3 (with Isaiah 24 as background); Ezekiel 37; and Hosea 13:14; 6:1–3.[12] Israel's great hope was that God would, in the end, restore her fortunes, free her from the domination of Gentiles, and bring restoration in justice and peace, even if this required an act of new creation. Out of this developed a belief and hope of a literal resurrection, a reversal of death. By the time of Jesus, Wright concludes, most Jews either believed in some form of resurrection or knew it was standard teaching.[13]

JOHN'S GOSPEL

If we look briefly at John's themes and purpose in writing, we will see that many of these come together in the unfolding of this last and greatest sign that we are examining.

While not exclusive to John (they occur eighteen times in Matthew, eight times in Mark, and nineteen times in Luke), the words "life," or "eternal life," appear forty-two times in the fourth gospel, marking a major theme. This idea is presented early in the prologue (1:4 "in him was life"). It forms one of the two major themes of "the book of signs," and it serves as John's summary for the main part of the book and his express purpose in writing, "These are written that you may believe," he says, "and that by believing *you may have life*" (20:31).

The basic meaning of "life" in the Old Testament is not immortality or life after death but God's gift of complete well-being in earthly existence, including a long and prosperous life with many children, security, peace, and fellowship with God.[14] As Jewish eschatology developed it came to mean the life of the age to come, the life of the resurrection. In John these two thoughts are fused—life is both a state of "shalom" or "life to the full" and the resurrection life (John 5:29; 10:10). This fusion is found very clearly in the revelation of Jesus to Martha at the tomb of Lazarus, *"I am the resurrection and the life."* This life is not to be found in Torah, as the Jews thought, but in Jesus (5:30–40; 6:33; 17:3).[15]

---

12. Wright, *Resurrection*, 85–128. See especially pp. 115–21. He notes that the hope of resurrection in the Hebrew Bible is actually rare. The Old Testament is not particularly concerned with life after death, still less with resurrection.

13. Ibid., 129. The exception, of course, were the Sadducees; see their "case study" in Matt 22:23–28.

14. Ladd, *Theology of the New Testament*, 291.

15. Mediated through the Spirit (3:6; 6:63; 7:38–39).

"Believing" is another concept that has a major part in John's theology. In fact it is hard to overstate the importance of this theme in the fourth gospel. The way to this abundant, or eternal, life is through believing in Jesus. In John, unbelief is the essence of sin (16:9). Whoever does not believe is already condemned, under God's wrath, and will perish (3:16, 18, 36; 8:24). To believe means to receive Jesus in the fullness of his person, work, and mission, and to *respond appropriately* (1:12). It is God's desire that all believe and, again, John's purpose in writing is expressly designed to create such belief (1:7; 11:42; 20:31). His whole message is that Jesus came to give life in all its fullness to those who would believe in him. The mighty works of Jesus, especially the raising of Lazarus, separated those who believed from those who would not (11:5–53).

A number of other important themes include "work" (4:34; 5:36; 9:4) and "water." While the other three gospels refer to water twenty-times in total, John uses the word twenty-two times in significant settings and with powerful metaphorical meaning.[16] Other themes that run through the gospel are truth, light, and glory.

While the Synoptics focus on the contrast between this age and the age to come, in John the contrast is largely between this world—the world below—and the world above.[17] This forms the essential background of both John's Christology and of the book itself. The Son, pre-existent with the Father, came into this world from the world above. The word became flesh, the light shone in the darkness, the bread came down from heaven (1:5, 14; 3:19; 6:33, 50–51. Cf. 1:10–11; 3:13; 6:38; 7:33; 8:23; 16:27; 19:11). When he finished the work that the Father sent him to do, thus bringing glory to the Father and making him known in the world, he ascended once more to the world above (17:4–5, 13, 26; 16:5, 28; 20:1). From there he sent the Spirit and from there he will return (14:3; 15:26; 16:7; 21:22). Jesus was sent into this world from the world above to "save" it in the fullest possible sense (3:17).[18]

This dualism does not lend support to the concept of the separation of "heaven" and "earth" (as discussed earlier in the book). Rather it is testimony

---

16. Following NIV.

17. Though John does also present a "this age/age to come" contrast, which is actually central to his overall theology. Jesus not only came into this world from the world above, he came also into *history*. In him, and in the Spirit he sent, "the age to come" invaded this age.

18. The "world" (cosmos) is used in different ways by John, which may be summed up as designating: a) the created world (God's world and therefore good, 1:11) and its people (e.g., 17:24; 12:19, loved by God, 3:16), and b) fallen humanity, those who are at enmity with God (e.g., 7:7). See Ladd, *Theology of the New Testament*, 261–63.

to the constant and ongoing interaction between the two. Jesus, enthroned in heaven, reigns over the whole creation. "All authority *in heaven and on earth*," he said, "has been given to me." God the Spirit is active in this world. The creation is one, and it is God's.

In John the *"ego eimi"* formula ("I, I am"—the pronoun adding emphasis) is used in different ways in the gospel and is obviously a theologically significant expression, echoing an extensive Old Testament background. Seven times the phrase is used by Jesus in combination with a particular metaphor:

I am the bread of life (6:35, 48; cf. 6:41, 51)

I am the light of the world (8:12; cf. 9:5)

I am the door (of the sheep, 10:7, 9)

I am the good shepherd (10:11, 14)

I am the resurrection and life (11:25)

I am the way, truth and life (14:6)

I am the true vine (15:1, 5)

John sometimes places these in the context of one of the seven "signs" or other action of Jesus—e.g., the "bread of life" with the feeding of the five thousand (cf. 6:26-27) and the "light of the world" with the healing of the blind man (cf. 9:39). In these cases "saying" and "sign" illuminate each other. In addition, the phrase is used absolutely as an identifying formula (6:20; 18:5, 6, 8) and as a particular claim to unique identity (8:24, 28; 13:19). Additional meaning is added with its use in John 8:58, "before Abraham was *I am*." This is a deliberate reference to Exodus 3:14, which the LXX translates *"ego eimi."* That this was clearly recognized as a claim to identity with God is evidenced by the Jewish reaction. They intended to stone him for blasphemy (8:59).

Many differences can be noted between John and the other gospels. The parables, for instance, are missing from John. There is no account of the nativity, nor of the baptism of Jesus, the casting out of demons, the transfiguration, Gethsemane, or the last supper. John has nothing to say about repentance. The Synoptics are largely set in Galilee, whereas John focuses on Jerusalem. The Synoptics mention only one Passover, whereas John mentions at least three. There is a difference also in Greek style.

One of the major differences has to do with the cleansing of the temple, which the Synoptics place at the end of Jesus' ministry and present as the culminating motivation on the part of the Jewish authorities for deciding he had to die. John places it at the beginning of Jesus' public ministry (John 2:12–17; he is more concerned with theology than chronology). In John it is the Lazarus miracle that is presented as the final and immediate reason for the decision to put Jesus to death.

THE RAISING OF LAZARUS

The story of the raising of Lazarus is the most astonishing and significant of Jesus' miracles and contains several unusual aspects. The resuscitations in the Synoptics were of those recently dead and unburied. There was some room for doubt perhaps. But Lazarus, it is stressed, had been in the tomb for four days (John 11:17, 39)[19] and the reluctance to open the burial chamber bears testimony to the presumed state of the dead body, i.e., beyond redemption. Then too, those other resuscitations had been in far-off Galilee. Bethany, where Lazarus lived, on the other hand, was on the doorstep of Jerusalem and bore the weight of significant messianic expectation. Those had been relatively private affairs; this was observed by many (John 11:45–46). Though all the resuscitations reveal Jesus' power over death, the raising of Lazarus is in many ways unique. The importance of the sign in John's overall scheme is made obvious by its location, its outcome, and by the sheer length of the account. It is the seventh and final of the signs—obviously the climax of what John is presenting through them—and brings to a head the opposition to Jesus.

The story is complex, tying together the themes, metaphors, and subplots of the rest of the gospel, bringing to a climax the seven signs of the first part and laying the foundation of what is to come. As with the blind man in John 9:3, this sickness of Lazarus is presented by Jesus as being for a greater good. It is for the glory of God to be revealed in the works of Jesus to the end, again, that the disciples might believe (John 11:4, 14). There is implicit in verse four also the real meaning of this final sign as pointing to the death and resurrection of Jesus himself. God's son is greater than death. When the potential danger of the situation is pointed out to Jesus, he is still willing to go. This miraculous resuscitation really does precipitate his death, but in that death Jesus surrenders his life for all who will believe; the good shepherd lays down his life for the sheep.

As we have noted, Martha understood that her brother would have a part in the future resurrection but Jesus had a much greater revelation to bring; *"I am the resurrection and life,"* he declared (John 11:26–26). This forms the highpoint of revelation in the gospel, the climax of everything

---

19. Burial on the day of death was customary for Jews. Beasley-Murray, *John*, 189.

that has come before and the preparation for what will follow. The longed for day of resurrection, Jesus declares, has arrived; the day of restoration is here, now. He is the resurrection power. Israel's exile is over, and the full life, the promised "shalom," the resurrection life, is given *now* to those who believe in him (John 3:36; 5:24; 6:40, 47; etc.). The raising of Lazarus confirms his right and authority to make such a claim. But it will also, in turn, be a picture of the final resurrection, the resurrection Israel has been hoping for, the new exodus. Jesus himself will lead this when he rises from the dead into a whole new level of existence. Jesus himself is the abundant life, the very principle of life; and just as light dispels darkness, so life triumphs over death, first in him and then in those who believe in him. They too will rise when he gives the final command (John 5:25; 1 Thess 4:16).

What Wright says of the mindset of Jesus in general is particularly relevant here. "Jesus believed," he writes, "that Israel's history had arrived at its focal point... that the *exile* had reached its climax... that he himself was the bearer of Israel's destiny at this critical time."[20] Israel's suffering would be focused in him. He would receive forgiveness for the nation, the true Israel who believed in him. He would lead them out of darkness of death back to life in the father's presence. The power of death would be broken, the curse removed.

In the first sign at Cana, at a wedding celebration, Jesus had begun to reveal his glory (John 2:11; 17:5). In the final sign, this time in a situation of mourning, the process is complete. In the victory over death and corruption Jesus' great glory is revealed for all to see (John 11 38-44; cf. 1 Cor 15:26). The day spoken of by Jesus when the dead would hear his voice and come out of their graves is seen to be already present in him, in his presence, in his person (5:24-29).

Lazarus serves also as a picture of Israel—bound in grave clothes, corrupt, seemingly beyond redemption, but not beyond the sound and power of Jesus' voice (John 5:28-29). Eventually, Israel too will be called from the tomb, the grave clothes will be removed, and "all Israel will be saved" (Rom 11:1-10, 25-32). The fullness of God's destiny for Israel, as promised and declared by the prophets, will be fulfilled in and through Jesus.

In the cleansing of the temple with which John opened the account of Jesus' public ministry (John 2:12-22), Jesus had shown that the temple was a *temporary* provision of God. Destroy it, he said, and I will raise up the new temple in three days (which, John tells us, he spoke about his body). John then closes the public ministry of Jesus with the raising of Lazarus, thus tying the two together. The new temple, the new dwelling place of God, is

---

20. Wright, *Challenge of Jesus*, 89.

the temple made without hands, made of living stones. From *this* temple, this living temple, will flow rivers of living water (John 7:38). The image of God is to be restored and he will dwell again with the image-bearers. Jesus' own death and resurrection will make this possible. There is much here that pictures that coming event also—the grave clothes, the tomb with the stone, the victory itself.

We reach the climax of John's believing motif in verses 45-53. What began in the prologue (John 1:11-12) is brought to a head through the raising of Lazarus. Some believe and receive, but some do not. He came to that which was his own but his own received him not. So the raising of Lazarus serves John as the catalyst for the firming of Jewish opinion against Jesus which is to result in his death.

Study of the miracles in their literary context, then, considerably opens up our understanding of these demonstrations of authority performed by Jesus. We can see in this case that the raising of Lazarus is the greatest of Jesus' acts of power and the center of John's gospel. It is both a wonder and a sign. It draws together the themes of the gospel and it points forward to what is to come, serving as a catalyst for Jesus' death through which he accomplished the even greater act of power in rising from the grave himself, the first-fruits of the resurrection promised by the prophets.

SUMMARY OF CHAPTER EIGHT

Jesus was widely known as a worker of miracles. These acts of power were demonstrations of who he was and why he came. They were evidence that a powerful prophet had again come to Israel and, even more, that the age to come had broken in upon those living in this present, evil world.

The literary contexts of the miracle stories reveal new levels of meaning. In John, the raising of Lazarus is the climax of the seven signs of the first part of the gospel and a bridge to what is to follow—the greatest sign of all—the death and resurrection of Jesus himself. In the great declaration that forms the central part of the story and the gospel, John reveals that the longed for time of the restoration of all things is here in the person and works of Jesus the Son of God. The exile of Israel is over, as the prophets predicted. The promised "shalom" is to be found in him, which John calls *eternal* life, or *abundant* life. The temple is not needed anymore, as the dwelling place of God will from henceforth be in the church, in the lives of those who believe in and receive the Son, indwelt eternally by the Spirit.

The long exile of the image-bearers is over. It is finished. The flaming sword has been sheathed for those who believe, and they may freely and boldly enter in once more to the creator's presence; they may freely eat of the tree of life, of the bread that came down from heaven. The coming of Jesus heralded the arrival of the kingdom of God and the breaking in of the age to come. A new order of things had begun. The new wine is served.

But the guardians of the old order were not pleased. A great prophet, mighty in word and deed, had risen in Israel. Some even believed him to be the promised messiah. "What are we accomplishing?" they asked. "Here is this man performing many signs and wonders. If we let him go on like this, everyone will believe in him and then the Romans will come and take away both our temple and our nation" (John 11:45–50).

Then one of them, named Caiaphas, who was high priest that year, spoke up, "You know nothing at all! You do not realize that *it is better for you that one man die for the people than that the whole nation perish.*" Jesus was too dangerous; if allowed to continue these acts of power, everything would have to change. He had to die.

Chapter Nine

JESUS AND THE FATHER

"Jesus often withdrew to lonely places and prayed . . ." (Luke 5:16)

OF ALL THE MYSTERIES of the incarnation, one of the greatest and potentially most instructive has to do with the relationship between Jesus and the Father, particularly in regard to the time Jesus spent in solitary prayer. What need has the second person of the Trinity for prayer? What is it that drives the Son of God to turn aside and spend time alone with the Father? What was the nature, the function, the purpose of this communion? Were they not in continual, uninterrupted relationship and communication? What need had he of these special times?

And wrapped up in the mystery of Jesus' prayer life is the general enigma of prayer itself. Why do we human beings need to pray? Especially puzzling is the place of petitionary and intercessory prayer—human beings making requests of God for themselves and for others, when, as Jesus himself said, "your Father knows what you need before you ask him" (Matt 6:8).

Jesus often withdrew to places where he could be alone to pray (Luke 5:16; 6:12; Matt 14:23; Mark 1:35). There was an aspect of his life, an aspect that concerned his communion with the Father, which was totally private. He invited all to come to him, he made time for small and great alike, and he was often the center of large crowds, but *"he often withdrew to lonely places"* to be alone with the Father. Sometimes he prayed, seemingly, where others could see him (Luke 11:1; Matt 26:36–45), but he prayed often in private (see Heb 7:25). How much of Jesus' prayer life was spent in prophetic intercession is not clear. On one occasion we are told he interceded for Peter (Luke 22:31–32) and, in what is sometimes called his "high priestly" prayer, he interceded for his disciples and for all those who would believe in him (John 17:6–26). His deep concern for Jerusalem (Matt 23:37–39) hints at other occasions for intercession also, and note Hebrews 5:7 and 7:23. In one sense, Jesus' whole life was an act of intercession for the fallen creation (Isa 53:12).

The prophets, of course, had their own devotional lives and often sought God in prayer (Exod 19:3, 8; 33:7–11; Num 11:11; 1 Sam 8:6, 21; Jer 32:16–25), but *intercessory* prayer, particularly, is a prophetic function (1 Sam 12:23). Abraham interceded for Lot and the cities of the plain (Gen 18:16–33) and, on another occasion, for Abimelech (Gen 20:17–18). Samuel interceded for Saul (1 Sam 15:10–11, 35) and for Israel (1 Sam 7:5, 9), as Moses often did also (Exod 32:11–14; 31–34; etc.). Elijah interceded for the widow (1 Kgs 17:20), Isaiah for the people of Judah (2 Chr 32:20), and Ezekiel for the remnant of Israel (Ezek 11:13). Amos interceded for the nation of Israel (Amos 7:2, 5), Jeremiah for the last remnant of Judah as they fled to Egypt (Jer 42:4–22), and Daniel prayed to God for the exiles (Dan 9:4–19). Jeremiah was instructed several times *not* to intercede for the people of Judah (Jer 7:16; 11:4; 14:11), indicating the natural propensity for doing so among the prophets. Much of the prophetic literature is intercessory in function.

The intercession of the prophets was often sought out (Exod 8:8; 10:17; 20:18; Num 12:10–13; 1 Sam 7:8, 12:19; 2 Ki 4:1; Jer 42:1–3), even by Israel's kings, who recognized that this was part of the prophetic function (1 Kgs 22:5–23; 2 Kgs 3:11–19, 19:1–4; Isa 37:1–4; Jer 37:1–3). This again indicates how common and prominent this part of their ministry was. The prophets not only spoke to the people on God's behalf, they also sought God on behalf of the people.

THE ENIGMA OF INTERCESSORY PRAYER

That prayer is required of us also in the New Testament prophetic community is immediately obvious. In the gospels we are instructed to pray (Matt 9:38), we are expected to pray (Matt 6:6), we are urged to pray (Matt 7: 7–8), we are instructed in prayer (Matt 6: 9–15), and we are given the example of Jesus who prayed (Mark 1:35; 6:46; Luke 3:21; 5;16; etc.). The importance of prayer is demonstrated to us (Matt 21:13) and indeed we are commanded to pray (Matt 5:44; 26:41; Luke 21:36; 22:40; John 16:24). The rest of the New Testament is in agreement: "devote yourselves to prayer" (Col 4:2), "pray continually" (1 Thess 5:17), "pray . . . on all occasions" (Eph 6:18), "I want men everywhere to lift up holy hands in prayer" (1 Tim 2:8).

That God is in control of all things is axiomatic. He is the "sovereign God." He is all-knowing, needs no instruction, is never surprised. He comprehends everything—all knowledge of all things and all history—in one great act of knowing. He knows what is needed before it is spoken. He is "all-wise," so he *understands* what is best. He is all goodness and all love, so he *desires* what is best for all. He is all-powerful and can *do* whatever is best. Nothing can thwart his purpose, nor is there anything he cannot do if he wills it or desires it (2 Chr 20:6; Ps 115:3; Ps 135:6; Gen 18:14; Jer 32:17, 27; etc.). He does whatever he pleases whenever it pleases him. The Bible clearly spells this out for us in a number of Old and New Testament references (e.g., Isa 46:10; Ps 135:6; Eph 1:11). So obviously (and thankfully), it is his sovereign will that must always, in the end, carry the day. How then to reconcile the two? How do we solve the apparent tension between these two facts? Why pray for people, events, situations, even for our own needs, if the sovereign will of God must always prevail anyway? What difference can prayer make? What does it matter what we, with our limited knowledge and imperfect understanding, think or desire? God has no need of instruction, nor has he need of urging to act. We will come back to this.

Not all interaction between human beings and God is prayer. Sometimes God acts to bless (Adam and Eve) or to convict (David confronted by Nathan). Sometimes he acts to judge (Adam and Eve driven from Eden, Korah swallowed by the earth, Ananias and Sapphira fall dead in church). Sometimes man curses God, or cries out against him ("crucify him!"). Prayer is the act of a human being who deliberately turns his or her heart and thoughts heavenward to reach out to God and to communicate with him. The amazing thing is that God has anticipated and (because he *is* sovereign) initiated such communication. It is implicit in the creation of the man and woman made "in the image of God" (Gen 1:26–27). They are made for interaction with God. They are made for communion with the creator. This communion is a large part of what makes them human, what they were created to be, how they were created to live. It is in this communion that they become truly human. It is in this communion that the image is fully realized.

Prayer is not asking only. It takes many forms; worship, thanksgiving, intercession, petition, confession, contrition, repentance, warfare, celebration, "seeking" God and more. The aspect that is relevant to our study here is petition, both on behalf of others and in our own interest. To this we will shortly turn. The other aspects of prayer mentioned here are not then part of our problem—so they become part of the answer. Human beings then must pray because prayer is all of these other things.

Worship is at the heart of the believer's prayer. Worship is commanded (Ps 29:2; 96:9; 99:5, 9) and indeed men and women were created to worship (John 4:23). But, in truth, worship is the *automatic* response of a human heart that is in a right relationship with God. In this sense we cannot help but pray. Meditation on the person and works of God leads to revelation and revelation gives birth to worship. *Confession* of sin is a part of repentance and again is commanded of us (1 John 1:9). *Thanksgiving* is urged upon us. "In everything give thanks—for this is the will of God in Christ Jesus concerning you" (1 Thess 5:18). Thanksgiving reminds us of God's goodness, it brings glory to God (Ps 69:30), and it brings life's difficulties into perspective. There is also *celebration*—the joyful expression of our love for God, a rejoicing in his presence, and the demonstration of our appreciation for his goodness to us. Celebration is often a *corporate* expression of worship or prayer.

The Bible refers also to "seeking" God (Ps 24:1–6; 27:4, 8). This is to deliberately reorient our lives to him, to draw aside from the mundane, the temporal, the distracting—all that cloaks the reality of God from our minds and hearts—to climb the mountain and do business with the Almighty. Often we are *driven* to such prayer by our needs and experiences—God's wise grace at work again. We are driven by inadequacy, by adverse circumstances, by powerful emotions—driven to seek God, to cry out to him for help. Abraham Lincoln once said, "I have been driven many times to my knees by the overwhelming conviction that I had nowhere else to go."[1] On these occasions we do not pause to ask "what is prayer?" "should I pray?" or "is prayer effective?" We *must* pray; we cannot help it—we are at the end of ourselves and must have help. Driven by some primeval knowledge, or drawn by infinite love, we turn again to our creator, to him who is greater, stronger, all-sufficient. We do not turn there in vain (Jer 29:13–14).

We must also seek God for guidance (Jer 10:23). He has given human beings many wonderful faculties and abilities, but not the ability to order our own steps or to walk independently of his guidance and instruction. Prayer is an admission of our dependent relationship with God, of our need for him. It is an expression of faith that he *is* and that he is willing and able to help. There is sometimes too an experience of a kind of "warfare" in prayer. In one sense, a lot of prayer is warfare—a battle that is fought first of all against our own spiritual inertia. One commentator says (on behalf of us all)

---

1. Quoted by Fosdick, *The Meaning of Prayer*, 15.

"it is a permanent mystery to me why I do not pray more."[2] We must pray as part of the battle to overcome the "flesh" and to be led by the Spirit. Then too there is some indication in the Bible that in prayer we sometimes engage spiritual forces, as with Daniel (Dan 10:12–13, 20–21). The armor of God (Eph 6:10) has to do with righteous living and knowledge of God's word but with this comes the command to "pray in the Spirit on all occasions with all kinds of prayers and requests . . ." (v 18). Prayer is surely a necessary part of the battle. All of these then *will* be done and *must* be done—and all of these are prayer.

The *pattern* for prayer was given to us by Jesus himself (Matt 6:9–13) in which the priority was to be—after the acknowledgement of our privileged relationship with him—intercession for the establishment of his eschatological kingdom on earth and its spread to all the nations: "your kingdom come, your will be done on earth as it is in heaven."[3] The prophetic church, as was Israel before it, is tasked with interceding for the nations (Isa 56:7). After that we are encouraged to petition God for our personal needs both physical and spiritual. Obviously then, there is a place for intercession and petition in the economy of human interaction with God.

To come back to our main question, these two related categories—petition and intercession—are the basic mysteries. How is it that a man or woman can dare to ask God to alter the laws of the universe for their benefit alone? How can the finite order the infinite? If the sovereign will of God prevails in all things, then what difference can our petition make? Perhaps the problem is best stated for us by C. S. Lewis when he asks, "Can we believe that God ever really modified his actions in response to the suggestions of men? For infinite wisdom does not need telling what is best, and infinite goodness needs no urging to do it."[4]

The problem is even deeper than this, though. I am one of several billions of people on the earth. The destinies of many of us are entwined. What I pray for, if granted, will impact the lives of many others, in turn affecting other lives in an ever-increasing circle. Many of those people are praying also—petitions of which I know nothing and which are possibly completely different, maybe even contradictory to mine. I am praying for sunny weather for the church picnic, the farmer down the road for rain.

---

2. Casey, *Towards God*, 103.

3. Note that Jesus' focus is on the establishment of the kingdom here on earth. The focus of much of modern Christianity is on heaven; but heaven is, of course, a temporary place of residence for those who die before Jesus returns. Jesus is coming back to reign on earth, and he will bring with him the souls of those who have died. There will be a resurrection to physical life on the new earth.

4. Lewis, *Subject and Structure*, 445.

Somehow God is working through the destinies of all these people, through all of their petitions (with his knowledge of their *real* needs, which may or may not be the same as those they are praying for), to somehow bring about an answer to *my* prayers, in which I may well be asking him to intervene miraculously in the created world and the answer to which may depend upon events already transpired or still to come. "Most of our prayers," to quote Lewis again, "if fully analyzed, ask either for a miracle, or for events whose foundation will have to have been laid before I was born, indeed, laid when the universe began."[5] Still another complicating factor is that God in his great love and wisdom will sometimes deny my request for reasons I may never understand and expect me to trust in his wisdom and foreknowledge. Not all petitions are granted. "In Gethsemane," Lewis says, "the holiest of all petitioners prayed three times that a certain cup might pass from Him. It did not."[6]

So of what use is this prophetic function of intercession? Why pray? What difference will my intercession make? How will my petition turn the mighty hand of the infinite God?

LESSONS FROM ADAM AND EVE

God created men and women to work. He created the world in such a way that Adam and Eve's labor was needed to complete it, or to cause it to yield up its treasures (Gen 2:15, 19–20; 2 Thess 3:10). God gives soil and seed, he sends rain and sun, but human labor is needed to sow and to reap. God lifts men and women to work at his side, the creator dignifies his creatures by requiring their partnership in the creation. God created the world to supply the needs of those made in his image, but they must *work* to release the fullness of the creative potential.

So God has seemingly purposed it in the spiritual realm also, building into his great redemptive plan the need for our prayer. "Ask," Jesus said, "and you will receive." God again requires the participation of human beings in his work. In prayer also, he dignifies the creature. God needs neither human work nor human prayer, but he has nevertheless ordered things in such a way that both are required to complete his work. An inconvenience to God, perhaps, but a wonderful, dignifying blessing for those made in his image. Prayer, it seems, is part of God's sovereign plan, one of the factors he has taken into account in the fashioning and outworking of his infinitely wise purpose for human beings. God has made room for men and women to

---

5. Lewis, *Miracles*, 189.
6. Lewis, *Subject and Structure*, 443.

work at his side. And just as unsown seed will never produce a harvest, so it is terribly possible that without the participation of men and women in prayer, certain aspects of God's redemptive program might not be realized in the lives of some individuals or situations. We must pray. We must accept the prophetic responsibility to interceded for people, for situations, and for the nations.

Our personal devotional life is also, in some measure, the restoration of the Adamic privilege of walking with God. When we first see the man and woman in the Bible, we see them as God intended them to be (Gen. 2:7, 15–22; 3:8). The fallen creatures we see in the world today are not what God intended. He created something much higher by far, much grander, much more wonderful. The man and the woman were the heads of God's creation, beings standing with one foot in both worlds—living in this "good" physical world, but in communion with the spiritual realm also. In the lives of Adam and Eve before the fall, we see a divine pattern that can be restored in our lives through prayer. Adam and Eve were in direct and regular *communion* with God (Gen 3:8—not stated, but implicit, I think, in the verse). They alone, of all the creation, walked and talked with the creator. They enjoyed the divine perspective on their lives. To all that they did, they brought the benefit of this regular and open communion with God. Their souls were daily enriched and refreshed as they drew spiritual power from this regular contact. Their hearts were filled with the peace, assurance, and encouragement, their entire beings with the dignity, authority, and joy that arose from spending time in the presence of the creator. And all of that, all the benefits of that regular communion, they brought to their God-given work and ministry over creation. The man and the woman, alone of all the created things, were able to intelligently commune with God, to *know* him and to speak his words and will into the creation. It was in this communion, there in the solitude of the garden in the cool of the evening, that the man and the woman were fully revealed in the image of God. They were never more human than in this encounter. There in God's presence, walking and talking with him, they were truly the sons of God.

So Jesus—representative man, the perfect image, the Son of God—must often withdraw to a solitary place to walk and talk with the Father. So we too, the sons of God ("for that is what we are," 1 John 3:1), must regularly seek out the solitary place to commune with the Father (Matt 6:6). There, in deliberate, intelligent, communion with God, are we truly the image of himself that God intended. On our knees we reach the highest.

Secondly, Adam and Eve lived in *dependence* on God (Gen 1:29; 2:8, 9, 15–16). They depended on him for their daily provision (channeled to them through their work) and for the fulfillment of their destinies. Thirdly, Adam and Eve lived in *submission* to God. (Gen 2:15, 19–20). They worked for God (Gen 2:17) and they lived under his commandment (Gen 3:1–10). So prayer too is, in essence, a submission to the will of God, an acknowledgment of his right to direct—"nevertheless, not my will, but yours be done." It is, in effect, an eating from the tree of life, a rejection of the tree of autonomy.

So we must pray *even if God never granted a single request*, because prayer lifts us up, completes us, consummates our creation and our existence. Prayer does not bring God down, but—wonderful privilege—it lifts us up to him. Prayer is the way we regain and maintain the divine perspective, enabling us to keep our lives in right order and balance. Through prayer there comes a harmonization of our will and character with God's. Prayer changes us. We become like him; we commune with. We must pray, we must intercede, we must work thus with the creator. We must fulfill our prophetic function and mandate to intercede for justice, righteousness, mercy, grace, and salvation. We must fulfill the requirement of the house of God to intercede for the nations, that all will be brought into the place of God's blessing.

SUMMARY OF CHAPTER NINE

Prayer is many things besides petition that do not in any way conflict with the sovereignty of God: some prayers are automatic, like worship; some are necessary, like thanksgiving, confession, and celebration. Some are inevitable, like warfare, and to the seeking of God we are often driven by great and wise grace. Prayer in essence is communion with God. It was the sovereign will of God that he give to his creatures the infinitely precious gift of communion with him in his rule over the creation.

Corporate prayer is required, beneficial, a wonderful expression of human fellowship with God. But it is the solitary walk with God in the cool of the evening, the oft withdrawing to lonely places to be alone with him, the personal face-to-face encounter in the tent of meeting, the time with him alone in the room with the closed door, the encounter in the secret place . . . these are the intimate times of communion that build and strengthen our relationship with God. If Jesus needed this, how much more do we need it?

Finally, we have seen that in petition and intercession God's grace has been extended to us, and rather than being in conflict with his sovereign plan, prayer is in fact part of that plan. In prayer, as in the physical labor of men and women, God has made room for, and in fact required, the cooperation of human beings with him in his work. It is a means he has initiated to give dignity to his creation. We have therefore a great responsibility to work together with God, especially in prayer, to intercede, to petition him, that his kingdom will come and that his will be done on earth as it is in heaven. Prayer is in fact a prophetic task and a channel for the kingdom to come on earth.

So Jesus "often withdrew to solitary places to pray." Last Adam and second man, he once again walks with God in the cool of the evening. The prophet like Moses, he regularly goes to the tent of meeting outside the camp. Representative man and perfect image, he does not seek autonomy from God but seeks regular personal and private communion with him. Sinless, he has no need to hide from God. The greatest of the prophets, he intercedes for those who will follow him into the new creation—the elect, the people of God.

In prayer we become "like him," made in his image. We share his concerns and his priorities for the people around us and for the nations. We become intercessors; we become the house of God where prayer is offered for the nations. We bear the mantle of this intercession for the nations; to this prophetic function the church is called. God forbid that the house grow silent, the cry of intercession fail, the praying hands be lowered. God forbid that we should fail to pray.

We cannot, of course, fully enter into the communion between Father and Son, but we can note, from that communion, that the Father loves the Son and the Son loves the Father. This is the song of the biblical revelation that we must learn to sing, that we must become—by choice—a part of. The Father seeks in all of the created order to glorify the Son and the Son seeks always to bring glory to the Father, and in a sense, the whole life of Jesus is a prophetic intercession for the fallen creation. He came to redeem it, and when he has completed that work he will hand it back to the Father, cleansed, perfected, and renewed, that "God might be all in all" (1 Cor 15:20–28).

Chapter Ten

JESUS AND THE SPIRIT

"These men are not drunk as you suppose. It's only nine in the morning! No, this is what was spoken by the prophet Joel..." (Acts 2:15)

CLOSELY ASSOCIATED WITH THE coming of the messiah in the prophets was the inauguration of a new covenant and the general outpouring of God's Spirit (see Jer 31:31–34; Ezek 11:19–20; 18:31; 36:26–27; 37:14; 39:29; Isa 32:15; 44:3). The messiah's coming would bring about the general fulfillment of the prophetic prayer of Moses, who desired that all of God's people might enjoy the intimate relationship with God through the Spirit that was afforded the prophets. For those made in his image (made to be like him, 1 John 3:2), the knowledge of God is the whole purpose of the divine revelation. That revelation culminates, of course, in Jesus, and it is the Spirit who brings about that knowledge (John 16:14). This intimate knowledge of the Father through the Word and the Spirit was always God's intention and will for all human beings and is the most wonderful of all creation's treasures, worth every cost and every sacrifice (Phil 3:7–11; Col 2:2–3).[1] Moses recognized this, and he desired that everyone might be afforded this great privilege. The outpoured Spirit made all of God's people prophets as

---

1. Why did God create? To lavish his goodness on a people made in his image so they could enjoy him. Behold the goodness of God.

he foresaw—men and women who would know God, hear from God, and speak for God.[2]

The point of Peter's sermon on the day of Pentecost was that this great blessing that God had intended, that Moses had desired, and that the prophets had promised was now fulfilled. *"This,"* he said (what was experienced by the Christians and the observable charismatic phenomena that accompanied it), "is the promised outpouring of God's Spirit, which proves Jesus must be the Messiah" (Acts 2:14–36). Many of those who heard this were convinced he was right and became followers of Jesus the messiah the same day (Acts 2:37–41). The Spirit leads to Jesus.

THE SPIRIT AND PROPHECY IN THE OLD TESTAMENT

In the Old Testament the Spirit was recognized as the source of the word of God (2 Sam 23:2; 1 Chr 12:18; 2 Chr 15:1; 20:14–15; 24:20; Isa 59:21; 61:1; Ezek 11:5; Mic 3:8; Zech 7:12). The Spirit was also clearly identified as the source of prophecy (1 Sam 10:5–6, 9–11; Num 11:25–26; 1 Sam 19:19–20, 23–24; cf. Gen 41:38; Joel 2:28–29).[3] He was the source of the prophetic ministry (Neh 9:30; Ezek 2:2; 3:24; 8:3; Mic 3:8; Zech 7:12) and of the visions given to the prophets (Ezek 11:24. Cf. also Dan 4:8–9, 18; 5:11, 14; Acts 7:51–53). This was acknowledged by both the earlier prophets like Elijah and Elisha (2 Kgs 2:9–15) and also later prophets like Isaiah and Ezekiel (Isa 61:1; Ezek 2:2; 3:12–27).

Isaiah reminded God's people that it was the Spirit who guided the history of Israel from the beginning (Isa 63:10–14). If they disobey the Spirit they would be opposed by him (Isa 63:10), but when they follow his leading, their lives and hearts would be transformed and purified (see Ezek 36:26–27). Their hope for the future is that God's Spirit will renew their relationship with him (Isa 44:3–5; Ezek 11:19–20) and send them a new ruler filled with wisdom and justice (Isa 11:2–5). So the Spirit was the driving force behind the whole Old Testament prophetic ministry and facilitator of Israel's relationship with God.

This has important ramifications for the New Testament preaching ministry; Spirit-anointed preaching of the word of God in the New Testament is "prophetic" in the sense of speaking to the church on behalf of God, or bringing the word of God to the people of God (cf. Luke 4:18). The

---

2. The anointing of the Spirit also made all of God's people "kings" and "priests" (1 Pet 2:9; Rev 1:6; 5:10).

3. Even the pagan prophet Balaam uttered oracles by the Spirit of God (Num 24:2).

preacher has spent time with God, has heard from God, and comes to the pulpit with what he or she believes is a word from God. This is a part of the prophetic function. This, in turn, will help our understanding of passages such as 1 Corinthians 14:1–32 (especially vv 1, 3–5; cf. vv 19, 24, 26, 29–31). The church is a prophetic community and the church service should be a place where the prophetic word of God is heard and received. In this way the church is edified, built up, and strengthened.[4]

JESUS AND THE SPIRIT

The life and ministry of Jesus are not to be fully understood without taking into account the part played by the Holy Spirit. As Word and Spirit worked together in the first creation, so they do in the new creation. As they acted inseparably in Genesis chapter one, so they worked inseparably in the gospels. The gospel story began when the angel Gabriel was sent to Mary with the message that she would conceive and bear a son. To Mary's question "How will this be?" Gabriel answered, "The Holy Spirit will come upon you and the power of the most high will overshadow you" (Luke 1:26–35). Matthew says, "[Mary] was found to be with child *by the Holy Spirit*" (Matt 1:18). This is immensely helpful in understanding the person and work of Jesus. He was born of a virgin, conceived through the overshadowing of the Spirit. Exactly how, we are not told, nor is it important; the fact is it came about through the power and agency of the Holy Spirit. He had a human mother but that mother was found to be with child by the Holy Spirit. So while he was perfectly human, he was at the same time fully God. Not half man and half God, but both at the same time, both at once, both human and divine.[5] Because he was born of the *Holy* Spirit he was holy; he was sinless. He came "in the likeness of sinful man" (Rom 8:3) but had no fallen nature.

At the dedication of Jesus (Luke 2:22–35) we see how the Holy Spirit directed operations as the child was presented at the temple. The prophets

---

4. The reason prophecy is preferred over tongues in this passage is not because tongues is inferior or somehow undesirable—verse 26 includes tongues in a list of things that must be done for the strengthening of the church, and verse 4 tells us those speak in tongues strengthen themselves spiritually. Paul is thankful to God that he speaks in tongues more than anyone else and declares he would like everyone to speak in tongues. Prophecy is preferred over tongues here for the simple reason that there is no need to interpret it as it is spoken in the common language. The motivation for these prophetic giftings is the strengthening of the church, and verse 5 makes it clear that, when interpreted, tongues messages function in the same way as prophecy.

5. Though we have to remember, too, that he existed before the incarnation (John 1:1–5, 14).

Simeon and Anna had been prepared by the Spirit for this day (Luke 2:26). Under the Spirit's anointing, Simeon prophesied that the messiah was here in Jesus and his work would affect Israel, would affect the Gentiles, and there would be an aspect that would also pierce the heart of his mother Mary.[6]

Each one of the gospel writers makes a point of telling us of the Spirit coming upon Jesus as a dove at his baptism (Matt 3:16–17; Mark 1:9–11; Luke 3:21–22; John 1:32–34). Mark notes the heavens were "torn open" as the Spirit descended, a reference to the cry of Isaiah: "Oh that you would rend the heavens and come down!" (Isa 64:1). The Spirit descended from the realm above, and he bought all the life and power of that realm into this. In the Spirit, heaven and earth were joined together. "The Spirit," John notes in reference to Jesus, then "remains on him." Jesus is, in all of the gospels, "the anointed one," the messiah, the Christ, God's anointed. The dove is an image taken from the original creation when "the Spirit of God was hovering over the oceans" (Gen 1:2), a symbol of immense power, of divine purpose, and of creative intent.

After his baptism, Jesus (now "full of the Spirit") was sent by the Spirit into the wilderness (Luke 4:1–2; Mark 1:12) where he was to be tested as Adam had been tested before him. Jesus' ministry is thereafter undertaken *in the power of the Spirit* (Luke 4:14–21). As prophesied by Isaiah (Isa 61:1–9), Jesus claimed a unique anointing of the Spirit to bring in the kingdom and the Day of the Lord. In Jesus, the king had come and the eschatological age of the Spirit had begun.[7]

The process of what the New Testament means by "salvation" is spelled out in Acts 2:38: "Repent and be baptized, every one of you, in the name of Jesus Christ for the forgiveness of your sins. *And you will receive the gift of the Holy Spirit.*" The end of God's saving plan is the dwelling of the Spirit in the lives of his people. In order for this to happen Jesus had to come and redeem those people. In theological terms, the intended eschatological result of the "Christ event" was that those made in his image would now also be filled with his Spirit. Jesus the redeemer would be Jesus the baptizer in the Spirit. John the Baptist identified Jesus (by revelation) as the source of the Spirit within the new creation (John 1:32–34), and Jesus himself confirmed this (John 7:37–39; 14:15–17; 16:7). It was from him that the river of living

---

6. Along with the great privilege of being the messiah's mother came a great cost. Prophecy prepared Mary for the great hardship that lay ahead. It's interesting that Mary had not been told this by Gabriel at first (that we are aware of). Prophecy of a great and glorious future does not necessarily tell the full story.

7. The work of the Spirit in Jesus' life also brought him into conflict with the demonic realm (Matt 12:28–29). Jesus came in the power of the Spirit to bind the strongman and plunder his house (see Mark 3:22–30).

water would flow, bringing life wherever it reached.[8] The new age would be the age of the Spirit. God's people would be a prophetic people; indwelt by the Spirit, filled with the Spirit, led by the Spirit, called by the Spirit, gifted by the Spirit, anointed by the Spirit and, as a body, prepared by the Spirit for the return of Jesus.

After his resurrection, Jesus instructed the disciples that they were to wait for the coming of the Spirit upon them before they entered upon their own ministry tasks. He was the *promised* (by the prophets) Spirit whom Jesus himself would send (Luke 24:45–49). New Testament ministry is to be undertaken in the prophetic power of the Spirit (Acts 1:4–8; Luke 24:49).

THE CHURCH AND THE SPIRIT

The New Testament church was born on the day of Pentecost when the Holy Spirit fell on the believers and they "spoke in tongues" (Acts 2:1–41), a form of ecstatic prophetic speech (cf. 1 Sam 10:9–10, etc.). Peter explained that this was the fulfillment of the prophecy of Joel 2:28–32.[9] Peter commanded those convicted by his words to repent and be baptized in order to receive the Holy Spirit as God had purposed and promised for all believers. The church then met regularly to receive instruction through the Apostles' teaching, to fellowship, to break bread, and to pray (Acts 2:42–47). They met publically in the temple and in private homes, and as they met together with the Spirit they experienced a sense of awe—with signs, wonders, and miracles taking place among them. There was a sharing of possessions, favor with other people, and a constant stream of conversions that swelled their numbers daily. The kingdom had come on earth and it was a Spirit-empowered kingdom.

Peter healed a lame man at the temple gates and explained what he did to the witnesses (Acts 3:1–26). He had healed the man by the power of Jesus, whom they had disowned then handed over to Pilate to be killed, but whom God had then raised from the dead (3:1–26). Peter exhorted them to repent and promised them forgiveness of sins and *"times of refreshing."* He cited Deuteronomy 18:15, 18–19 as fulfilled in Jesus; he was the predicted prophet like Moses. All of these things, he said, fulfilled the promises and predictions of all the prophets and are the fulfillment of God's covenant with Abraham. What God had promised to Abraham 2,000 years before,

---

8. Then they would flow consequently from all believers; see John 7:38.

9. He also cited Psalm 16:8–11 as fulfilled by Jesus' resurrection ("you will not abandon me to the grave, nor will you let your Holy One see decay").

he brought to fulfillment in and through Jesus and the infilling of the Holy Spirit.

PAUL AND THE SPIRIT

The Spirit played a core role in Paul's understanding of the gospel. For him it is the Spirit who makes effective in the world, church, and believer everything that Jesus accomplished in his life, death, and resurrection. The Spirit is the key to everything in the Christian life, from conversion to the ongoing work of change and growth, to revelation, and to gifting and empowerment for ministry. It is the Spirit who reveals truth, who gives anointing and power for miracles, and the Spirit is at the center of the shared life of the new community.

That the Old Testament formed the foundation for Paul's theology of the Holy Spirit and his work is shown by the many quotations from, and allusions to, the Old Testament Scriptures in his writings. For example, the body is the "temple" of the Holy Spirit (1 Cor 6:19), believers corporately form that temple (I Cor 3:16; 2 Cor 6:16; Eph 2: 21–22), and those who worship by the Spirit are the true circumcision (Phil 3:3).

Paul saw the Spirit as the fulfillment of the Old Testament eschatological hope, as is evident from his references to the "promised" Holy Spirit (Gal 3:14; Eph 1:13). He also speaks of the Spirit writing on the human heart (2 Cor 3:3), referencing the Old Testament promises of a new covenant; and again in Romans 7:6 Paul speaks of the "new way" of the Spirit. References to the Old Testament language of a "pouring out" of the Spirit are seen in Paul also (Rom 5:5; Titus 3:6). For Paul, the way to God's abundant life is no longer through observing Torah (the law) but by believing in Jesus and being led by the Spirit.

There are two discernible aspects to the Old Testament promises of the gift of the Spirit. Some of the prophecies speak of an *internal* work of sanctification and renewal (Ezek 11:19–20; 36:25–27; Jer 31:31–34), others of an *external* outpouring and empowering resulting in supernatural manifestations (Joel 2:28–32; cf. Isa 32:15; 44:3; Ezek 39:29). While Luke makes much of the external aspect in Acts, in Paul the predominance of direct references to the Spirit are to his internal work of personal transformation in the life of the believer. He is the "Spirit of holiness" (Rom 1:3), or the "Holy" Spirit (Rom 5:5; 14:7; 15:13; etc.), who sanctifies the believer (Rom 15:16; 1 Cor 6:11; 2 Thess 2:13). He is the one who circumcises the heart (Rom 2:29). He is the one who mediates the love of God to the heart of the believer (Rom 5:5). It is he who opposes and overcomes the sinful nature in the life of the believer (see Rom 8), who gives wisdom and revelation (Eph 1:17; 3:5). He washes and renews (Tit 3:5) and brings understanding of the deep things of God (1 Cor 2: 10–15). The character, or ethical qualities, of the Christ-life which believers were to live out are described as the "fruit of the Spirit" (Gal 5:22–25). It is obvious that for Paul the Spirit, not Torah, was now the key to the whole inner, sanctifying work of God in the lives of believers. This was in fulfillment of the prophetic promises to Abraham and to Israel.

Of course Paul does refer to the "external" work of the Spirit also. Though not at first as evident as his references to the Spirit's internal sanctifying ministry, it nevertheless obviously formed an important part of his theology. "Paul's understanding of the Spirit," a commentator writes, "is what might today be called a "charismatic" understanding. He is in the Old Testament tradition, in which the Spirit comes on individuals powerfully and visibly to inspire prophecy and mighty actions (e.g., Jdg 14:6; 1 Sam 10:10). Only now this is not restricted to the occasional experience of the few, but is for all who are in Christ."[10] In the new creation all have received the Spirit, the Church is a charismatic and prophetic body.

Thus Paul sees the Spirit at work not only *in* the believer but also *through* the believer in supernatural ways, in spiritual gifts, and especially in prophetic utterance, by means of which God speaks to believers to encourage, strengthen, and to guide. Paul makes it clear that all believers, men and women, may participate in this part of the Spirit's activity (1 Cor 11:4–5; 14:31. Cf. Acts 2:17–18). In the coming of the Holy Spirit the new eschatological age has arrived and it is a Spirit-anointed, Spirit-led, Spirit-empowered age.

In 1 Corinthians Paul deals with the supernatural "manifestations of the Spirit" at some length. Some might say that were it not for the problems that arose in Corinth in this area, Paul's writings would be almost devoid of reference to this side of the Spirit's activity so it was obviously not important to him. However, it could in fact be argued the other way round, that Paul dealt so much with the internal aspect because this was the "problem" area, the one that needed his attention—the early Christians having no "problems" when it came to the external, experiential, aspect of the Spirit's work because it was very much taken for granted as the common experience of Christians at that time. The first century Christian community into which Paul came, as is evident from Acts, was a group of people for whom the Holy Spirit was more than a mere theology or doctrine. He was for them a present, experiential reality, and the supernatural manifestations of the

---

10. Wenham, *Paul*, 231.

Spirit were not only common, but indeed in some ways defined the Christian community.

There were several ways in which the early Christians experienced the Spirit, a commentator says: in the perception of God's imminence during worship, in the working of miracles, in the inspiration of prophecy, the experience of boldness and wisdom to proclaim the gospel, and in the feeling of joy.[11] So the Spirit *experienced* was the accepted and taken-for-granted milieu, or environment, in which Paul found himself upon conversion. The outpoured Spirit was the matrix from which the new people of God emerged. The experience of Pentecost formed the paradigm under which the early Christians operated in their Christian mission.

J. D. Dunn outlines what he sees as three strands to Paul's theology—justification, "Christ mysticism," and the gift of the Spirit. The first two, he says, were distinctively Pauline, whereas the third was characteristic of the broad spectrum of early Christianity. "The sect of the Nazarenes," he says, "was evidently marked out within first century Judaism by its claim to have been given the Spirit of God in a new and exceptional way."[12]

In Paul's debate with the Galatians, his argument starts with the fact that they received the Spirit (Gal 1:2-3) as was evidenced by the supernatural results that followed (Gal 3:5). Possession of the Spirit was the defining mark of the Christian (Rom 8:9) and was evidence of inclusion in God's eschatological people (Rom 8:14). The Spirit empowered Paul's own mission work, again with supernatural manifestations (Rom 15:19). The supernatural gifts so evident in Corinth were "manifestations of the Spirit" (1 Cor 12:7-11; 14:1-40). There was an "anointing" of the Spirit as well as an inner residence (2 Cor 1:21). As part of Christian worship there is a "filling" of the Spirit, which is suggestively contrasted by Paul with getting drunk on wine (Eph 5:8). In Paul's experience the power of the Holy Spirit accompanied the preaching of the gospel, producing deep conviction and then joy when responded to (1 Thess 1:5-6). It will be seen that most of these references are allusions to the Spirit's work that evidently require no explanation. So, as Dunn writes again, "the degree to which Paul could assume that his imagery [of the Spirit] would resonate with his audience's own experience is itself indicative that the first Christian talk of the Spirit referred to what they all had experienced when they first believed."[13]

---

11. See Paige, *Dictionary of Paul and His Letters*, 405.

12. Dunn, *The Theology of Paul*, 440. They were "justified with God, bonded with Christ, gifted with the Spirit."

13. Dunn, *Christ and the Spirit*, 428.

It is evident from all of this that for Paul the *experience* of the Spirit was *the essential evidence,* and the great privilege, of the Christian life. To become a follower of messiah Jesus was to receive the Spirit, with all that that meant. Christians were people of the Spirit; they had received the Spirit, they walked in the Spirit, they were led by the Spirit, and they spoke by the Spirit. God sent his Spirit, says Wright, "to make his people truly what they were before only in theory and in hope—his own children, heirs of the world."[14]

It is important for us to note that while the gifts and outward manifestations of the Spirit were important to Paul,[15] he was aware that these were temporary, for "between the times" only. The lasting work of the Spirit was that which took place in the heart (1 Cor 13:8–13). The character produced by the Spirit, not the outward manifestations, wonderful and necessary as they were, was the important thing (1 Cor 13:1–7). Thus, we see in Paul that the Spirit was essentially involved in major areas of theology and practice—in sanctification, in adoption (as sons/heirs), in liberation, in illumination, guidance, power, in the proclamation of the gospel, in charismatic gifting, and in the shared life of the new community.

For Paul, the Spirit formed the essence of this shared community life. The believers were corporately the dwelling place of the Spirit (Eph 2:22) and they were baptized by the one Spirit into one body (1 Cor 12:13). Thus in the Spirit (as in Christ) all differences of race or status or gender became of no theological importance and the Spirit himself was the living water from which they corporately drew life (1 Cor 12:13b). The Spirit was the gift in which all the believers shared. He was the force that drew them together. He it was who bound the community together in peace, and every effort was to be made to maintain that unity of the Spirit (Eph 4:3–4). This peace in the Holy Spirit was to Paul one of the hallmarks (along with righteousness and joy) of the kingdom of God itself (Rom 14:17). The shared life of the Spirit was extremely important to the apostle, and he strongly warned those who would seek to destroy the body corporate (1 Cor 3:16) or grieve the Spirit by behaving in a way that damaged personal relationships within the community (Eph 4:30). The best gifts, Paul stressed, are those that strengthen the community (1 Cor 14:1–5, 12). The *fruit of the Spirit* encapsulated the lifestyle conducive to community peace, a lifestyle in step with the Spirit and contrasted with the sinful nature that produced passions that would

---

14. Wright, *Gospel in Paul*, 230.

15. 1 Cor 14:18 makes it plain that speaking in tongues was very important for him personally, if prophecy was most important in the gathered community.

destroy the community (Gal 5:13–26). The people of God were to live in the unity of the Spirit.

Christianity, for Paul, was not the individualistic, private, religious experience it is for many today; it was essentially a communal sharing of the life of the new age, and at the heart of it was the shared experience of the Holy Spirit (2 Cor 13:14; Phil 2:1). A shared experience of his imminent presence, grace, and power. A shared experience of the life and powers of the coming age in fulfillment of the promises and predictions of the prophets.

THE ESCHATOLOGICAL SPIRIT

There has been a lot of debate over the "center" of Pauline theology. Was there one overarching concept that bound all of his theology together, one concept under which it could all be summed up? Was there one central reality on which he based his theology? This debate has thrown up a number of possible alternatives such as justification by faith, reconciliation, incorporation in Christ, Christ himself in his saving work, the antithesis of Spirit and letter of the law and so on. These proposals each have their supporters but others argue that they are all too narrow. One commentator notes that only a wide-angle perspective that sees God the Father planning, superintending, and consummating redemption can gather all aspects of Pauline theology into such an integrated unity.[16] There is a consensus among many scholars now that the only perspective large enough to contain all the Pauline motifs and emphases is to see the true center in the eschatological nature of Paul's understanding of the work of God in Christ.

We have seen that the Old Testament view of God's redemptive program involved two ages, the present evil age and the age of righteousness to come (cf. Matt 12:32; Luke 18:30; 20:34–35; Eph 1:21). Paul indeed reflects this in his writing, speaking in some places of "this age" (1 Cor 1:20; 2:6; 2:8; 3:18; 2 Cor 4:4; cf. 1 Tim 6:17; Titus 2:12), the "present evil age" (Gal 1:4), and the present world that is passing away (1 Cor 7:31). He contrasts also the present and the future (Rom 8:8, 38; 1 Cor 3:22; cf. 1 Tim 4:8) and the "temporary" with the "eternal" (2 Cor 4:18). It is plain, however, that Paul believed that the future age (the new creation, Gal 6:15; 2 Cor 5:17) foretold by the Old Testament prophets had in fact begun with the death and resurrection of Jesus, or rather—in a radical change to the prevailing dualistic view of the "ages"—that the future age had broken into the present age so that there is in fact an overlap. We live now "in between the times," awaiting the return of Christ for the fulfillment and consummation of God's

---

16. Howell, *Bibliotheca Sacra*, 70.

redemptive program (see Rom 8:23). This "already / not yet" eschatology integrates almost everything in Paul's writing and all of the other suggested "centers" can be fitted into this larger category. Gordon Fee goes so far as to say that it seems impossible to understand Paul without beginning with this already / not yet eschatological understanding as the essential framework of his theology.[17]

For Paul, the "already" that has broken in is the *Spirit*. The new age has come in the person of the Holy Spirit. This can clearly be seen in his contrasting of the sinful nature ("flesh") and the Spirit (Rom 8:5-17; Gal 5:16-26; 6:8), the circumcision in the flesh with the circumcision of heart by the Spirit (Rom 8:29), the old way of the law and the new way of the Spirit (Rom 7:6; 8:2; Gal 1:2-4), the temporary ministry of the letter that brought death and the lasting ministry of the Spirit which brings life (2 Cor 3:7-11). For Paul the gifted Spirit was evidence that the age to come had invaded the present age. Salvation then, in this new age, is not merely to be understood with the mind, it is appropriated experientially in and through the Holy Spirit. He is the deposit which guarantees the final outcome, and he is both the essence and source of life "between the times."

So for Paul the Spirit is a "seal" (Eph 1:13; 4:30; cf. 2 Cor 1:22), the "first-fruits" (Rom 8:23), a "deposit" and "guarantee" (2 Cor 1:21; 5:5; Eph 1:14; cf. 2 Tim 1:14), a "down payment" in the lives of believers on the wonderful life that will be theirs in full at the return of Christ.

THE SPIRIT AND THE SONS OF GOD

In a long argument that takes up the first twelve chapters of Romans, the apostle Paul lays out the essence of his gospel. This is what he received by revelation and this is what he preaches. This is his understanding of what it means that Jesus came and died and rose and ascended. The caricature that passes for the gospel in the understanding of much of the church today, "the good news that Jesus died for my sins so I could be forgiven and go to heaven when I die," bears little resemblance to what Paul lays out here. To Paul, the gospel is the whole saving plan of God, embracing the history of Israel, the whole of creation and the new creation, and includes the consequences for his life of what God has accomplished in Jesus. And for Paul it all leads to the infilling of the Holy Spirit and the creation of the Spirit-filled community.

---

17. Fee, *God's Empowering Presence*, 13.

In the introduction to this argument (Rom 1:1–5), Paul lays out the framework upon which he will build in the following chapters. In these verses we see that for Paul, the gospel—

- was promised beforehand by the prophets.
- is laid out in the Scriptures (i.e., the Old Testament).
- is about Jesus
  » who was descended from David (he is the Jewish messiah, anointed king of Israel).
  » who was declared to be the son of God, with power, through the Spirit, by his resurrection from the dead.
  » who is now Lord (ascended and enthroned)
  » who appointed Paul an apostle to the work of bringing in the Gentiles, work which will culminate eventually in the restoration and salvation of Israel.

We cannot unpack all of this here, but it is clear for a start that Paul's gospel was "promised beforehand by the prophets." That is, it is in line with the prophetic message, the promises and the predictions made by Old Testament prophets. What he is presenting in his preaching is not something new, it is not as though God failed with his plan for Israel and so starts again with Jesus and the church (see Rom 9–11). What God has done in Jesus and the Spirit is the fulfillment of what he has been doing all along in and through Israel. The prophets had talked about righteousness and justice, about a new covenant, a new heart, and a general outpouring of the Spirit. They had devoted large parts of their message to the coming of the kingdom of God in these ways. All of these are foundational to Paul's gospel.

The prophets' understanding of the "end" of the world included, from Daniel, a physical resurrection and, from Isaiah, a new, physical creation. They looked forward to the redemption of the present physical order. The world God created was "very good," including the physical aspects of human existence. The understanding of some in the church today of human beings as "spiritual beings" that "have bodies" derives from gnosticism rather than from the Bible, from the Greek philosophers rather than the Hebrew prophets. God did not create a "spirit" and then fashion a body for it; he created a body and breathed into it the breath of life (Gen 2:7).[18] Human beings were made as an indivisible creation. Made with physical bodies to be part of this present, "very good" creation, they were also made in God's image—with a conscious soul or spirit. It is only through death that the physical and in-

---

18. As he had done also with the animals (Gen 1:24, 30; 2:19).

corporeal aspects of a human being are separated and that was never meant to happen. Death is the ultimate abomination in the creation, the last and greatest enemy, whose defeat must mean, then, the permanent reuniting of the physical and the spirit/soul (1 Cor 15:26 in context).

The "end" of Paul's gospel, the place where everything is fulfilled and complete, comes with the revelation of the sons of God (Rom 8:19). This includes the physical resurrection the prophets had predicted (Rom 8:23) and the comprehensive renewing of the physical creation (Rom 8:20–22). Paul knew nothing of the present Christian understanding of existence through eternity as being some kind of "spiritual," disembodied state in heaven. Paul taught resurrection (1 Cor 15, etc.), he taught a new creation, he taught a renewed physical existence for those who put their faith in Jesus. He did talk about being away from the body and at home with the Lord (2 Cor 5:8), but that was a temporary state until the return of Jesus and the resurrection (1 Cor 15:50–54). He did talk about a *natural* body and a *spiritual* body (1 Cor 15:44), but that spiritual body is in the same form as the body of Jesus after his resurrection (1 Cor 15:49). Jesus was raised with a physical body. "Look at my hands and feet. It is I myself!" he said to the disciples after rising from the dead. "Touch me and see; *a ghost does not have flesh and bones, as you see I have.*" After that, to further drive the point home, he asked them for some fish and ate it before them (Luke 24:38–43). The resurrection life will be a life in a physical body. That, after all, is the point of resurrection—the defeat of death within the creation. Resurrection is meaningless if existence afterwards is some kind of out-of-body nebulousness. Death is not defeated without a physical resurrection and a continued physical existence within a new (physical) creation.

It has always been God's intention to have many sons (Gen 1:28; Rom 8:29; cf. Heb 2:10) in the image of *the* son Jesus (Rom 8:28–30; cf. 1 John 3:2). This plan includes Israel (Rom 9:26; Hos 1:10), and the outworking of this plan is the work of the Holy Spirit (Rom 8:1–17). In Romans 7, Paul speaks (representatively rather than autobiographically) as a man who is awakened to sin by the law (Rom 7:7b). He is now dissatisfied with his old life, he sees he is a sinner, displeasing to God, in breach of God's commandments. He now wants to please God and gain life as the law requires and describes. But he realizes that he is fatally weak; that which he wants to do he cannot do, that which he wishes to attain he is too weak to attain.[19] That which is demanded of him, and which he agrees is good (Rom 7:16), is beyond him (Rom 7:14–20). His conscience is now violated by his own actions. The light of the law not only reveals the moral truth to him, it also

---

19. Sin is, in essence, weakness.

reveals his awful plight. His "flesh" is fatally flawed; it is, in effect, a "body of death" to him (Rom 7:24). With the coming of the law, awareness of his sin sprang to life in him (Rom 7:9). The very light the law has brought to him has, in effect, condemned him to death. Thus the law cannot redeem but only condemn him, it cannot release but only frustrate, it cannot bring life but it can only mean death (Rom 7:10).[20]

He cries out in his desperation, where can release be found? Is there anyone who can help? He looks for someone to help him, to save him, and finds that savior in Jesus Christ. How can he be released from the terrible dilemma the knowledge of the law has brought him? Only through Christ. The righteousness that could not come by the law is now his by faith in Christ. The law has fulfilled its purpose; it has driven him to Christ. Surely that is the whole thrust of Paul's argument through these early chapters (cf. 7:6), which then flows seamlessly and triumphantly into Rom 8:1-4, "Therefore, there is now no condemnation for those who are in Christ Jesus, because through Christ Jesus *the law of the Spirit of life set me free from the law of sin and death.*"

Jesus died in order for the creation to be redeemed, and it is the "Spirit of life" who carries out that redemptive, renewing work. The sons of God are those who are filled with, and led by, the Spirit (Rom 8:14). The new creation is Spirit-infused and empowered just as the original creation was. Paul's gospel leads to the indwelling of the Holy Spirit. God's plan is fulfilled; there is a prophetic community.

SUMMARY OF CHAPTER TEN

The Old Testament prophets had predicted a new age of the Spirit for God's people and in the book of Acts we see this actualized in the experiences of the early church. The violent wind of the Holy Spirit's coming blew away the old paradigm and produced a new prophetic community in which all could know God personally and intimately, all could receive revelation, all could prophesy, and all could speak in God's name.

The Holy Spirit was to dwell, from now on, not in a temple made by human hands but in a new temple composed of living stones. His purpose was to work *within* the lives of believers to produce Christ-likeness and to work *through* them to bring wholeness and healing to the world. It involved working *with* them to extend the kingdom of God in the world by bringing in the Gentiles as God had always intended, that the new temple might be completed.

20. Though sin, not the law, is the real "killer" (Rom 7:13).

The Church is the new Spirit-filled community brought into existence by the life, death, resurrection, and ascension of Jesus and through the outpouring of the Spirit. The shared life of this community is the fellowship of the Spirit in which all differences of race or gender, of politics or place in life, become of no importance. The infilling of the Spirit thus given to the members of the new community is a "deposit," guaranteeing the fullness that will come with the return of Jesus.

The Spirit is preparing the "sons of God" to be finally revealed when Jesus does return. This—the Spirit-filled and Spirit-anointed community of prophets, priests, and kings—is the "end" of the world towards which all of God's plans and purposes are working, when the sons of God will be revealed, when they will take their place again as kings and priests in the new creation.

Chapter Eleven

THE KINGDOM ON EARTH

> *"This is what was spoken by the prophet Joel: 'In the last days, God says, I will pour out my Spirit on all people. Your sons and daughters will prophesy, your young men will see visions, your old men will dream dreams. Even on my servants, both men and women, I will pour out my Spirit in those days, and they will prophesy'"* (Acts 2:16–18)

ACTS 2—THE DAY OF Pentecost—is a major dividing line between the old and new covenants. The anointed of the Lord had come, the presence of God had returned to Zion, Israel's story had begun to reach its fulfillment, the servant had suffered at the hands of sinful men, the Son of David had begun to reign. He had dealt with evil and with death, and he had made possible the forgiveness of sins. The kingdom of God had come upon the earth. The predictions and promises of the prophets of a new age and a general outpouring of the Spirit had at long last come to pass. The age of the Spirit had begun.

One of the results of this end-time outpouring of the Spirit was a general release of prophecy in the church (Acts 2:17). All of God's people were anointed, all could prophesy, all could know God intimately through the Spirit. The Spirit's anointing—evidenced by prophecy, by a sense of his immediate presence, by demonstrations of the miraculous—would now be the distinguishing mark of the people of God. So, in the book of Acts, in the life of the new eschatological community, it is possible to see glimpses of what the kingdom of God on earth really looks like, what it means when the king reigns and his people are filled with the Spirit (Acts 2:1, 14, 41–47; 3:23; cf. 1:13–14, 15).[1]

NEW TESTAMENT PROPHETS

The writers and preachers of the New Testament and their early audiences were part of a theological culture whose eschatological expectations were formed in large part by the writings and ministries of the Old Testament prophets. Added to this, the release of prophecy that had come as a result of the outpouring of the Spirit at Pentecost formed part of their shared experience—the common background of the exciting time in which they found themselves—and its nature was self-evident to these early Christians. Because of this, there is very little discussion on the nature of prophets and prophecy and their place in the church by the New Testament authors. There is no need to discuss something that everyone is familiar with and takes for granted. What *is* clear is that prophets were important figures in the early church and prophetic activity (both true and false) is mentioned in almost every book of the New Testament. Prophecy is considered the most important of the spiritual gifts—vital, indeed, for the building up of the church (1 Cor 14:1–5, 29, 39; 1 Thess 5:20).

From the instructions given in these passages it seems that the presence of prophets (a number of them) and the practice of prophecy in all the churches was common. Despite the general release of prophecy in the church as outlined above, the *office* of the prophet continued to operate among the people of God as it had under the old covenant (see Eph 4:11). Interestingly, as in the Old Testament, the prophets are sometimes mentioned in groups (Acts 13:1; 11:27; 15:32; 1 Cor 14:29).[2] There was a group in Jerusalem (Acts 11:27–28; 21:10), at Antioch (Acts 13:1), and at

---

1. This new community had several distinguishing features—it was obviously a *saved* community (2:38–40; 3:19. Cf. 2:24; 2:1–4; 2:38; 4:12), it was a *praying* community (2:42; 3:1. Cf. 1:14), and of course it was a *Christ-centered* community (2:22–36; 3:12–16. Cf. 2:42). It was an *egalitarian* community in every sense (2:3–4, 17–18) and it was a *healing* community (3:1–10; 2:43). It was a *worshipping* community (2:11, 46–47), a *teaching* community (2:42), a *missionary* community (2:40; 3:25–26. Cf. 1:8; Matt 24:14; Rev 7:9–14; 2:5–12), and consequently a *growing* community (2:41, 47). It was time to bring in the Gentiles. Underlying all of these other attributes, this new expression of the people of God, as we have seen, was a *Spirit-filled* community (2:1–4, 38) and because of this, it was a *prophetic* community (2:4, 11, 17–18). It was a people living by the word of God and filled with the Spirit of God.

2. Though this was not always the case (Acts 21:10).

Caesarea (Acts 21:8). Some of these prophets travelled to other locations where they were readily accepted and had a strong ministry influence (Acts 11:27–28; 15:22–32; 21:10). It seems that the office of a prophet was in some instances itinerant to a certain extent, speaking to the church at large rather than speaking to a church in a specific location (as with some of the other ministry gifts).

The church recognized the office and ministry of a prophet as a distinct New Testament ministry calling and gifting. Prophets operated at a level of senior leadership in the early days of Christianity (Acts 13:1–3; 15:22–32; cf. 1 Cor 12:28; Eph 3:5; 4:11), second only to apostles, with whom they are bracketed together as the foundational ministries of the New Testament church (Eph 2:20; 3:5; Rev 18:20; cf. 1 Cor 12:28–29; Eph 4:11; Luke 11:49). The church was built on an apostolic-prophetic foundation, functioning together under the gifting and direction of the Holy Spirit.[3] In the New Testament, church leadership is usually corporate (see Eph 4:11)[4], though the first twelve apostles maintained a senior role, as we see in Acts.

The nature of the New Testament prophetic ministry in the early church, for reasons mentioned above, is not easy to define exactly. It can, perhaps, be seen most clearly in terms of the prophetic *practice*—what the New Testament prophets actually *did* and how they ministered. Firstly, like the prophets of the Old Testament, their primary ministry was to the people of God. They spoke in the first place to the unique historical situation they found themselves in. The Old Testament prophets spoke into the first creation, to the people of the old creation, whereas the New Testament prophets spoke into the new creation, to the New Testament people of God

But there is an important caveat to this. Like the Old Testament prophets again, the prophetic church recognized that God (in Jesus now) was Lord not only of the church but of the whole world, and the prophets were his representatives. Just as Jesus had confronted the Jewish leaders and Pilate, as the representative of the world powers, so there were occasions when those same world powers—manifested in either antagonistic Jewish or imperial Roman guise—needed to be confronted also. "Judge for yourselves," Peter and John said to the rulers and elders of Israel, "whether it is right in God's sight to obey you rather than God" (Acts 4:1–20). Stephen loses his life when he is brought into confrontation with these same powers

---

3. In Acts chapter 13, we read of prophets and *teachers* as church leadership (Acts 13:1).

4. The seeming exceptions of Timothy in Ephesus and Titus in Crete were temporary situations. Their apostolic charge in both cases was to bring order to the churches and appoint elders—*plural*. See 1 Tim 1:3–3:15; Titus 1:5. The two men were also part of Paul's apostolic *team*.

(Acts 6:8—7:60). Paul confronts an attendant of the proconsul on Cyprus (Acts 13:4–12), and he is later brought into confrontation with the Jewish leaders (Acts 22:30–23:11), the Roman governors Felix and Festus (Acts 24:1–25:12), King Agrippa (Acts 25:13–26:32), and eventually the Roman Emperor himself (Acts 25:12; 27:1–28:30). Note should be taken that these world powers were both violent and corrupt, and part of the confrontation with them involved suffering—both for Jesus and his prophetic representatives. This has always been the way when God's prophets confront injustice and ungodliness (Matt 23:29–39; Acts 7:51–53). Jesus said his witnesses could expect the same treatment from the powers of this world also (Luke 11:49).

Secondly, the prophets of the New Testament were not as involved in the formulation of theology as the Old Testament prophets had been. Jesus was now God's final word to his people (Heb 1:1–2), and it was the apostles who would now compose the documents of the New Testament (Acts 2:42), explaining the implications of his life, death, and resurrection. The Holy Spirit would now convict (John 16:8). Judgment had fallen on Jesus and the new covenant had been internalized, based on promises now rather than commandments (Heb 8:6). But the prophets worked closely with the apostles and continued to God's representatives among his people, reminding them that he was sovereign and holy and that he had a plan. All of this was being directly guided by the Holy Spirit.

To the apostles and prophets was given the understanding of the mysteries of God's new creation work in Christ (Eph 3:4–6). The apostles contributed to the emerging church in terms of providing it with a Christian theology (Acts 2:42) and powerful supernatural witness (Acts 4:33). This theology and witness were both again focused on revealing how the Old Testament promises and prophetic eschatology were fulfilled in Jesus. They taught the Old Testament in the light of the life and death and resurrection of Jesus. The prophets, on the other hand, provided an immediate voice of revelation (1 Cor 14:30; Eph 3:4–5), encouragement (Acts 15:32; 1 Cor 14:31), direction (Acts 13:2), and prediction (Acts 11:28; 20:23; 21:10–11). Prophets also provided instruction (1 Cor 14:31; cf. Acts 13:1) and served as channels for the impartation of spiritual gifts (1 Tim 4:14). The prophets also provided a critique of what was spoken into the church (1 Cor 14:29–33). What is spoken should be "weighed carefully," Paul taught. Everything is to be tested, he told the Thessalonians (1 Thess 5:19–21). Part of the function, or the result, of prophecy (and by inference the prophet) in the church was also to bring a sense of the holiness of God through the uncovering of sin, producing contrition and repentance (1 Cor 14:24–25).

The prophet is concerned for the holiness of the church and for the integrity of the Christian teaching, ministry, and leadership.[5]

As with the Old Testament (Jer 6:13–15; Ezek 13:17–23; etc.), there would be false prophets in the church also. Jesus cautioned against accepting and following them (Matt 7:15–23; 24:11, 24). Paul warned of "savage wolves" that would come among the flock (Acts 20:29–30). John warned the church that there were many false prophets in the world (1 John 4:1–6). In light of this fact, John said, there must be a testing of the spirits, a discerning between the true and the false.

How then are prophets and prophecy to be weighed and tested? In the Old Testament, we saw that there was a prophetic truth test (Deut 18:21–22). If what a prophet predicted came to pass, he or she was a genuine prophet. The true prophet hears from God, the false prophet does not. There was a qualification to this though, as we have seen (Deut 13:1–5), in that prophecy must be in agreement with previous revelation. These are still good guidelines for judging prophecy in the New Testament. John says also that true prophets will exalt the person and work of Jesus (1 John 4:1–3; Rev 19:10). Jesus also said prophets could be tested, or sorted, by their fruit—the results of their ministry, their reputation within the church (Matt 7:15–23. Cf. 1 Tim 3:2, 7, 10). Are they well-spoken of among God's people?

PROPHECY IN THE CHURCH

It is clear that there were people who were widely recognized as prophets in the early church. The question in 1 Corinthians 12:29, "are all prophets?" obviously distinguishes between some who were and those who were not. However, Paul is writing to the whole Christian community in Corinth (i.e., not just to the recognized prophets there) when he says "Follow the way of love and eagerly desire spiritual gifts, especially the gift of prophecy" (1 Cor 14:1–25). The passage seems to indicate that there was a more widespread use of prophecy as a kind of inspired message to the church, something that all could participate in (1 Cor 14:24). "You can all prophesy in turn" (1 Cor 14:31), may have been written to the prophets in the church but again may have wider application. Prophecy is listed among the general gifts of the Spirit (1 Cor 12:7–11). Because all are anointed, all can potentially prophesy (Acts 2:17–18, 38–39; 1 Cor 14:31). There is no gender difference here in the new community; both men and women may prophesy (1 Cor 11:4–5).

---

5. One aspect, perhaps, of the lessening of the importance of the prophetic office in the church is a lessening of the emphasis on the need for holiness.

Prophecy is considered the most important and desirable of the spiritual gifts (1 Cor 14:1–5, 29, 39), essential to the life and health of the church. It is the primary gift of the Spirit to the eschatological people of God, evidence of the age of the Spirit, confirmation of the new covenant, the prophesied result of the Spirit's general outpouring, the evidence that all can now enjoy an intimate knowledge of God (Heb 8:10–11). Through prophecy (preaching as well as the charismatic gift) the church is strengthened, encouraged, and comforted (1 Cor 14:3; cf. Acts 14:22; 15:32). Prophecy is associated with teaching (1 Cor 14:6, 31; cf. Acts 13:1). In the life of the church, the operation of this charismatic gift should be ordered (1 Cor 14:29–32) and is to be used in proportion to the level of faith given to each believer by the Lord (Rom 12:3, 6).

Tongues and prophecy are very closely related in the Acts record (Acts 2:4, 11, 17; 10:44–47; 19:6). Tongues is a kind of ecstatic prophetic declaration that seems to have been used in two ways: Firstly, in public worship, in a similar way to prophecy, as a means of bringing an immediate message of encouragement from God to the church. In this case these messages obviously needed to be interpreted into the common language so they could be understood by all (1 Cor 14:5). Secondly, tongues are used as a kind of private language of prayer and praise (see 1 Cor 14:2, and compare 1 Cor 14:18 where Paul claims to speak in tongues more than anyone else). This has the result of edifying the speaker (1 Cor 14:4, by inference).

NEW TESTAMENT USE OF OLD TESTAMENT PROPHECY

The New Testament uses the Old Testament prophets in a number of ways. We have seen already the extensive use the gospel writers make of the prophets to support their contention that Jesus was the messiah, and we have seen something of the considerable use Jesus made of the prophets, identifying with them in their message and mission. There are one hundred and five direct quotes from the prophets in the New Testament.[6] Sixty-five of these are from Isaiah; six each are from Jeremiah, Hosea, and Zechariah; five are from Joel and Amos; three from Ezekiel, Habakkuk, and Malachi; and one each from Daniel, Jonah, and Haggai. On top of this, there are an estimated five hundred or more *allusions* and verbal parallels, mainly from the Major Prophets. Many of the Old Testament prophetic texts quoted in the New Testament obviously apply directly to Jesus, but others refer to the

---

6. Aland et al., "Index of Quotations," in *The Greek New Testament*, 887–890.

things that follow—the birth of the church, the inclusion of the Gentiles, the present unbelief of Israel, and the future salvation of Israel and the nations.

Interestingly, the quotations and references from Isaiah in the New Testament (applying to both Jesus and to the people of God) are drawn from both major portions of the book without any distinction being drawn between them.[7] The most significant use of Jeremiah in the New Testament is the new covenant passage of Jeremiah 31:31-34 (Heb 8:8-12; 10:16-17), but Paul twice refers also to Jeremiah 9:24 about boasting in the Lord rather than anything else that that may seem personally important (1 Cor 1:31; 2 Cor 10:17).

There are an estimated one hundred and thirty allusions to Ezekiel in the New Testament. Half of these are found in Revelation, which as we will see, contains no formal quotations from the prophets but nevertheless references the Old Testament more than any other New Testament book. One of the major ways Daniel is used in the New Testament is seen in the gospel writers' references to Jesus as *the Son of Man* (Dan 7:13-14. See also Ezek 2:1, etc.). The other major use of Daniel is in Revelation where, as noted elsewhere, it is the most alluded to of the prophetic books.

There are also significant quotations from the Book of the Twelve in the New Testament. The three Synoptics, for instance, all use Malachi 3:1 in reference to John the Baptist, "See, I will send my messenger who will prepare the way before me" (Matt 11:10; Mark 1:2; Luke 7:27). Matthew also, by way of example, again quotes from Micah, Hosea, Jonah, and Zechariah. The other gospels and many other New Testament books reference them also. It is obvious, again, that the New Testament writers consider themselves to be living through events predicted by the prophets of the Old Testament.

WOMEN IN THE PROPHETIC COMMUNITY

There needs to be some comment made here on the inclusion of women in this new community, as it is an issue that is particularly significant and relevant for many in the church today (where there are often more women than men). The church, as we have seen, is an egalitarian community. "Through the gospel," Paul tells us, "the Gentiles are heirs together with Israel, members together of one body, and sharers together in the promise in Christ Jesus" (Eph 3:6). In the church, he writes further, "there is neither Jew nor Gentile, neither slave nor free, *nor is there male and female*, for you are all one in Christ Jesus" (Gal 3:28). One of the remarkable aspects of the prophecy of Joel quoted by Peter about the church on the day of Pentecost

---

7. Strengthening the case for its unity.

was that in the age to come the Spirit would be poured out on *all* flesh, including women. "Your sons *and daughters* will prophesy," God promised through the prophet. "Even on my servants, both men *and women*, I will pour out my Spirit in those days, and they will prophesy" (Acts 2:17–18). Even though there were a few women prophets in the Old Testament world, this is still remarkable in first century cultural terms.

The world of that time, as it has often been, was a difficult place for women, according them a largely secondary status and restricting their contribution to society and to the religious life of the people of God. The gospels and Acts present a world in which the status of women varied. There were obviously women who enjoyed a measure of freedom and influence—even financial independence (cf. Luke 8:3; Acts 16:14; 17:4, 12). These, though, were possibly of the upper class, and the lot of women in general was far from good. The historical picture of women in Palestinian Judaism of the time is of a class generally subordinate to men.[8] First century Israel was a patriarchal society. Women were often treated more like chattels than persons, usually had no say in who their marriage partners would be, and had little opportunity for education or employment equal to a man's. The husband was master of his wife. He could divorce her, but she could not divorce him. A daughter could be sold into slavery by her father.[9]

This difficult lot was true in the wider world also. One historian tells us that "In much . . . Greek literature woman is despised, ridiculed, and denigrated. Although she fares better in Roman perspective, even there she is little more than a sex object."[10] It was a man's world; women were subject to scorn and penalty, and abuses were common and sometimes overwhelming. Contempt for women was fairly common in Jewish literature of the time. A woman passed from her father's authority to that of her husband. It was difficult and unusual for a woman to inherit property.[11] The legal system largely devalued their testimony, rating them, in most cases, unfit as witnesses.[12]

In the religious realm they were also discriminated against in Israel, being excluded from the heart of Jewish religious life and practice. They could not be priests.[13] They were forbidden in certain parts of the temple,

---

8. Wilson-Kastner, *Faith, Feminism, and the Christ*, 71–72.
9. Faxon, *Women and Jesus*, 11–12.
10. Stagg, *Women in the World of Jesus*, 123, 130.
11. Witherington, *Women and the Genesis of Christianity*, 3–4.
12. Bauckham, *Gospel Women*, 269.
13. Stagg, *Women in the World of Jesus*, 29–30. Stagg says the exclusion of women from the priesthood in Israel may have been due to the long struggle between Yahwism and the fertility religions and/or to reproductive realities that regularly rendered them

and even those parts to which they had access (the women's court), they must enter through special gates. They were exempt from studying Torah.[14] A woman's sphere of influence was largely limited to her home and domestic duties. She played little part in the public realm, in which contact was very limited. Jewish men and women did not mix in public. Although some question this negative picture, the overall consensus of commentators and historical witness is strong—a low view of woman is observable in much of the world of the time.

One of the ways in which Jesus deliberately challenged the prevailing customs, indeed the worldview, of his day was in this area of the unjust and unloving treatment of women. Never do we hear of him speaking (and he was not a man to mince words) of male headship, women's subordination, or of differing gender roles. This is surely strange if these are important, foundational, "creation" truths governing the relationships between men and women, as some claim. In fact much of what Jesus said and did—indeed his whole attitude—called these teachings into question. The gospel story is amazing and convincing in its inclusion of women—from the birth narratives (where they are presented as of more noble and obedient character than their male counterparts) to being numbered among Jesus' disciples and being among the witnesses to Jesus' death on the cross (where they perhaps alone represent the disciples of Jesus) and on to the resurrection. Against the prevailing attitudes of the day, God chose a group of women to be the first witnesses and heralds (i.e., preachers/apostles) of the resurrection. This is surely deliberate and therefore hugely significant theologically. The presentation of women in the gospels is remarkable for its favorable treatment. For Jesus, women were social equals. He talked publically with them (John 4:6-26), included them among his disciples (Luke 8:1-3), and counted them among his close friends (John 11:5). His attention was given to women of all social ranks and situations—married and unmarried, Gentiles, women of standing and also those who were considered unclean and immoral (Luke 8:2-3; Mark 5:25-34; 7:24-30; Luke 7:36-50; etc.). Jesus challenged the prevailing religious and cultural understandings of his day in this area, not always by open criticism but simply by treating women with respect, as responsible *people*, equal with men in every way. He also treated them with a special tenderness in recognition that their lot in life is at times

---

ritually unclean. Women participated in other ministries—the prophetic, judging, ruling—which were not tied to ritual cleanliness.

14. Though some were able to become learned in both oral and written law and tradition. Witherington, *Women and the Genesis of Christianity*, 7.

particularly difficult and onerous.[15] A close look at some of his interactions with women will show the radical nature of those encounters.

Jesus actually taught women. Rather than choosing the temple in Jerusalem as the usual place for his ministry and teaching, most of it took place in public places where there was no division between women and men. And even when Jesus did teach in the temple, he chose the public areas where women were allowed.[16] He also taught women in private settings. Luke 10:38–42 is the story of Martha's complaint against Mary and Jesus' positive response to Mary's action. He treated her in a way that normally would have been restricted to men, commending her choice and affirming her as a genuine student and disciple. This was contrary to the cultural norms of the day, as most Jews considered it improper to teach women the Scriptures. Jesus' actions were a deliberate decision to break this discrimination. Just as the male disciple had to be absolutely single-minded about his following of Jesus, so too the woman has to pursue the only thing necessary, the message of Jesus—even if that means neglecting her traditional responsibilities, leaving the kitchen and sitting at Jesus' feet as rabbinical students would sit at the feet of the great scholars. This kind of study had been for men only, the woman being expected to follow Martha's example in serving the men while they talked.

There is also the story of the woman at the well (John 4:7–42) who preaches to the people of her village, including men, with no remonstrance from Jesus. He accepted and defended his anointing by the woman at Bethany as the prophetic or priestly action it was (Matt 26:6–13). And we must bear in mind, in light of John 21:25, that these are probably just a few examples of many that the gospel writers had to choose from. Jesus' attitude to women, his obvious concern for them and his appreciation of them as important human beings, was revolutionary. Not only did he deign to speak to them, he revealed to them new spiritual truths, confident in their ability to understand what he was teaching. Some of his most profound revelations about himself and the Father were given in private teaching to women (See John 4:13–26; Luke 10:42; John 11:25; 20:17; etc.). Of note too is the obviously deliberate inclusiveness of the teaching of Jesus. Men and women are treated as equals in everything. He does not give separate "teaching for women." Both women and men are used as examples for all disciples in

---

15. This can lead to misunderstanding. Some see romantic love between Jesus and Mary Magdalene, but this is crass and unimaginative in the extreme. This is the creator, God, the all-sufficient one, the Almighty, come from the heights of unimaginable power and glory to the creature, lost and blind and hopeless. There is no possibility of romance here; the thought is absurd.

16. Cunningham and Hamilton, *Why Not Women?*, 119.

his parables and general teaching. The parable of the Mustard Seed and the Leaven, for example (Luke 13:18–21), and the Lost Sheep and the Lost Coin (15:3–10), are paired in using men and women in their differing domestic roles.

The account of a woman crippled for eighteen years, who Jesus healed in a synagogue during a Sabbath service, is instructive (Luke 13:10–17). She would presumably have been in an area reserved for women where she must remain silent, segregated from the men and from the main ritual. Jesus called her down, actually touched her, and healed her dreadful infirmity. As a result, she began to praise God aloud. When the synagogue ruler cruelly spoke out against this act of mercy, Jesus powerfully denounces and humiliates him and those who supported him. "Hypocrites!" he said to them, "cruel, selfish, legalistic men! Should not this woman, *a daughter of Abraham*, be set free . . ." It was a surprising, even shocking title, giving her (and thereby all women) equality of spiritual status with men (the "sons of Abraham") among the people of God. Can we imagine the reaction in the women's gallery? Is it any wonder that no opposition to Jesus from women is recorded in any of the gospels?

Why is it, then, that the twelve were all men? Why were twelve men and no women chosen? Commentator Kevin Giles offers two probable reasons: They were counterparts of the twelve patriarchs, and their main work was to be witnesses, something women could not legitimately do in Jewish society at the time.[17] Men were also perhaps better suited physically for an itinerant ministry and outdoor preaching. To have called a single woman could have been culturally and morally unacceptable and married women were most often constrained by the demands of children and family.[18]

The teachings and example of Jesus are all-important to the establishment of a correct understanding of the relationship between women and men in the church and of the eligibility of women to take places of leadership in the new prophetic community. Jesus' example served as the foundation of the early church's attitude to women—as can be seen by the very fact of the inclusion of these stories by the gospel writers—and they must surely inform our approach today. His teachings and attitudes served as a foundation upon which was constructed the doctrine and practice of the early Christian community in this area. They regarded the redemptive work of Jesus as gaining a new and equal status for all human beings in the sight of God and providing the groundwork for overturning all discrimination. The

---

17. Giles, *Trinity and Subordination*, 204.

18. Yet there were occasions when Jesus' travelling group did include women. Luke 8:1–3; cf. Luke 23:49, 55.

phraseology of the account of the prophesied Pentecostal outpouring deliberately emphasized the inclusion of women on an equal basis with men in the new community. The new Spirit-filled status was, again, for "all people," for both "sons and daughters," for "both men and women." They would all be filled; they would all prophesy (Acts 2:17–18).

The early Christians followed the lead of Jesus in their treatment of women. The New Testament records the active part played by many women in the spread of Christianity and their acceptance by everyone in the new community, even in places of leadership (Acts 6:11–15; 18:18; Rom 16:1–7, 12, 15; Col 4:15). The Christian church was a new community in which everything was different, including the status of women, guided now by the obvious example and teaching of Jesus and the common reception of the Spirit-gift by all on an equal basis. It is this new community attitude and understanding that must then provide much of the theological and literary context for interpreting the "difficult" passages in Paul (e.g., 1 Cor 14:34; 1 Tim 2:11–15).[19] There were women who were recognized for their gifts of prophecy (Acts 21:9). The gift of the Holy Spirit was to be for the whole community, including women. An equal status is afforded them in the church. If Adam is forgiven and restored to fellowship with God, so too is Eve. She stands once more at his side and takes her part in the God-given work. Within cultural parameters, a woman can prophesy, can bring the word of God in the meetings of the church (1 Cor 11:4–5); she too can know God intimately, and she too can speak for God.

SUMMARY OF CHAPTER ELEVEN

The new community, the New Testament church—because of the promised outpouring of the Holy Spirit in fulfillment of Old Testament prophecy—is by nature a prophetic community. Prophets and prophecy are a core part of its identity. It is clear from the book of Acts that prophets played a key leadership role in the establishment of the new community and the gift of prophecy was accounted desirable and even essential to its continued health and strength. All were anointed and all were encouraged to participate in this prophetic ministry. Women were, within cultural boundaries, received into the prophetic community on the same basis as men.

These are difficult issues for some parts of the church today. Is the Acts record to be considered normative, that is, setting guidelines for Christian practice today? Are leadership and worship patterns seen in that record

---

19. There are the social and cultural contexts to consider also when interpreting these passages—and the OT scriptures also, of course.

desirable or necessary today? Is reform needed in some areas? Gender equality needs to be re-emphasized; women taught, encouraged, and released to own their own destinies in God both within and through the church. They need to be able to bring their own kind of contribution and style of leadership to the church so that the image is fully revealed and restored.

The "prophetic edge" needs restoring, whatever that may mean in practice and however it may be expressed in the life of the church. The prophetic role is missing from the leadership of much of the church today, and, Scripturally, the church must be the weaker for it. The expression of the gift of prophecy itself is not found in much of the church. Even in Pentecostal streams, the tide has gone out on prophecy, and the gift that Paul taught was essential for the building up of the body does not often find expression in carefully choreographed services except when it comes from the pulpit.

In the New Testament, the prophet attended the apostle as he did the king in the Old Testament. The church is built on the apostolic/prophetic foundation. If there is one thing postmodernism has taught us about the human condition, it is that there is always a tendency towards the misuse of power. If church leadership positions itself beyond the reach of any prophetic critique, the position of authority may be abused and the church damaged. Even apostles can act in ways that are not Christian, as is clearly revealed by the situation outlined in Galatians 2:11–21. If what is taught in the church is not subject to some kind of collective prophetic critique also, the church again will be weakened. It is truth that brings life and freedom, not just persuasive preaching. The prophet needs to stand with the apostle and bring God's counsel, guard the purity and holiness of God and the church, and declare God's purpose into the new creation. And the prophet still speaks the purpose and blessing of God into existence. If prophecy is missing from the church and the prophetic ministry is missing from church leadership, it can only mean that much that is purposed does not in fact take place. *The Lord does nothing without revealing his plan to his servants the prophets.* Only that which is spoken will take place.

Finally, the church is—or should be—a prophetic voice to the powers of the world in the face of injustice and ungodliness. The church has been very good at times in addressing injustice in practical ways but not always good at speaking up about it. God's prophetic representatives should not accept the political falsehood of the separation of church and state and so retreat into an inward-looking, isolated little world where they adopt a self-congratulatory stance over their "contemporary relevance" when the huge percentage of the world immediately around them is unaffected by their message. Where are the prophets and church leaders speaking into the great issues of our time? Has the church nothing to say to those issues? Jesus is

Lord of the whole world and commands all people everywhere to repent. The church is tasked with discipling the nations. Will we be silent—and so complicit— in the face of injustice and unrighteousness? We work towards that final victory of righteousness and justice in the world that will be fully established at the return of Jesus. To the end of the story we now turn.

Part Three

THE END OF THE WORLD

"Then the angel I had seen standing on the sea and on the land raised his right hand to heaven. And he swore by him who lives forever and ever, who created the heavens and all that is in them, the earth and all that is in it, and the sea and all that is in it, and said,

'There will be no more delay! But in the days when the seventh angel is about to sound his trumpet, the mystery of God will be accomplished, just as he announced to his servants the prophets.'"

—Revelation 10:5–7

Chapter Twelve

LISTENING TO REVELATION

"The revelation of Jesus Christ, which God gave him to show his servants what must soon take place . . . Do not seal up the words of the prophecy of this book, because the time is near . . ." (Rev 1:1; 22:10)

WE HAVE SEEN THAT the eschatological predictions of the prophets revolve around two interrelated concepts, the kingdom of God and the day of the Lord. The first concept led naturally to the gospels, to the coming of Jesus and the events surrounding his life and ministry as he announced the arrival of the kingdom and set about establishing it on earth. The cataclysmic and climactic events predicted of the "Day of the Lord" lead us finally to the book of Revelation, which claims to present, as we will see, the events surrounding the return of Jesus to finally and fully establish his rule over a new creation. The gospels declared the arrival of the kingdom of God with the coming of Jesus, Revelation describes the unfolding of God's final act of judgment and salvation in the Day of the Lord, culminating in the return of Jesus. The two concepts are obviously interconnected in the prophets and are sometimes difficult to separate in their actual outworking in history, but two concepts there are. The king and the kingdom have come already, and clearly the end has not yet come. So, in the final section of this book we turn to a brief study of the last book of the Bible.

THE OLD TESTAMENT IN REVELATION

The book of Revelation contains more Old Testament references than any other book in the New Testament. In his major commentary on Revelation G. K. Beale gives the numbers as anything between 195–1,000, depending on what criteria are used.[1] Revelation uses no direct quotes from the Old Testament, nor are there any overt claims to the fulfillment of Old Testament prophecy or prediction, but it does contain many verbal and textual allusions, some clear, some not so clear, but all probable to differing degrees. M. C. Tenney gives the number as ten per chapter,[2] but others go even further—Steven Moyise says there is about one allusion to the Old Testament for every verse of Revelation.[3] Some of those allusions might reference two or more Old Testament scriptures. Even much of the phraseology of Revelation is Old Testament in origin. The author is obviously someone whose thoughts and whose concepts are soaked in the Old Testament text and eschatological story.

At least twenty-four of the Old Testament books are alluded to in Revelation, including each of the books of the Pentateuch plus Judges, the two books of Samuel, the two books of Kings, Psalms, Proverbs, Job, Song of Solomon, and there is extensive use of both the Major and Minor prophets.

Around half of the references are from the five books of Psalms, Isaiah, Jeremiah, Ezekiel, and Daniel. These last two are the books most alluded to (especially Daniel 7), with some of Zechariah's images also featuring prominently. Many of the predictive prophecies of the Old Testament are found in these books, indicating a direct and *intentional* relationship between the Old Testament prophetic promises of judgment and restoration and the message of Revelation. Like the Old Testament prophetic books, Revelation is composed of more than one literary genre and includes a number of prophetic oracles (cf. 2:1–3:22). Like the Old Testament prophetic books, major themes are judgment and restoration. As with some of the Old Testament prophetic books, Revelation contains a great deal of symbolism and imagery.

INTERPRETING REVELATION

Because of this extensive use of fantastic imagery and symbols, its twisting plot, and its long history of misinterpretation, the book of Revelation is held

---

1. Beale, *Revelation*, 77.
2. Tenney, *Interpreting Revelation*, 101.
3. Moyise, *Old Testament in the New*, 117.

by many to be too difficult to understand. This means that many Christians, even preachers, effectively ignore the book except as a source of proof-texts for innovative eschatological schemes. But the book is a part—a very important part, as we will see—of the biblical cannon and needs to be read and studied as much as any of the other books. Though some of the details may be difficult to interpret and understand, the broad message, general thrust, and outline are no more difficult than some of those other biblical books.

There are four different approaches generally advanced as interpretive options for the book of Revelation.

1. *Preterist:* Preterists basically hold that Revelation belongs to the genre of "apocalypse" and refers to events in John's own time, the late 1st century AD. Apocalyptic literature generally presents a hidden reality behind the events taking place in the world through the medium of dreams and visions and the use of cryptic symbols and numbers. Preterists interpret Revelation historically, as a message in coded language written to encourage Christians in a situation of persecution under the Romans. Revelation, in this view then, is a prophecy of the fall of the Roman Empire.[4] Thus, the book had direct application only to the particular historical situation that produced it, though it may contain principles that apply more widely.

2. *Historicist:* This school of interpretation holds that Revelation is a symbolic prophecy of the entire church age, from the time of its composition right up until the return of Christ and the end of the present age. Parallels are sought between historical events and the unfolding drama described in the text, a task that must obviously be quite subjective, so there are a range of opinions as to how it applies.

3. *Idealist:* It is held by these interpreters that Revelation is a symbolic portrayal of the spiritual conflict between good and evil, between the kingdom of God and the kingdom of darkness. No direct connection is sought, in this instance, between the visions and symbols of Revelation and particular historical events. There is not necessarily any final end to history.

4. *Futurist:* Those interpreting from this vantage point see Revelation as largely a prophecy of future events leading up to the end of the present age. Connections are often sought between its images and contemporary events, which is again a necessarily subjective enterprise.

---

4. Or "the destruction of Israel and Christ's victory over His enemies in the establishment of the New Covenant Temple." Chilton, *The Days of Vengeance*, 23.

Most approaches to unfolding the meaning of the twisting plot and confusing imagery of the book of Revelation are based on various permutations of these four interpretive approaches.

How then to interpret? Which approach do we use? How do we decide? How do we avoid a purely subjective approach? How do we avoid the almost universal tendency to read our own preconceptions into the text? All kinds of meanings and messages have been read into this book, from a secret rendezvous between Christ and the church to coded references to Emperor-worship, dispensational divisions, and more, because interpreters have so often approached it with presuppositions. This carries the danger of stifling the actual voice of the text itself and of consequently limiting our understanding of what it is saying. For instance, if we come to the text with the *a priori* understanding that it is an example of apocalypse, and that books in that genre are written to encourage people in historical situations of persecution, we immediately limit the scope of possible meanings.

So before we impose any imported hermeneutical framework on the text we need firstly to attempt to treat it with enough integrity to let it speak for itself, to allow it its own voice, to listen to what the text is telling us, and to permit it to tell its own story.[5] Secondly, we need to allow the text its place in the whole panorama of the biblical story. What is the *text*, in the larger biblical *context*, actually saying to us?

GIVING THE TEXT A VOICE

Firstly, then, Revelation is a general message to seven historical churches of John's time (1:11), and for each of the churches Jesus gives a personal introductory greeting in the form of a prophetic oracle (chapters 2–3). I will return to this later. The text claims to be about certain events that are future to the time of the author (1:1–3; 4:1; 17:10; 22:6). They are *"near"* and they are to take place in the prophetic period *"soon."* This prophetic "soon" is also used of the time of the return of Jesus: "Behold, I am coming soon! My reward is with me, and I will give to everyone according to what he has done" (cf. 22:7, 12, 20). The prophesied events in Revelation, then, are not only of immediate application to the historical period of the book's writing, but are related in some way to the return of Jesus and the final judgment.

The claim is made by the text to be an account of a revelation of, and from, Jesus Christ (1:1). It is a supernaturally given message revealed in vision form to the author, John. This directly relates it to the experiences of

---

5. We all bring presuppositions to all interpretation, but we can and must attempt to be as neutral as possible.

the Old Testament prophets, to the words and works of Jesus, and to the experiences of other biblical characters like the Apostle Paul as related in Galatians 1:12 and 2 Corinthians 12:1–4. In other words, this is not merely the cleverly-coded composition of a human author only, but a written record of supernatural visions given to the author by Jesus Christ. Such is the claim of the text. This is prophetic literature; these are the words of a prophet, received from God and written down for the instruction of God's people.

Revelation several times claims to be prophecy (1:3; 22:7, 10, 18, 19; 22:10, 18, 19) and it claims, in fact, to be a message revealed by the same Lord who inspired the prophets (Rev 22:6). "There will be no more delay!" an angel pronounces, "but in the days when the seventh angel is about to sound his trumpet, the mystery of God will be accomplished, *just as he announced to his servants the prophets . . .*" (Rev 10:6–7; cf. 11:18; 16:6; 18:24; 21:1–5; 22:6, 9–10). The author claims to be a prophet with a mandate from heaven. "I was told," he writes, "*You must prophesy again* about many peoples, nations, languages and kings" (Rev 10:11). He is included by an angelic messenger in a group with the other prophets (Rev 22:9) and he claims that his prophecy brings to completion their message and ministry.

The text, then, claims to be in some way directly related to the message and ministry of the Old Testament biblical prophets. And it claims to be the conclusion and consummation of the "mystery of God," the purpose of God in creation that was previously hidden but has now been revealed by the prophets and now here in this final revelation also. So what I am proposing in this book is an alternative to the four interpretive methods outlined above, that is, interpreting Revelation as the fulfillment of the prophetic eschatology, rooted in, and bringing culmination and completion to, the biblical meta-narrative—*Revelation as the unfolding of the prophetic Day of the Lord.*

The text informs us that the author was on four occasions *"in the Spirit"* (1:10; 4:2; 17:3; 21:10), presumably indicating some kind of ecstatic state. On each of these occasions John received a supernatural communication in the form of a vision, so Revelation is a record of these four visions.[6] The first vision is the account of John's divine call and commission (1:10—3:22). This again identifies him with the line of important Old Testament prophets—Isaiah, Jeremiah and Ezekiel—who also report significant commissioning experiences (Isaiah 6; Jeremiah 1; Ezekiel 1). John is tasked by the glorified Jesus with writing down what he is about to be shown and sending a copy to the seven churches, with an individual word of admonition for each one.

6. See Ladd, *Revelation*, 14.

The second vision is the account of three series of seven judgments which are sent upon the earth (4:1–16:21). Each of the three series concludes with the end of the age and the fulfillment of God's prophetically declared purpose for the world (6:12–17; 10:7; 16:17–21). The third vision details the end of the old creation: the fall of "Babylon," the return of Christ, the final defeat of Satan, the resurrection and last judgment, and, finally, the descent of the New Jerusalem onto a new earth (17:1–21:8). The fourth vision, finally, is a "close-up" view of the New Jerusalem where God's people dwell in his manifest presence forever (21:9–22:7). So reads the text.

REVELATION IN THE BIBLICAL CANNON

Secondly, as already noted above, we need to allow the text its place in the biblical meta-narrative. Interpreters are often approaching Revelation as a stand-alone text outside of the general context of the whole biblical story. There is again a measure of interpretive value in that approach, of course, in helping to understand critical issues of authorship, dating, and historical setting, etc. But Revelation is also the last book of the biblical canon, and it contains material that is obviously supposed to reflect that position. If Genesis is the book of origins and beginnings, Revelation is the book of endings, of conclusions, of completions.

The last few chapters of Revelation in particular are so obviously a summation and conclusion of the biblical story that we would be doing great damage to the text not to recognize this and treat them as such. The interrelationship of the early chapters of Genesis and the closing chapters of Revelation (noting there were no chapters in the original, of course) are obvious.

Genesis	*Revelation*
Creation (Gen 1:1)	New creation (Rev 21:1)
Heaven and earth created (Gen 1:1)	Earth and sky flee away (Rev 20:11)
Night and day created (Gen 1:3–5)	No more night, sun not needed (Rev 22:5)
Sea created (Gen 1:2, 9–10)	No more sea (Rev 21:1)
Creation of sun and moon (Gen 1:16)	Sun and moon not needed (Rev 21:23)
God's people in the garden (Gen 2:8)	God's people in the city (Rev 21:23–27)
Tree of life in the garden (Gen 2:9)	Tree of life in the city (Rev 22:2)
River flowing in Eden (Gen 2:10)	River flowing in the city (Rev 22:1)
A bride for Adam (Gen 2:21–23)	A bride for Christ (Rev 21:9–10)

Satan appears (Gen 3:1)	Satan destroyed (Rev 20:10)
Curse pronounced (Gen 3:14–19)	Curse removed (Rev 22:3)
Death pronounced (Gen 3:19)	Death removed (Rev 21:4)
Banished from God's presence (Gen 3:23)	Restored to God's presence (Rev 21:2–4)
Access to tree of life blocked (Gen 3:22–24)	Access to tree of life restored (Rev 22:2)

This interconnection between the two passages is so clear as to be obviously deliberate on the part of the author. Note also that several times in Revelation Jesus is presented as the alpha and omega, the beginning and end, the first and the last (cf. Isa 48:12). This concept first appears at the beginning of the book (1:8) and then is repeated near the end (22:13; cf. 21:6), framing all that takes place between them. What was begun in the sanctuary of the Edenic garden is brought to completion in the sanctuary of the holy city. All that began in Genesis is brought to a conclusion in Revelation.

There are many other connections between the two books also; for instance, note:

Genesis	Revelation
Image of God created (Gen 1:27)	Image of beast made (Rev 13:14)
God gives breath to his image (Gen 2:7)	Breath given to beast's image (Rev 13:14–15)
The serpent deceives Eve (Gen 3:1–13)	Serpent deceives the whole world (Rev 12:9)

Or further, as noted above, in Genesis God created a bride for Adam, in Revelation a bride for Christ (the church). Eve was taken from Adam's side, and in order for the woman to be thus created the man had to be "wounded" and put into a "deep sleep"—a picture of death. Likewise, the church was brought into being when Christ was "wounded for our transgressions" (Isa 53:5 KJV, "pierced" NIV). Is that why Jesus was thrust in the side with a spear—a picture of the wound in Adam's side (or vice versa)? The first woman in the garden is thus a beautiful picture of the bride of Christ for which he died (see Eph 5:25–32) and who appears now in the final pages of the Bible's story. In Genesis the heavens and earth are created as a home for this first man and woman; in Revelation a new heaven and earth are created for the new man who has been created through faith in Jesus.

These are further examples of the interweaving of illustrations, types, and parallels that so fill the pages of the Bible, strengthening again the case for a biblical meta-narrative.

Again, as we listen to the text itself we note the many ways in which Revelation summarizes and completes the biblical story. It presents:

- The completion of the prophetic message and biblical plan of God (Rev 10:7)
- The return of Jesus (Rev 19:11–16)
- The final and complete wrath of God poured out on the earth (Rev 15:1)
- The end of the old creation and the beginning of the new (Rev 21:1)
- The end of Satan (Rev 20:7–10), of sin (Rev 21:27), and of death (Rev 21:4)
- The general resurrection (Rev 20:4–6; 11–13)
- The final judgment (20:11–15)
- The New Jerusalem as the end of God's work (Rev 21:2, 12, 14)
- God's people restored to God's presence (Rev 21:3; 22:3)

In so many ways, then, the text is claiming to be the capstone of the story that began with the creation of the heavens, the earth, and the first man and woman. All the great biblical themes and motifs are brought to fulfillment in Revelation, including those of the prophetic books:

- The final judgment of the earth and its unrepentant people
- The defeat of death and evil
- The final and ultimate restoration
- The triumph of the kingdom of God
- Messiah Jesus reigning in victory over a sinless and perfect new creation
- The blessing of God covering the earth

So, the book claims to bring to completion the message of the prophets, the story of Israel, and the story of creation itself.

SUMMARY OF CHAPTER TWELVE

In interpretive circles today, Revelation is generally labelled as apocalyptic literature (because of its style and content). It is compared with other (often non-canonical) apocalyptic literature of that period and said, like them, to be a symbolic representation of events within its own historical situation. It must have been understood thus, it is claimed, by its original audience, so we too must interpret it in that light. It cannot be about future events, it is said, or it would have had no immediate relevance to its original audience.[7]

However this may be, Revelation actually claims to be, in every conceivable way, the climax of biblical prophecy and to present the climactic conclusion of the biblical story. Several passages in Daniel (Dan 2:45; 8:19, 26; 10:14; 11:35; 12:1, 4, 9) show that it is possible for prophetic and apocalyptic literature to concern future events, even distant events, and thus be not immediately related to a current historical situation. The original audience will then understand it in the same way as interpreters of every age understand it, in the same way we understand it. Every generation will inevitably look for application to its own historical situation and will find some parallels, but the text claims to have a much bigger and wider application. While speaking directly to its historical situation in regards to the letters addressed to the seven churches and offering the encouragement of God's sovereign control of events on earth, much of the material in Revelation claims to deal with the climactic end of God's purposes and of human history in this age.

Revelation purports to be the summation and conclusion of all biblical prophecy, hence its relevance to the purpose of this book. It claims to show the full and complete wrath of God poured on the unbelieving world, the destruction of the anti-God world system, the return of Jesus, and the final and complete establishment of God's kingdom on a new earth—both complete judgment and complete salvation. If we are to take the text as it stands, then, it is clear that Revelation depicts the events of the prophetic Day of the Lord as described in chapter four of this book.

There is a divinely purposed and controlled end to the creation, a complete fulfillment, a renewal, a cleansing, a completion, and a restoration. God's power and purpose are bigger than human frailty and destructive satanic interference. What began as very good will be brought to completion, and it will be even better than when it started.

---

7. Jewish apocalyptic literature often pretended to be long-term prophecy from ancient times that was about to be fulfilled.

Chapter Thirteen

READING REVELATION

"Blessed is the one who reads the words of this prophecy, and blessed are those who hear it and take to heart what is written in it, because the time is near..." (Rev 1:3)

REVELATION IS NOT DIFFICULT to understand if we read the text in the light of the previous chapter, that is, as it claims to be the conclusion of the prophetic message and of the wider biblical story. Some of the details are difficult, to be sure (as are some details in the other prophets), but the broad structure, meaning, and message are fairly clear. In these last three chapters we again want to listen to the text as it unfolds its message. We want to let the text tell its own story—bearing in mind, of course, the symbolic and pictorial nature of the language used and the difficulty in interpreting some of it. We attempt to take the text, first of all, at face value.

Revelation is written in the form of a letter (see 1:4-9; 22:18-21), though as we have seen, the book itself claims to be prophecy (1:1, 3; 22:18-18) and John classes himself among the prophets (1:1; 22:9; 10:11). There is much apocalyptic content in the form of visions, fantastic imagery, and symbolism. Like Ezekiel and the second half of Daniel, Revelation is composed of four visions, each of which begins when John is "caught up in the Spirit" (1:10; 4:2; 17:3; 21:10). Ezekiel used a similar phrase when he said, "the Spirit lifted me up" (Ezek 3:12, 14; 8:3; 11:1, 24; 43:5). The unfolding of the four visions is preceded by an introduction (1:1-9) and followed by a conclusion (22:8–21). The four visions follow an interesting pattern, in that each is a development of something mentioned in preceding verses:

- Mention of Jesus Christ towards the end of the introduction (1:5) sets the stage for the first vision, which begins with a description of the glorified Jesus.
- Mention of the throne towards the end of the first vision (3:21) serves as an introduction to the second vision, which opens with a more complete description of the throne of God.
- Similarly, mention of "Babylon the great" at the end of the second vision (16:19) flows through into the third vision which opens with a description of this "Babylon the great."
- Mention of the New Jerusalem towards the end of the third vision (21:2) prepares the stage, then, for the fourth vision, which begins with a description of the heavenly city.

THE FIRST VISION

John, on the island of Patmos in the Mediterranean, is caught up in the Spirit and has a vision of the now glorified Jesus (Rev 1:9–3:22). No longer veiled as he was when he walked on earth, Jesus is seen now as he really is—Daniel's "Son of Man" (with features of Daniel's "Ancient of Days" also) who is given the everlasting kingdom and all authority (cf. Dan 7:13–14). He is ancient and wise and glorious, fearful and irresistible. He holds the churches in his hand, and his words are like a double-edged sword, laying bare all falsehood and misunderstanding. John falls before him as though dead (Rev 1:17. Cf. Dan 8:17–18; Ezek 1:28). This vision forms the background to all that follows in the rest of the book, providing an essential foundational truth that must be borne in mind through the pages that follow. Jesus is Lord; he is in control. The book of Revelation is not first of all about the antichrist or "the tribulation," not about secret codes and hidden meanings; it is about Jesus and the triumph of his redemptive plan for the world. He is in control of all events and of all destinies; he is alpha and omega. It is he who controls the great story and guides it towards its pre-ordained outcome.

Jesus holds the seven stars in his right hand (1:16) and walks among the seven golden lamp stands (1:13; cf. 1:20). These are interpreted for us as representing the seven churches and their "angels." The churches are under his care, under the power of his protection. He is the head of the churches, and he is both aware of, and is concerned about, what is happening in them and to them. The keys (1:18) symbolize his authority, and the sword (1:16) the power of his word as he speaks into each situation. Jesus commissions John to write down what he is about to see, hear, and experience, and to send it to the seven churches. The seven introductory addresses take the form of prophetic oracles, each following a similar pattern:[1]

1. Each letter is addressed to a particular church.
2. Each begins with the prophetic "Thus sayeth the Lord" formula ("these are the words").
3. Each one begins with a description of the one sending the message.
4. Most contain a specific commendation, where appropriate.
5. Some contain a "I have one thing against you" formula and a call to repentance.
6. Some contain an admonition as to the consequences of failing to repent.
7. Each finishes with the "he who has ears . . ." formula.
8. Each contains a promise to those who overcome.

Some claim to see here a dispensational message to the church through various ages, each letter being addressed to the church in a particular "dispensation" or historic period. There is nothing in the text itself to suggest this. That the letters are nonetheless an important part of Revelation and its message is clearly shown by the space afforded them—two and a half chapters out of the twenty-two that make up the book.

These are seven historical churches of that time, but why these seven churches? There were other churches in the region—why were these chosen? We need to note, in answer, the repetitious and symbolic use of certain numbers in Revelation.

The number two	*The number 10*	*The number seven*
2 resurrections (20:4–15)	10 horns (12:3)	7 lamp stands (1:2)
2 witnesses (11:3)	10 horns (13:1)	7 stars (1:6)
2 beasts (13:1, 11)	10 crowns (13:1)	7-fold Spirit (1:4)
2 horns (13:11)	10 horns (17:3)	7 letters (2:1–3:22)
2 deaths (20:11–14)		7 churches (1:11)
2 judgments of Satan (20:2, 10)	*The number 12*	7 promises (2:7–3:21)

---

1. See Witherington, *Revelation*, 90–91.

2 women (12:1; 21:2)	12 gates (21:12)	7 seals (5:1)
2 cities (17:5; 21:2)	12 angels (21:12)	7 angels (15:1; 8:2)
	12 tribes (21:12)	7 plagues (15:1)
The number four	12 foundations (21:14)	7 trumpets (8:2)
4 visions (1:10–21:7)	12 apostles (21:14)	7 bowls (16:1)
4 living creatures (4:6)	12,000 stadia (21:16)	7,000 killed (11:3)
4 faces (4:7)	12 jewels (21:19)	7 heads (12:3)
4 judgments (6:8)	12 pearls (21:21)	7 heads (17:3)
4 angels (7:1; 9:14)	12 fruits (22:2)	7 hills (17:9)
4 horses (6:1–8)		7 kings (17:10)
4 winds (7:1)		7 thunders (10:1–4)
4 corners (20:8)		

As can be seen, the number "seven" is used of these churches of chapters two and three, of the lampstands and stars of chapter one, the seven seals of chapter five, and much more. The number seven, in fact, appears fifty-two times in the book and is used symbolically to denote the idea of fullness or completion. These are seven real, historical churches that existed at the time of writing, and the particular prophetic oracle given to each one had specific reference and application to the historical situation to which it was addressed. That is clearly the import and intention of the text. But in the context of the symbolic use of the number seven in the book, the fact that this number of churches are chosen clearly implies that something more is involved. These are seven historical churches, but they are also seven representative churches. The overall message appears to be addressed to the church in all its fullness or completion, to the whole church across the ages. These seven particular churches somehow represent the wider church (cf. Rev 22:16). Jesus, in sending this message to the church as a whole, chooses seven real churches to be representative of the whole church body. In each instance, for example, the letters are concluded with the admonition, "He who has an ear, let him hear what the Spirit says to the *churches* . . ." indicating a more general application. Likewise, the promises given to those who overcome are surely not specific only to the members of the particular historical churches to which they are written. The introductory autobiographical words of Jesus to each of the seven oracles obviously speak to the church of all ages.

If Revelation is written by the apostle John towards the end of the first century,[2] then it is sixty or seventy years since Jesus died. Jerusalem, the temple, and the nation of Israel are all gone. The center of church life has now moved to Asia. John is in his nineties and all of the other apostles are dead. The rest of the New Testament is already written and only John's writings are left to complete it. The churches referred to here are forty or fifty years old. They have become well established and have had time to develop characteristics that Jesus either commended or condemned. The things that Jesus found to *commend* in the churches were attributes and practices that are commendable in any age, such as perseverance and endurance (2:2, 3, 19; 3:10), faithfulness (2:10, 13; 3:8), the discerning and rejecting of false doctrine and practice (2:2), love and faith (2:19), hard work, and willing service (2:2, 19). These are the things that please the heart of the Lord of the churches.

The things he found to *condemn* in these representative churches were the cooling of Christian passion (the "forsaking of the first love," or being "lukewarm," Rev 2:4-5; 3:14-20), the tolerance of false doctrine and practice, and disobedience (2:14-16; 2:20-25; 3:1-3). These are things that are undesirable in any church at any time.

These are all obviously traits that have a universal application to Christians and churches of all historical ages and all locations. Jesus is Lord of the church. He holds the churches in his hand; he walks among them and is very concerned with their well-being. Note must be taken by all churches of the things that please him and those that are unacceptable to him.[3]

Each of the seven letters ends with a promise given to those who overcome:

1. "To him who overcomes *I will give the right to eat from the tree of life*, which is in the paradise of God" (Rev 2:7, cf. 22:2).

2. "He who overcomes *will not be hurt at all by the second death*" (Rev 2:11; 20:14; 21:8).

3. "To him who overcomes *I will give some of the hidden manna. I will also give him a white stone with a new name written on it*, known only to him who receives it" (Rev 2:17; cf. 3:12).

4. "To him who overcomes and does my will to the end *I will give authority over the nations—'he will rule them with an iron scepter, he will dash them to pieces like pottery'*—just as I received authority from my

---

2. This, of course, is disputed by some.

3. As with the occasional material found in the NT Epistles, for example. Note that preterists treat all of Revelation in this way.

Father. *I will also give him the morning star*" (Rev 2:26–28; 12:5; 19:15; 22:16).

5. "He who overcomes . . . *will be dressed in white*. I will never blot out his name from the book of life, but will acknowledge his name before my Father and his angels" (Rev 3:5; 7:9; 20:12, 15).

6. "Him who overcomes *I will make a pillar in the temple of my God.* Never again will he leave it. *I will write on him the name of my God* and the name of the city of my God, the New Jerusalem, which is coming down out of heaven from my God; and I will also write on him my new name" (Rev 3:12; 21:2; 3:12).

7. "To him who overcomes *I will give the right to sit with me on my throne*, just as I overcame and sat down with my Father on his throne" (Rev 3:21; 5:6, 13; 7:17; 22:1, 3).

From this list we are firstly reminded of what was said in chapter six, that the kingdom of God in this age is often advanced through trial and suffering. These promises are given to those who have "overcome," and obviously for that to be possible there needs to be something to overcome. The letters themselves supply some of these things—false teaching, wickedness, slander, suffering, sexual immorality, apostasy, persecution, the cooling of spiritual passion, etc. In each case, those in the churches addressed are expected to be overcomers, and it is to these, the ones who conquer temptation and trial and remain faithful to the end, that the promises are given.

Secondly, we notice that these seven promises lay out for us the *end*, or the intention, that God has in mind for his people. This is describing, in a sense, "the manifestation of the sons of God" (Rom 8:18–21). Some of the references are mysterious, it is true, but what *is* clear is that these are staggering promises spelling out the immense purpose of God for his people, besides which everything else pales into insignificance. These promises speak of things so great as to be difficult to conceive of. "No eye has seen," Paul writes, "no ear has heard . . . no human mind conceived, *the things God has prepared for those who love him*" (1 Cor 2:9; cf. Eph 3:20). "When Christ appears," John also writes, *"we shall be like him . . ."* (1 John 3:2). Amazing.

SUMMARY OF CHAPTER THIRTEEN

Revelation is a record of four visions given to John while on the island of Patmos, "because of the word of God and the testimony of Jesus." In this first vision, John is instructed by the now glorified Jesus—particularly designated here "the Alpha and Omega" and "the Almighty"—to write down all that he is to be shown and to send the account to seven representative churches. These visions are given to make known (not to conceal—we are *supposed* to read and interpret Revelation) to the servants of Jesus "what must soon take place" (Rev 1:1). Each time, John is caught up in the Spirit and receives a vision that focuses on a particular scenario or series of events. John considers himself to be ministering in the line of the Old Testament prophets and claims to be presenting in this correspondence to the churches the culmination and fulfillment of the prophetic promises and predictions—the end of the Bible's story, the final accomplishment of the plan of God.

The first vision has served as a kind of introduction to what we are now going to read. In it we are reminded that there was a beginning and there is an end to God's purpose for this age and that there is one who controls the unfolding of that purpose. He is the one who declares the future and decides all destinies. We are reminded that history is not a meaningless, random unfolding of unrelated events; the universe is not out of control, evil has not won the day and will not prevail. There is one who holds the destiny of the churches and of the nations in his hands. There *is* a great story and he *will* bring it to completion.

He is the one who has been given the supremacy in all things. He is the "Son of Man" to whom the eternal kingdom is given. He is the Lord of the churches, disciplining the recalcitrant and rewarding those who overcome. This is essential background to the events that are about to unfold in the next few pages. All things are under his control, and in the end everything will work out for good for those who love him and are called according to his purpose.

Chapter Fourteen

THE TIME OF DISTRESS

"For then there will be a great distress, unequaled from the beginning of the world until now—and never to be equaled again." (Matt 24:21)

THE SECOND VISION (4:1–16:21) is the most difficult of the four to interpret, and this chapter should be read with an open Bible nearby. This vision unfolds a time of great distress coming upon the earth and is filled at times with dark imagery and dreadful symbols. Earth's sin has reached its fullness and God again calls time on the rebellious creation (2 Pet 3:5–7). The imagery and symbolism are complicated and at times difficult to follow, but the overall picture is clear enough as it outlines three series of seven judgments against the unrepentant world. There are the judgments of the *seals* in chapter six and eight; the *trumpets* in chapters eight, nine, and eleven; and the *bowls* in chapter sixteen. Between the three series of judgments, the text contains certain interludes describing various events taking place both in heaven and on the earth during this period.

Between 6th and 7th Seals	Between 6th and 7th Trumpets	Between 7th Trumpet and Bowls
Two groups	Two scenes	Two battles
1. The 144,000	1. The angel with the scroll	1. In heaven
2. The great multitude	2. The two witnesses	2. On earth

The third interlude, between the trumpets and the bowls, is expanded to include several other events taking place during this period also:

- There appear a woman and a dragon (12:1–6)
- There is war between the dragon (revealed as Satan) and the archangel Michael (12:7–17)
- Two beasts arise (13:1–18)
- The Lamb is shown with 144,000 redeemed followers (14:1–5)
- Three angelic heralds are seen (14:6–13)
- The harvest of the earth is described (14:14–20)

Each of the three series of judgments concludes with the end of the age and the end of God's prophetically declared purpose for the world (cf. 6:12–17; 10:7; 16:17–21), so they obviously do not follow each other chronologically. It is not altogether unusual for the Bible to cover the same time period more than once, or to look at the same event from different angles; for example, see:

- Genesis 1:26–30 and 2:4–25, showing two accounts of the creation of human beings
- The books of Kings and Chronicles cover the same historical period, Kings dealing with the history of both Judah and Israel, Chronicles with the history of Judah alone.
- The four gospels each cover the life and ministry of Jesus from different angles.

So, it is quite possible for the three series of judgments to occur over the same time period, though they seem to intensify towards the end. Robert Guthrie suggests something like this:[1]

```
1 2 3   4   5     6     7   Seals    }
        1 2 3 4 5  6     7  Trumpets } The end.
                  1234567   Bowls    }
```

Again, *seven* as used in Revelation equates to completeness or fullness, and the *three* series of seven serve to intensify this sense of completion. With these judgments, *all* of the promises, predictions, and prophecies of God's wrath against the unrepentant world are fulfilled and brought to completion. This describes the *fullness* of God's wrath, the completion of it, the end of it.

---

1. Gundry, *Church and Tribulation*, 75.

THE VISION UNFOLDS

This vision begins with a scene centered on the throne of God. We are reminded again that above everything that transpires on earth, above all adversity, above all despair, above all confusion and lack of understanding, there is a throne, and he who is seated on that throne is the one who was, and is, and is to come. Witherington calls the throne, "the central theological symbol of Revelation," which is written, he says, to answer the question, "to whom does the earth belong? Who is the ruler of the world?"[2] The throne is mentioned thirty-five times in Revelation, and this scene again sets the context from which to view all that follows and should always be borne in mind when reading the book—God is in control. There *is* a throne and the one enthroned there controls all history and all destinies, and he is good.

There is no description of the person on the throne (vv2–3). He is indescribable; there are no human words to convey the glory of him who sits enthroned between the cherubim. John can only try to tell us something of that glory in terms of the purity, brilliance, and beauty of precious jewels. God is awesome beyond words, and that sense of awe and fear should be maintained in interpreting what follows (see 1 Tim 6:16).

A rainbow encircled the throne (4:3). Ezekiel had a commissioning vision that bears remarkable similarities to John's in some respects (Ezek 1–3). He also saw a throne in his vision and similarly said of the one who sat on it that "brilliant light surrounded him . . . *like the appearance of a rainbow in the clouds on a rainy day,* so was the radiance around him" (Ezek 1:27–28).

Both John and Ezekiel describe four living creatures around the throne, their descriptions being similar in some ways but different in others, as would be expected of two different people trying to describe something completely outside of human experience, or perhaps two people seeing different aspects of the same supernatural scene. Ezekiel calls these angelic beings cherubim (Ezek 10:2–14). Isaiah describes seeing similar creatures in his commissioning vision and he calls them seraphs (Isa 6:2–4). The creatures in John's vision are covered with eyes (Rev 4:6; cf. Ezek 10:12) speaking perhaps of their all-seeing powers of perception and discernment. Nothing is hidden from their sight; they are constantly looking upon God and all he is doing in the universe. This in turn prompts continual worship from their lips, born of continual revelation.[3] They are joined in this worship by

---

2. Witherington, *Revelation*, 113.
3. This is not their only function. See Rev 6:1, 6; 15:7.

twenty-four elders, probably angelic beings also,[4] and by an innumerable angelic host.[5]

John tells us there was "a sea of glass, clear as crystal" before the throne. Ezekiel saw in his vision an expanse above the four living creatures that was "sparkling like ice" (Ezek 1:22). In Exodus, the seventy elders of Israel saw the God of Israel and under his feet was something like a pavement made of sapphire, "clear as the sky itself" (Exod 24:10). This is perhaps alluding to the purity of God in his remoteness and perfection, or it may be a more direct reference to the Holy Spirit (cf. Rev 22:1). It is the heavenly counterpart, perhaps, of the basin in the tabernacle that was made from the bronze mirrors of the women who served at the tent of the meeting (Exod 38:8).

THE SCROLL

Then John notices a *scroll* and the only one who was worthy to open it (Rev 5:1). The scene now changes and focuses on the *Lamb*, another picture of Jesus. In chapter four we saw the majestic sovereign God, seated on the throne, forever different from and above his creation. In chapter five we see at the center of that throne the lamb, the one who entered into and became part of the creation and who was slain in order to redeem it. The salvation of human beings was accomplished by God himself; he provided the sacrifice, the Son of God was himself the sacrifice (cf. Gen 22:13–14). The Lamb has seven eyes, also speaking perhaps of his complete vision and perception—nothing is hidden from him (Heb. 4:13). He has seven horns, indicating complete power—nothing is too hard for him.

From the things that happen as the seals are broken we can see that the scroll is the record of God's final judgment and redemption of the earth. It is a book of destiny, a book of final events, a book of righteousness and justice. It is written on both sides, speaking perhaps of the completeness of God's purposes. Nothing is left to chance, God is in complete control of the events of history. Seven seals protect its contents; it is completely sealed up and its contents hidden from every eye until revealed by God (cf. Acts 1:7 and Matt 24:36). Daniel had been told to seal up his prophetic scroll until "*the time of the end*" (Dan 12:4). Jesus now begins to open the seals on this scroll, inaugurating the final scenes of redemptive history, the prophetic day of the Lord.

---

4. See Ladd, *Revelation*, 75.

5. Compare again 1 Chronicles 24 and 25, where the temple priests and musicians were organized into twenty-four groups by David and the prophets.

As the seals are opened the first of the three series of judgments is let loose upon the earth. That these events are historically climactic and refer to the end of the age is evident from the context. For example, Revelation 6:12-17 describes the end of the age (cf. Isa 13:9-11; 34:2-4; Joel 3:14-16; Matt 24:29-31; etc.) and the great multitude of 7:9-14 come out of the *"great tribulation"* (cf. Dan 12:1-4; Matt 24:21), a term that seems in the Bible to have special application to the time immediately preceding the conclusion of the age.

The imagery of the four horses that constitute the judgments of the first four seals is taken from Zechariah 6:1-7 (cf. Zech 1:8-11) where they are explained as four spirits sent out across the earth from the presence of God. The first here in Revelation is a spirit of conquest, a militant spirit; people rise up intent on imposing their will on others. The second horse represents a spirit of open warfare, the third a spirit of economic hardship. As this judgment spreads across the earth, food is available (even luxury food) but at a very high price, so that many suffer hardship. The fourth horse represents a spirit of death, affecting one quarter of the earth's population, and many die by the "four judgments of God" (cf. Ezek 5:17; 14:21; etc.). These are the conditions that will prevail on the earth during the time of these four judgments. The fifth seal suggests that as well as God's judgments falling on the earth's unrepentant people, there will also be widespread persecution and even martyrdom experienced by the people of God through this time. This is not God's judgment or wrath affecting God's people, rather it is a result of the anger of Satan (Rev 12:12) and the final expression of the kingdom principle we looked at in chapter six, that the followers of Jesus have the privilege of sharing in his suffering. The opening of the sixth seal brings us to "the great day of . . . wrath," the final great cosmic judgment that affects the whole of the creation and ushers in the end of the age with the appearing of Jesus (cf. Isa 24).

FIRST INTERLUDE

Chapter seven is an interlude in the unfolding story of judgment (see table 5 above). It describes two companies, firstly a group of 144,000. This is a symbolic number, 12,000 each from the 12 tribes of Israel (cf. 14:1-3). No one knows why Dan has been substituted by Manasseh. These are sealed to protect them from judgment (cf. Ezek 9:4-6). They symbolically represent literal Israel or perhaps the church (cf. 7:3, Israel no longer existed as a nation at the time of writing). The second company is a group of the redeemed standing before the throne in heaven. John is told that "these are those who have come out of the great tribulation" (7:14). They number "a great multitude that none can count, from every nation, tribe, people and language" (7:9). They have "washed their robes and made them white in the blood of the Lamb" (7:14). They are Christians.

There are echoes here of the elders' song of Revelation 5:9-10 and there are allusions to Old Testament passages which reveal the purpose of God for the creation. The first man and woman were told to "fill the earth" with the image of God (Gen 1:27-28) and Abraham was told that his offspring would number as many as the dust of the earth or the stars in the sky (Gen 13:16; 15:5; cf. Heb 11:12), the point being that both are uncountable. These images all find fulfillment in this "great multitude that none can count." This suggests that they represent the church in all its fullness, the "church universal." But the fact that the angel describes them as coming out of "the great tribulation," implies also that there will be, during the time of these judgments, a great spiritual revival resulting in a great and final harvest of the earth's people and that the task that Jesus set the church will be completed (Matt 24:14; 28:19; Luke 24:47; Acts 1:8). The phrase the angel uses here, "the great tribulation," is the same phrase (in the Greek) as that used by Jesus in Matthew 24:21 when he talks about the time of unequalled distress that will close out the age, a reference to Daniel 12:1. The opening of the seventh seal (Rev 8:1) brings silence in heaven for a short time, perhaps marking the solemnity of the occasion (see Amos 8:3; Hab 2:20; Isa 41:1; Zeph 1:7; Zec 2:13). The seven trumpet judgments are about to begin.

THE SEVEN TRUMPETS

As with the first four seals, the first four trumpet judgments form a subgroup. As they are sounded one after another, one third of the earth is blasted with fire; one third of the sea, its creatures, and its ships destroyed; one third of the rivers and springs are poisoned; and one third of the heavenly bodies are darkened. This results in great loss of life (Rev 8:11).

When the fifth trumpet is sounded, an angel opens the *Abyss* and something like a demonic plague is released upon those who do not have the seal of God on their foreheads. There is some evidence in the Bible that the Abyss is a place where certain demonic spirits are imprisoned (Luke 8:31; 1 Pet 3:19; 2 Pet 2:4; Jude 6; and Rev 9:11). This is also the origin of the spirit that drives the "beast" of Revelation 11:7 and 17:8. The sounding of the sixth trumpet results in what is perhaps another, more severe, demonic plague, but if this is compared to the events of the sixth bowl judgment

THE TIME OF DISTRESS

(16:12-16) it would seem that the human armies are also involved. This judgment too affects one third of the people on earth.

SECOND INTERLUDE

Chapter 10:1-11 begins another interlude between the sixth and seventh trumpet that describes two scenes. The first involves a little scroll which John receives from a great angel. This is perhaps a record of the further visions and prophecies that were to follow (v 11). He is told to eat the scroll and it is sweet in his mouth (cf. Ezek 2:9-3:3) but turns bitter in his stomach. This may refer to the fact that what was to follow, the things that John was still to prophetically announce, would be a mixture of blessing and woe. Also, the words of God are sweet to some and bitter to others—life to those who love him, judgment and death to those who stand against him.

The interlude continues with the account of two witnesses (11:1-12). John is told first of all to measure the temple. This is difficult, but is probably speaking of some form of protection for the people of God through this time (cf. 11:2). But it seems the *Holy City* (Jerusalem? See 11:8; 21:2) will be "trampled on" for a period of time—forty-two months, or three and a half years (cf. Luke 21:24; Zech 12:1-3; 14:1-2). The two witnesses—whether two literal individuals or symbolic of a larger group of believers (see Luke 10:1, where the disciples are sent out two by two)—have a prophetic ministry in Jerusalem for 1,260 days, or three and a half years. They have been identified by some with Old Testament figures, particularly Moses and Elijah because of the similarity of the miracles they perform (cf. Mal 4:4-5). But again there is nothing of this in the text. It seems better to regard this as another example of the repetition and interweaving of themes and parallels as discussed in earlier chapters. When their ministry is over, the "beast" attacks and slays them, then after three and a half days they are raised to life and taken up to heaven. This is the first mention in Revelation of the *beast*, who will be seen to take a prominent part in events related in the chapters ahead.

The seventh trumpet again brings us to the end. Victory is proclaimed and the signs that mark the end of the age appear on the earth. An angel announces that this last trumpet brings to completion the message given to the prophets (10:7). Judgment is finished and God begins to reign (11:15). This adds to the evidence that Revelation is describing the prophetic day of the Lord, the time of climactic judgment and final salvation.

THIRD INTERLUDE

Another interlude is formed by chapters 12–14, this time between the judgments of the seven trumpets and those of the seven bowls. They relate a great heavenly battle and the results of that battle on the earth. John sees two "signs" or images (Rev 12:1–9), firstly a woman, "clothed with the sun, with the moon under her feet and a crown of twelve stars on her head." This image has been variously interpreted as representing the church, Israel, Mary, the people of God, and more. The imagery here only appears elsewhere in the Bible in Genesis 37:9, where Joseph describes his dream, saying, "the sun and moon and eleven stars were bowing down to me," symbolizing Jacob, Rachel, and his brothers. It seems best on this basis to interpret this woman as representing Israel.[6] From out of Israel then comes the "male-child," probably speaking of the messiah, who will rule all nations with an iron scepter (see Ps 2:7–9; Gen 1:26, 28; 49:10; Ezek 20:33; Dan 7:13–14; Mic 5:2; Zech 9:10; Rev 19:11–16)[7] and who is attacked by Satan but is taken up to the throne of God, the place of authority (cf. Rev 5:6).

Secondly, John sees a dragon (Rev 12:3) identified as Satan, the ancient serpent of Genesis chapter three (Rev 12:9). He is "crafty," totally opposed to God and all that he loves and plans to do. His only and every motivation is to "steal, kill, and destroy" (John 10:10). The dragon has seven heads, seven crowns, and ten horns. Seven again speaks of completeness. Heads in the Bible speak of ruling; horns speak of power; and crowns speak of authority, conquest, honor, or reward. This is a powerful being who has made himself the enemy of God and of God's people, a being who has held sway over many of the kingdoms of this world.[8] Again he has power here over one third of the stars, and this is taken by some to indicate that in his own fall he affected a great number of other angelic beings (12:7–9; cf. Jude 6; 2 Pet 2:4). There is great conflict in the heavens; Satan is defeated. He is thrown to the earth and in great anger he pursues the woman, who is protected for "a time, times and a half a time"—three and a half years. There is great difficulty but also some measure of special protection for Israel—or the people of God again—through this time it seems. Satan, then, in his anger turns on Christians, "those who hold to the testimony of Jesus."

---

6. Or the people of God, a larger category.

7. But compare Rev 2:26–27.

8. Satan claimed to have been given authority over all the kingdoms of the earth (Luke 4:6). He is a liar and the father of lies (John 8:44).

THE TWO BEASTS

As this interlude continues, the dragon Satan stands on the shore of the sea and summons from there a terrible beast having seven heads with blasphemous names and ten horns bearing ten crowns, identifying it closely with the dragon itself—from which it draws its power and authority (Rev 13:1–10; 17:7–14). As it appears here in chapter thirteen the beast is seen first of all to be a kingdom or an empire. The imagery is drawn from Daniel 7, where Daniel had a vision of four beasts—a lion, a bear, a leopard, and a fourth, unidentified, beast—which are interpreted for him as four kingdoms that would arise in the earth. This beast of Revelation 13, *"resembles a leopard, had feet like a bear, and a mouth like a lion,"* so combines elements of Daniel's first three beasts/kingdoms (Dan 7:2–7, cf. 7:17) and it seems to be the fulfillment of the fourth.

Concerning the last beast, Daniel wrote, "in my vision at night I looked, and there before me was a fourth beast—terrifying and frightening and very powerful. It had large iron teeth; it crushed and devoured its victims and trampled underfoot whatever was left. It was different from all the former beasts, and it had ten horns" (Dan 7:7). The ten horns, Daniel was told, "are ten kings who will come from this kingdom" (Dan 7:19–25). Nebuchadnezzar's vision of the giant statue (Dan 2:40–43) is again interpreted as representing four empires, the last of which may again shed light on this beast/empire of Revelation thirteen. Daniel 2:40 and 7:7 seem to be referring to the same beast. The empire of Daniel 2 has ten toes and the beast of Daniel 7 has ten horns. In the time of both empires, it is declared, God will set up his eternal kingdom (cf. Dan 2:44; 7:13–14, 26–27).

These two comparisons are important because they help perhaps to give us an idea of the location of this end-time empire. Daniel's four beasts arise out of "the great sea," probably referring to the Mediterranean Sea and so to the Mediterranean area.[9] The first three empires of Nebuchadnezzar's vision were all centered in the same area—around Babylon in the Middle East. The statue stands in Babylon and may suggest the empires will occupy the same general area. In fact all of these first three empires (Babylon, Media-Persia, and the Greek empire of Alexander the Great—see Daniel 8) at some stage had Babylon as their capital city. So the fourth empire will perhaps arise in the same area. This is the arena of Old Testament biblical prophecy. It was the nations that surrounded Israel that naturally had a direct effect upon Israel's destiny.[10]

---

9. But, perhaps referring to the world in general.

10. Greece, for instance, only appeared in the Bible story when it moved into this arena.

Further background is supplied by Daniel 8:1–26 where Daniel is given visions of kingdoms and events relating to "the time of the end" (8:17), "the time of wrath," and "the appointed time of the end" (8:19). Here, a ram with two horns depicts the empire of Media-Persia, and a goat with a prominent horn the Greek empire of Alexander the Great (Dan 8:20–21), who is replaced with four lesser leaders.[11] Later, *in this area*, another king will arise who will cause "astounding devastation" and destroy the people of God (Dan 8:23–25). Prophecy again telescopes events of different time periods.

THE FIRST BEAST

The beast/empire of Revelation 13 has seven heads. These are identified for us as seven hills and seven kings (Rev 17:9–10). Hills in the Bible are figurative of royal or political power. So, the seven heads speak of seven empires and the kings who ruled over them.[12] This empire, then, is the final stage of what we might call the super-historical "kingdom of the dragon Satan," which down through the ages has had seven main identities or stages.

In what is meant, perhaps, as a dreadful mockery of the death and resurrection of Jesus, one of the heads suffers a fatal wound but recovers to the astonishment of all. It is difficult to determine if this is meant physically, politically, or in some other way.[13] We are told that this beast has had a previous existence in the past; there is a time when it does not exist, and yet it will have a future manifestation (Rev 17:8), so perhaps this is the meaning.

This empire, then, seems to have two phases. It has arisen on the earth, seems to have suffered a fatal setback, and then arisen again as strong as ever, causing widespread astonishment (Rev 13:3, 17:8). This fatal wounding of the beast is obviously significant in understanding its identity as it is mentioned three times (13:3, 12, 14). In the last reference it is described as a sword wound, something received in combat of some sort. So the text here appears to be talking about a kingdom or empire that has appeared on the stage of history, has been mortally vanquished, but then arises again as

---

11. History records that at Alexander's death, his empire (now centered in Babylon, where he died) was divided up between his generals. So true is this to history in fact, that those who cannot accept a predictive element to Biblical prophecy must assign a late date to Daniel, i.e., after the events here described with such precision.

12. The mention of the seven hills sometimes lead to the interpretation that Rome is being referred to here, because Rome was traditionally built on seven hills. But that interpretation is unimaginative and based on an external geographical reference rather than internal scriptural comparisons.

13. And cf. Gen 3:15.

powerfully as before, causing all who witness it to be amazed. Or, it may be that this is speaking more personally in some way of one of the kings.

Five of these seven empires belonged to history; they had come and gone at the time of John's writing (Rev 17:10). The sixth, probably Rome, ruled in John's time. The seventh kingdom, though, at the time of writing, is still to come. When it does come it will last "a little while" (v 10), or "one hour" (v 12). This last empire of Revelation has ten horns, which are identified for us in Revelation 17:12-14 as ten kings. These ten kings come together and form an alliance, the last manifestation of this "kingdom of Satan." This final empire is centered in the biblical prophetic theatre, the area we call the Middle East. That each of these ten nations has a "blasphemous" name reveals that in some way they share an anti-Christ nature. There is something about them that is irreverent and insulting to God and their power and authority is Satanic in origin. This empire is given wide-ranging power and control over the world's nations (13:7) and attracts both the admiration and the adoration of the world's peoples (13:3-4, 8).

This empire is given "a mouth to utter proud words and blasphemies." Compare this again with Daniel's vision of the fourth beast that had ten horns. "While I was thinking about the horns," he writes, "there before me was another horn, a little one, which came up among them; and three of the first horns were uprooted before it. This horn had eyes like the eyes of a man and a mouth that spoke boastfully . . ." (Dan 7:8, 11-12).

This appears to be speaking now of an individual (or perhaps a smaller influential group) that arises among the ten nations. So what the text appears to be saying here is that an empire seemingly lost to history will reappear on the world stage and out of that empire will emerge an individual who will attain worldwide authority and power. Some see here a reference to the expected anti-Christ figure of New Testament prophecy (2 Thess 2:3-4), a man who would appear in the last days and strongly oppose the Lord and his people. This antichrist was a seemingly well-known concept in the early church (2 Thess 2:1-6, esp. v 5; 1 John 2:18).

THE SECOND BEAST

The text then records a second beast arising out of the earth (Rev 13:11-18). This seems to be referring to an individual this time, and he is called, significantly, the "false prophet" (Rev 16:13, 19:20; 20:10). This man "looked like a lamb, but spoke like a dragon" (v 11). His outward appearance gives the impression of being a harmless man of peace, perhaps a religious man (hence "false prophet"), but his words betray where his heart really is and where the real source of his power lies. "Watch out for false prophets," Jesus warned, "they come to you in sheep's clothing, but inwardly they are ferocious wolves" (Matt 7:15).

Here then, at the end of the age, arises the ultimate false prophet whose objects are to deceive and to enslave. The fact that he looked like a lamb (a sacrificial animal) may, in some sort of way, be meant again as mockery of Jesus (Rev 5:6, etc.). He is given satanic power to perform great and miraculous signs (Rev 13:13–15), thereby deceiving a great many people. This sounds very similar to Paul's warning (to which it surely alludes) to the church in Thessalonica (2 Thess 2:9–12).

Amazingly, this false prophet then sets up an image of the first beast, to which he gives breath and which he causes to speak. He then forces everyone to worship the image. All who refuse are put to death. The imagery in this passage is drawn from Genesis, where we are told, "God created man in his own image" (Gen 1:27) and "breathed into his nostrils the breath of life" (Gen 2:7). It is also shot through with imagery from Daniel 3:1–6 where the king of Babylon sets up a golden image and forces everyone to worship it on pain of death.

We now have a kind of trinity of evil—the dragon, the beast, and the false prophet (cf. 16:13)—and an "image" of the beast. There is continued satanic imitation and mockery of the creation story here, again linking this last book of the Bible with the first.

THE "MARK OF THE BEAST"

The mockery continues as he (the false prophet or the image) forces everyone to receive a *mark* on his or her right hand or forehead, without which they cannot buy or sell. This is imitation again of the 144,000 followers of the Lamb who are sealed with the name of God on their foreheads (Rev 7:3; 14:1). This may in turn refer back to Ezekiel's vision where the righteous are sealed on their foreheads with a "mark"[14] (Ezek 9:4).

This "mark of the beast," which everyone is forced to receive, is "the name of the beast or the number of his name . . . it is a man's number . . . 666" (Rev 13:17–18). The number of proposed solutions to this puzzle is almost as high. If we look to the Old Testament to help solve the problem, we find that the only two similarities are with Nebuchadnezzar's golden image that was sixty cubits high and six cubits wide (Dan 3:1), and that Solomon received 666 talents of gold each year (1 Kgs 10:14). There are perhaps some clues in those references. Is it something to do with "gold" or finance? Or

---

14. The Hebrew letter *taw*, which originally looked like an "x."

idolatry in some way? Solomon had problems with both idolatry (1 Kgs 11:4) and greed (Deut 17:16-17; 1 Kgs 10:23-29), and the New Testament ties these two together (Col 3:5).

However, the mark placed on the foreheads of the followers of the Lamb is fairly obviously a metaphorical mark, whereas the "mark of the beast" may include, as well, something more tangible because of the forced economic element involved. Furthermore, whenever the beast's mark is mentioned it is always associated with the worship of the beast, so it serves both a religious and economic purpose (see 13:15, 16; 16:2; 19:20; 20:4). It somehow demonstrates an allegiance to the beast. The *forehead* and *hand* may be metaphorical in some way.

Some see in this an example of gematria, where in some older languages numbers were written with letters, or letters had a numerical value—for instance, A=1, B=2, C=3, etc. Using this method, interpreters have arrived at a long list of possible candidates for the beast, from the Roman emperor Nero of John's time to various political or religious figures and world leaders of our own time. However, no other numbers in Revelation are used in this way; instead they are used metaphorically, figuratively, or symbolically. G. K. Beale sees the number six as representing "incompleteness" in Revelation (in contrast to seven representing completeness), and the triple repetition as adding intensity to this idea of incompleteness or failure.[15] Using this suggestion, this is a failure of a man, a man of sin, a man who falls short of God's intention. It is perhaps best understood as the equivalent of Paul's "man of lawlessness" (2 Thess 2:3, "man of sin" KJV. Cf. 1 John 3:4).

THE COMPANY IN HEAVEN AND THE THREE ANGELS

A company of 144,000 of the redeemed in heaven is then described (Rev 14:1–5). We are not told a great deal about them. Are they the same company of chapter seven? Perhaps they are representative of all believers, or perhaps of a leadership group—144 is 12 x 12 and twelve seems to speak of God's governance in the Bible (twelve tribes, twelve apostles etc.).

Three angelic heralds then appear (Rev 14:6–13). One proclaims the gospel and calls for repentance, the second proclaims the destruction of "Babylon" and the third proclaims judgment on those who worship the beast and take his mark. These three things are taking place on the earth at this time: judgment, destruction, and salvation—the marks of the prophetic Day of the Lord.

---

15. Beale, *Revelation*, 722.

THE HARVEST OF THE EARTH

Then is described the "harvest of the earth" (Rev 14:14–20). There are actually two harvests here, or a two-phase harvest that speaks again of the final judgment. The first is by Daniel's "Son of Man" (cf. Dan 7:13–14). Some see this as a gathering in of the righteous at the return of Jesus (cf. Matt 24:30–31; Mark 4:26–29). The second harvest is carried out by an angel. The imagery of sickle, harvest, grapes, and winepress are taken from the prophet Joel where it is a picture of God's final judgment against the nations on the Day of the Lord. "Let the nations be roused; let them advance into the Valley of Jehoshaphat, for there I will sit to judge all the nations on every side . . . Swing the sickle, for the harvest is ripe. Come, trample the grapes, for the winepress is full and the vats overflow" (Joel 3:12–13; cf. Joel 3:1–3, 14–16).

Those who are victorious over the beast are then seen in heaven (Rev 15:2–4). Are these the same people as the great multitude of Revelation 7:9–17, or are they martyrs who have given their lives for Jesus? In the end we see that the beast has power only over men's bodies (cf. Matt 10:28). This has always been the weakness of those who would persecute men and women for their faith in God. Death is the limit of their influence and power. But for the followers of Jesus, the very act of martyrdom is a victory. For them, death is not the end; they have been "faithful unto death" (Rev 2:10 AV), and he who was himself obedient unto death has conquered that enemy, and they will share in his victory at the resurrection.

THE SEVEN BOWLS OF WRATH

The seven angels with the seven last plagues are then seen in heaven (Rev 15:1, 5–8, and we are told that with these seven judgments God's wrath is completed (Rev 15:1; cf. Nah 1:5–6; Zeph 1:14–18). This yet again indicates that Revelation is intended to refer to the Day of the Lord, the time when all things are brought to completion and conclusion, the time of final judgment and final salvation.

Both the trumpet and bowl judgments are carried out by groups of seven angels first seen in a temple setting (Rev 16:1–21; cf. 8:2; 15:5–8). These judgments are reminiscent of the plagues on Egypt (Exod 7–12)[16] except that here they are of worldwide scope. The "great distress" is, in a way, another picture of the exodus, as God's people are delivered through a time of darkness when God's wrath falls on the unrepentant of this world

---

16. Again illustrating the interweaving of concepts and themes that occur throughout the Bible narrative.

and their gods. The first four in each set of judgments are similar, covering the divisions of earth, sea, rivers, and sky, except that the bowl judgments are generally more intense.

Trumpets	Bowls
One third of the earth is blasted with fire.	Land and followers of the beast are struck.
One third of the sea, its creatures, and ships are destroyed.	All of the sea and its creatures are destroyed.
One third of the rivers and springs are poisoned.	All fresh water turns to blood.
One third of the heavenly bodies are darkened.	The sun scorches people with fire.

There are several things to note here: The judgments are aimed at the followers of the beast (the enemies of God's people and of God's prophets) and the unrepentant (Rev 16:2, 6, 9). God again is in complete control and it can be seen that part of the reason that God punishes people is so they will repent and turn to him for forgiveness (cf. Amos 4:6–11). Even in God's wrath there is always the element of grace for those who will repent, though many at this time will not (Rev 9:20–21).

The fifth angel pours out his bowl on the throne and the kingdom of the beast, plunging it into darkness (16:10–11). Earlier we were told that the beast was given "authority over every tribe, people, language, and nation," and now there is worldwide judgment against his kingdom (Rev 13:7–8, 12–16). The sixth bowl (vv 12–16) reveals the demonic activity behind the events that are taking place on earth as the armies of the world gather together for the last great battle (Rev 9:13–21; Joel 3:9–16). Again, here we see the text clearly using the terminology of the prophetic Day of the Lord as it talks of world leaders being gathered together for battle "on the great day of God Almighty" (16:14). In the middle of this judgment is a warning of the suddenness and unexpectedness of Jesus' return, so it appears that at this stage in the unfolding drama he has not returned to earth. This final war will end with his appearing (Rev 19:11–21).

As the seventh angel pours out his bowl of wrath, there is a shout, "it is done!" The last bowl brings us again to the end of the age. If we compare the ends of each of the three series of judgments we can see that each brings us to the same conclusion. We are not dealing with chronologically continuous or sequential events in this vision.

Sixth seal	Seventh trumpet	Seventh bowl
Rev 6:12–17	Rev 11:15–19	Rev 16:17–21
Great earthquake	Earthquake	Severe earthquake
Sun darkened	—	—
—	Hailstorm	Hailstones
Moon turned blood red	—	—
—	Lightning and thunder	Lightning and thunder
Stars fall to earth	—	—
Sky recedes like a scroll	—	—
Mountains and islands removed	—	—
God revealed	God begins to reign	"It is done!"
Day of wrath has come	—	Wrath on "Babylon"

Each of the three series references a concluding earthquake, *great* under the seals and *severe* under the bowl judgments, in fact so severe that there has never been another earthquake like it in human history. Further cataclysmic and cosmic events occur also; huge hailstones, thunder and lightning, the heavenly bodies affected, all of it leading to the end of the age and the return of Jesus.

Background to all of this is supplied by a large number of Old Testament references, many of them in the prophets. Ezekiel describes a huge earthquake and hailstones occurring "in that day" and "at that time" (Ezek 38:14–23), revealing the greatness and holiness of God to the nations. In other prophets also, cosmic signs indicate the arrival of the Day of the Lord (Isa 13:9–11; 24:21–2; and Joel 2:30–32; 3:14–16). The seventh plague upon Egypt involved hailstones, thunder, and lightning (Exod 9:22–25). In other passages too, thunder and lightning indicate the presence of the Lord (Exod 19:16; 2 Sam 22:13–14; Ps 18:12; Ps 77:18; Ezek 1:13). Once again, this is the language of the Day of the Lord.

SUMMARY OF CHAPTER FOURTEEN

John's second vision presents a sobering picture of the events that take place immediately preceding and leading up to the end of the age. The vision begins, deliberately, before the throne of God, reminding us that through all that is to be described in the following revelation there is a throne. Jesus is seated on the throne, and all that is about to transpire is according to his purpose, revealed ahead of time through the prophets, and under his control. It must, therefore, be ultimately good. A great deal of emphasis is placed on this (indicated by the space given to it), and the throne is referred to again and again throughout Revelation. It is therefore vital background to the rest of the vision and all that happens through the rest of the book. There is a throne, and its foundations—as the prophets constantly reminded us—are righteousness and justice. There is a throne, and the earth belongs to him who is seated on it. This is central to the theology of Revelation.

The imagery and symbolism of this section of Revelation is very complicated and at times confusing, but there are some things that emerge fairly clearly through it all. The text describes three series of seven judgments, and we are told that with these judgments the full extent of God's wrath has been poured out on the unrepentant peoples of the earth. This surely unfolds the "great distress, unequalled from the beginning of the world until now," spoken of by Jesus (Matt 24:15–22) and by the prophet Daniel (Dan 12:1–3), and the awful and unequalled "day of Jacob's trouble," spoken of by Jeremiah (Jer 30:7) and other prophets. Many references and allusions again and again make it plain that this is the fulfillment of the prophetic Day of the Lord spoken about so often through the prophets. Huge sections of the world's population will perish through these judgments, which are aimed primarily at the unrepentant and those who worship the beast. There is a tunnel through which the church and the world must pass before all things are completed and renewed.

It appears, if we are reading the text correctly, that during this time a Satanically-inspired coalition of ten nations in the biblical prophetic arena will take control of the world's trade and financial system and compel the nations of the world to yield it their allegiance and some form of religious worship.[17] It will also persecute both Jews and Christians. Although sealed by God to protect them against the effects of his wrath being poured out as above, many Christians will lose their lives as martyrs through this period (Rev 6:9–11). The preferred method of execution of Christians by the beast seems to be beheading (Rev 20:4). This may of course be symbolic of violent death in general.

It must be borne in mind that the length of this period of judgment is limited. The text refers to various periods of seven years and three and a half years. These should be taken as indicating a limited time rather than literal years necessarily. The text also talks of *a short time* and *one hour*. Jesus too spoke of this time of judgment as being "cut short" for the sake of the elect. If this was not the case, he said, no one would survive (Matt 24:22).

---

17. One of my reviewers made the comment that this sounds more like interpretation than letting the text speak for itself. While this may be, it seems relatively clear to me in the light of many other biblical texts.

At the same time, in line with the Day of the Lord in the prophets being a time of both judgment and salvation, a great spiritual revival will take place on the earth which will result in an uncountable number of people "from every nation, tribe, people and language" becoming Christians (Rev 7:9-17). The end of the age, then, is marked by cataclysmic and climactic events—both on the earth and in the heavens above, both in the natural realm and in the spiritual realm, both judgment and salvation—in a great and final "Day of the Lord."

Chapter Fifteen

THE END AND THE BEGINNING

"For he was looking forward to a city with foundations, whose architect and builder is God..." (Heb 11:10)

JOHN'S THIRD VISION (REV 17:1–21:8), if we allow the text its voice, tells of the destruction of "Babylon the Great" and the final establishment of God's rule on the new earth, the end of the present sinful age and the beginning of the age to come. After the great distress and dark imagery of the previous vision, hope and salvation are seen anew. The story that began in Genesis is brought to its predetermined end in Revelation.

This third vision is the tale of two cities, "Babylon the Great" and the "New Jerusalem." It is the story of two women, the "Great Prostitute" and the "Bride of the Lamb." It tells of the two judgments of Satan, the first in which he is bound in the abyss for 1,000 years and the second in which he is thrown into the lake of fire at the end of that time. It is the story of two resurrections, the first before the 1,000 years and the second after it.

THE WOMAN ON THE BEAST

As the vision opens, John is shown a woman who is described as "the great prostitute" seated on a fabulous beast. She is also described by the angelic interpreter as seated on *many waters*, which is interpreted for us as representing "peoples, multitudes, nations and languages" (17:15). Whoever, or whatever, this woman represents is spread across the nations. The beast she sits astride resembles a combination of the dragon of chapter twelve and the beast from the sea of chapter thirteen as can be seen in the following table:

Chapter twelve	Chapter thirteen	Chapter seventeen
Red dragon	Beast	Scarlet beast
Seven heads	Seven heads	Seven heads
Ten horns	Ten horns	Ten horns
Seven crowns	Ten crowns	—
—	Blasphemous names	Blasphemous names
Satan	World empire	Babylon

Who is this woman and what does she symbolize? The text tells us she is satanically empowered (see 12:3–9), and in some way she is linked also with the Beast and his kingdom. She is clothed in great luxury and splendor (17:4). Purple and scarlet in the ancient world were expensive dyes, and these colors were worn by the rich and powerful. She is named "Babylon the Great" (17:5).

Babylon

Babylon and the New Jerusalem in Revelation are symbols rather than two literal cities. "Babylon" represents the great rebellious *world system* that holds power over the nations, what Ben Witherington refers to as "the bastion of paganism."[1] It began with the first humans in the garden when they, in response to the voice of the serpent, decided that they did not need to live under the rule of their creator. They would be independent, make their own decisions, map out their own destinies, they would be self-determining. It found expression later at Babel, a city built in pride and in defiance of the divine will. Babylon is the city of human beings in rebellion against God. Its spirit is clearly shown by the declaration of King Nebuchadnezzar. "Is this not great Babylon," he said, "that I have built . . . by my mighty power and for the glory of my majesty?" (Dan 4:30). Babylon symbolizes the world opposed to the rule of God.

Babylon was the nation that carried Judah into captivity for seventy years, the city and empire the prophets warned the nation about, God's instrument of chastisement for his rebellious people. It was the city of banishment from God's presence and from his blessing. It has come to stand

---

1. Witherington, *Revelation*, 189.

for the whole anti-God world system (17:6). It reaches its zenith in these last days of history as recorded in Revelation, the great world-wide system of commerce (18:3, 11–19), industry (18:22), politics, and entertainment (18:22) that leaves God out of consideration. It stands in opposition (sometimes openly and even mockingly, but always there, even if covertly) to his plan and purpose in the world. It captures the hearts of men and women and lures them to destruction. It is "the great city that rules over the kings of the earth" (17:18).

This passage in Revelation describes the end of this city, the end of the "world" that John spoke of in his first epistle. "Do not love the world," he wrote, "or anything in the world. If anyone loves the world, the love of the Father is not in him. For everything in the world—the cravings of sinful man, the lust of his eyes and the boasting of what he has and does—comes not from the Father but from the world. The world and its desires pass away, but the man who does the will of God lasts forever" (1 John 2:15–17). In words reminiscent of Nahum's prophecy against Nineveh (Nah 3), John describes the fall and destruction of this ancient city in preparation for the revelation of the Bride of the Lamb and the final establishment of his kingdom on earth. Its judgment is swift and complete and causes great rejoicing in heaven but great dismay for the inhabitants of the earth.

"Woe! Woe to you, great city, where all who had ships on the sea became rich through her wealth! In one hour she has been brought to ruin! Rejoice over her, you heavens! Rejoice, you people of God! Rejoice, apostles and prophets! For God has judged her with the judgment she imposed on you . . . With such violence the great city of Babylon will be thrown down, never to be found again" (Rev 18:1–19:10).

Here is described the collapse of what seems to be the global trade and economic systems, brought about by the Beast and his confederation of nations who initially seemed to give their backing to it. They used it for their own purposes (13:16–17) but actually despised it and eventually destroyed it (Rev 17:15–18). Evil is always, in the end, self-destructive.

THE COMING OF THE KING

The text then describes what is taken by many commentators to be the return of Jesus to the earth, this time not as servant but now openly as king (19:11–21).[2] He has come to rule, not veiled as previously, but now clothed in glory for all to see, bringing justice and executing judgment on all who

---

2. It must be noted that this is not the only possible interpretation of these verses, but the passage includes many elements used elsewhere of the climactic return of Jesus.

stubbornly oppose him (cf. 2 Thess 1:6–10). In language borrowed from Isaiah, his robe is stained with the blood of his enemies, and he is accompanied by the armies of heaven (cf. Isa 63:1–6).

The beast has gathered his armies together to fight against God's people. This seems to be the same situation as those related in both 6:15–17 (the sixth seal) and 16:12–16 (the sixth bowl) and perhaps 9:16 (the sixth trumpet). The nations gather at "Armageddon," which might be a physical location (*Har Magiddo* or "the mountain of Megiddo"[3]) or a symbolic name in some way. The battle is decided by the direct intervention of Jesus (cf. Rev 9:16; 2 Thess 2:8; Zech 14:1–9). The beast and the false prophet are taken and thrown into the lake of fire and their followers overthrown.

THE MILLENNIUM AND THE NEW JERUSALEM

The first half of this third vision detailed the final judgment of the "world system." The second half then details the establishing of the visible kingdom of God on the earth, which takes place in two stages. In the first stage, Satan—that ancient serpent and enemy of all that is good, the power behind the beast, the false prophet, and "Babylon"—is himself seized and bound in the abyss for 1,000 years (Rev 20:1–3). From there he is unable to work his wickedness and the earth is free from his temptations and accusations. The final and physical establishment of God's kingdom on earth then begins with the first resurrection (Rev 20:4–6). The text suggests here that only those opponents and victims of the beast have a part in this resurrection but 1 Corinthians 15:51–57 and 1 Thessalonians 4:13–18 shed light on this event also and make clear that all those who have died in Christ will be resurrected at this time, together with those Christians who remain alive, whose bodies will be changed. This is the resurrection and the defeat of death prophesied and promised by both the Old Testament prophets and by Jesus, and it takes place on his return to rule finally on earth. All who have followed him will gain a perfect and glorious victory and share with Jesus as he reigns on earth for 1,000 years. This thousand-year reign is generally referred to as the Millennium (which just means 1,000 years), which is probably best taken as meaning a period of time, rather than necessarily being an exact designation.

---

3. Barker, *NIV Study Bible*, note on Rev 16:16.

THE RAPTURE

The "rapture" is a common element in the eschatological teaching of some evangelical and most pentecostal Christian streams today. In its classic form it refers to a "snatching up" of the church before an expected "tribulation," or time of trouble, immediately preceding the return of Christ. Jesus descends (it is taught) into the air, living Christians are caught up to meet him, their bodies changed, and they ascend with him again into heaven. The church then remains in heaven while on earth the "great tribulation" runs its course, after which the church returns with Jesus to reign on earth and the first resurrection takes place. There are problems, however, with this teaching that need exploring.

There is no mention in the prophets, for instance, of this currently popular evangelical concept and it seems altogether impossible that such an important eschatological event would be omitted altogether from the proclamations of the prophets were it true. "Surely the Sovereign Lord does nothing," Amos says, "without revealing his plan to his servants the prophets" (Amos 3:7). The prophets are silent on the subject of the rapture.

Jesus never once mentioned a rapture. His focus for the final victory was always on the resurrection of the dead, which would happen when he gave the command (John 5:25; cf. John 6:39-40, 54) as he had demonstrated before the tomb of Lazarus. Jesus often talked about the resurrection (Mark 12:25-27; Matt 22:30-31; Luke 14:14; 20:35-36), and it is clear that this was the common understanding and expectation of the time (John 11:24).[4] Never do we hear Jesus encouraging people to prepare for, strive for, or expect some snatching up before the resurrection. The passage in Matthew 24:36-41 is sometimes given as an example of Jesus talking about a rapture, but such an interpretation is only possible if these verses are completely lifted out of their context, which is clearly that of Jesus returning in great glory and power, accompanied by cataclysmic signs that affect the sun, moon, and stars, and "a loud trumpet call" (Matt 24:26-31). This hardly describes a secret coming to steal the church away to a place of safety. Jesus also made it clear that the church would play a prophetic intercessory role on the earth through the time he called the great distress (Matt 24:21-28; cf. 2 Tim 2:10; Tit 1:1; with Rom 1:5; 11:3; Gal 2:8; 1 Tim 2:7).

Paul's hope was in the resurrection, not a rapture (Acts 23:6; 24:15; Rom 6:5; 1 Cor 15:12-13, 21, 29, 42). "I want to know Christ," he wrote, "and the power of his resurrection and the fellowship of sharing in his sufferings, becoming like him in his death, and so, somehow, *to attain to the*

---

4. Excepting, of course, among the Sadducees.

resurrection from the dead " (Phil 3:10–11). This was his aim, his hope, his goal. In his teaching among the churches, he taught the resurrection, not the rapture (1 Cor 15:20–54; 1 Thess 4:13–18; 2 Tim 2:18).

There is no mention of a rapture in the book of Revelation. Some claim to see it in 4:1 or 11:12 but there is nothing of it in the actual text,[5] nor is there any clear, unambiguous mention of it anywhere else in Revelation. This is hard to credit in the book that purports to be about the final eschatological events of the age. Revelation, on the other hand, as with many other books in both Testaments, very clearly presents the resurrection as the event which marks the defeat of death at the return of Jesus (19:4–6). So the biblical Christian hope is not in a snatching away from the world before the time of distress, but in the resurrection from the dead at the return of Christ (cf. Rom 8:11, 23) as foretold and promised in the prophets.

The rapture is completely missing also from the major Christian creeds. These great statements of Christian faith and belief are entirely silent about any secret coming of Jesus for the church. When talking about the return of Jesus they each focus instead on the resurrection. The Nicene Creed—product of the first general church council—says, "*We look for the resurrection of the dead, and the life of the world to come.*"[6] The Apostles' Creed likewise closes with the statement, "I believe in the Holy Spirit, the holy catholic church, the communion of saints, the forgiveness of sins, *the resurrection of the body*, and the life everlasting." The Athanasian Creed, in turn, states, "At His coming, *all men are to arise with their own bodies*; and they are to give an account of their own deeds." It is the resurrection that has been awaited by the church throughout history, not a secret rapture.

The focus of all victorious biblical eschatology is on the resurrection, not some "snatching away" (Matt 22:28–31; etc. Cf. Luke 14:14; 20:35–36; John 11:24–25; Acts 1:22). It is a resurrection that was promised by the Old Testament prophets. It was the resurrection that was the focus of the New Testament preaching, not a rapture (Acts 4:2, 33; 17:18, 32; Heb 6:2). It was the resurrection that was the focus for those men and women of faith listed in Hebrews who suffered for their beliefs. "Others were tortured and refused to be released," it says there, "so that they might gain *a better resurrection*" (Heb 11:35). In Revelation 20:4–6 it is those who have a part in

---

5. These two texts are specific (in context) to the people directly addressed. Nor can both texts support the concept of a rapture. If one does the other cannot, yet both are supported by different groups.

6. The ecumenical, or general, councils were gatherings of church leaders and theological experts from all over the world called together to discuss and settle matters of church doctrine and practice. The first of these councils met in the city of Nicaea (Iznik in present-day Turkey) in AD 325.

the resurrection who receive heaven's approbation, not the participants in some supposed snatching up. There is no explicit teaching in either the Old or New Testaments on a "rapture" as a separate (or previous) event to the resurrection.

Those who advance the concept of a rapture frequently quote 1 Corinthians 15:20–52, and 1 Thessalonians 4:13–18 as key passages supporting their teaching, but even a cursory examination will reveal that these passages are about resurrection, not a pre-resurrection "rapture." "Listen," Paul writes in the Corinthian passage, "I tell you a mystery: We will not all sleep, but we will all be changed—in a flash, in the twinkling of an eye, at the last trumpet. For the trumpet will sound, *the dead will be raised* imperishable, *and we will be changed.* " The "changing" of those who do not sleep (i.e., those who are still alive when the last trumpet sounds) clearly takes place after, or in conjunction with, the dead being raised, that is, as part of the resurrection. In Thessalonians Paul is even clearer:

"Brothers," he writes, "we do not want you to be ignorant about those who fall asleep, or to grieve like the rest of men, who have no hope. We believe that Jesus died and rose again and so we believe that God will bring with Jesus those who have fallen asleep in him. According to the Lord's own word, we tell you that we who are still alive, who are left till the coming of the Lord, *will certainly not precede those who have fallen asleep.* For the Lord himself will come down from heaven, with a loud command, with the voice of the archangel and with the trumpet call of God, and *the dead in Christ will rise first.* After that, we who are still alive and are left will be caught up together with them in the clouds to meet the Lord in the air. And so we will be with the Lord forever."

This is straightforward—the dead will rise first. *After that* those redeemed people who remain alive at Christ's return will be caught up (*"raptured,"* from the Latin translation of the Greek word used here) together with those raised from the dead. This is the first resurrection. It is difficult to see how this can be inverted to place the "catching up" as a separate event taking place *before* the first resurrection. It is plain from these passages that those who remain alive at the return of Jesus will be changed and caught up *as part of the resurrection*. There is no separate rapture taught in the Bible.

The conclusive argument against the idea of a pre-resurrection rapture lies on the deep level of biblical Christian theology and worldview. N. T. Wright sees the rapture concept as a manifestation of the Gnosticism that has infected large parts of the church today.[7] It is both "escapist" and

---

7. Wright, *Creation, Power and Truth*, 12–13.

it reveals a typically gnostic dualism—the physical world is bad, and the spiritual world / heaven is good.

The worldview, or rationale, behind the concept of the rapture is completely foreign to New Testament Christianity and is exactly contradictory to the express will and purpose of Jesus for his church. Jesus does not want Christians to escape the world—he commanded his followers to go out *into* it and redeem it, transform it, and bring the nations under his lordship. The gospel of the kingdom is victory, not retreat. In the concept of a snatching away of the church out of harm's way, defeat is already admitted and assumed. The ground is yielded to the beast, to the dragon, to the forces of darkness and death.[8] Those left alive in the world are abandoned to the wrath of the evil one.

How does this bring glory to the one who laid down his life for his friends, who, for the joy that was set before him, endured the cross? It stands in direct opposition to the life-through-death principle we talked about in chapter six, the very principle of the cross at the center of Christianity. The mandate of the church is to *win* the world, to take the battle to the gates of hell (Matt 16:18). If in pursuit of that aim Christians are made uncomfortable (perish the thought), suffer persecution, or even be required to lay down their lives for their Lord—isn't that what they are called to do?[9] Isn't that what they are destined for? Isn't that the very heart of Christianity? Isn't that in line with the pledge they made to Jesus? Should they not rejoice with the apostles and prophets that they are privileged to suffer for the name of Jesus? The end, after all, is already decided, and it is *victory* over all that opposes God. That victory came at great cost to Jesus and it sometimes comes at great cost to those who follow him. The Christian has yielded his or her life up to Jesus, if he should choose that we lay it down for him (as he laid his down for us), that's his right and his call to make. We have seen already that the book of Revelation directly addresses the question of who the earth belongs to and who rules over it. The Bible very clearly answers that the earth is the Lord's. Jesus came and established his kingdom here and it is not to be abandoned.

---

8. Where now is the authority Christians claim in the name of Jesus? Where now is the bold assertion "I can do all things through Christ who strengthens me"? Where now is the victory we proclaim each Sunday in our triumphant and contemporary services?

9. We are not talking about "suffering the wrath of God" here. Proponents of the rapture concept point to scriptures like 1 Thessalonians 5:9 "God did not appoint us to suffer wrath . . ." (cf. Rom 5:9; 1 Thess 1:10). Because the time of distress is a time when God's wrath is being poured out on the earth, the church cannot be on the earth at that time, they maintain. But, as shown when God brought Israel out of Egypt, he is well able to judge the ungodly and protect his people at the same time.

The physical world is not a bad or evil place. It is the creation of a good God and it was declared by him to be very good. It is the place created for human beings, it is the home address of those made in his image. True, it is marred by the sin of those same human beings but God's intention is to renew it, not do away with it. God is not about to abandon the good earth to the power of the evil one, not about to withdraw his people and cede control to darkness and evil. The earth belongs to Jesus; it was made by him, through him, and for him. He already came for that which was his own, why would he yield it up again? The kingdom of God is already here on earth, Jesus already reigns, and his reign on earth is mediated through the church, his people. Theirs is the victory, theirs the earth (see Rev 5:10; Matt 5:5). If that victory is sometimes claimed by laying down their lives for Jesus, it is victory nonetheless—even more so, as it is victory of the very same order that he himself won through the cross. In fact, that is the very nature of the kingdom as we have seen, it is advanced by his people sharing in his suffering. We have redefined "the abundant life" that is ours through Jesus as "the comfortable life" to the point that we expect to be "evacuated" before we reach the place where we might be required to really live the cross-life. But suffering for Jesus is portrayed in the pages of the New Testament as victory.

The resurrection that is to take place at his coming and by his command (which includes the catching up of those Christians who remain alive at his coming) is the great declaration of that victory. It is not to be preceded by a demonstration of impotence and failure. The very concept of a rapture is foreign to the biblical Christian worldview.

So, though it is widely believed in some Christian circles, the rapture teaching is actually a misconception that threatens to leave the church unprepared for its hour of greatest trial and opportunity and to rob it of the power of its victorious testimony (Rev 12:11).[10] It is scripturally unsupportable and it is logically impossible to maintain—requiring two *last* trumpets, two *second* comings, two *first* resurrections, two churches, and two gospels.

It also runs counter to the concept of Christian love and compassion as it presents "the saints" celebrating in heaven while family, friends, and millions of others are experiencing great suffering on the earth below, where they could be helped, comforted, and guided to faith in Jesus by those same saints, were they more concerned for others than themselves.

Besides all of this, Jesus clearly indicated that the end would not come until the task of bringing in the Gentiles is complete. "This gospel of the kingdom," he said, "will be preached in the whole world as a testimony to all nations, *and then the end will come*" (Matt 24:14). The end will not come

---

10. It is sincerely believed, perhaps; but it is possible to be sincerely wrong.

for the church until the task of gathering in the nations is complete, and we have seen that this task proceeds *through* the time of great distress.

There are deeper theological issues involved, seldom referred to. What, for instance, of the fate of children who are still under the age of discretion, incapable of making serious eternal decisions? If these children die, are they forever condemned or are they received by the Lord, not on the basis of being of themselves fit for heaven, but because the Lord died for all? If so, how will such children fare in the rapture? Will all children be taken out of the world? What of the unborn, those still in the womb? What about children born after the rapture?

What, again, of those people who are mentally incapable, for one reason or another, of making decisions concerning eternal issues? Are they forever beyond the reach of God's grace, or can they too be received by the Lord on the basis of Jesus' saving work? Will they too be participants in the rapture?

What of those who might come to salvation during the time of distress that proponents of the rapture theory say will follow the snatching up? Will they too be immediately caught up, or will they have to suffer through the time of distress from which those caught up in the rapture are exempt? If so, why should this be? That raises too the whole question of why many Christians throughout church history have suffered and been persecuted for their faith but a generation of their fellows will be exempted by being caught out of the world.

It is resurrection, not rapture, that is, and always has been, the hope of the people of God when this age comes to an end and the world is renewed. There is no "rapture" in the Bible as something prior to, or separate from, the resurrection.

AFTER THE MILLENNIUM

The text then tells us that when the thousand years have ended, the devil is released. He goes out to the nations again and among those now living on earth he somehow finds many to join him in the final rebellion and battle against God and his people. The events following the millennial reign of Christ on earth reveal that the real root of man's sin is not poverty, not poor social conditions, not a bad environment, but the rebelliousness of the human heart. After the 1,000 year reign of Jesus on earth, still, when Satan is loosed he will find human hearts responsive to his seductions. He is easily defeated however;[11] his army is destroyed and he himself is taken

---

11. Evil in the end is arrogant and delusional.

and thrown into the "lake of fire"—the second death and the final judgment (Rev 20:7–10).

There is, it must be noted, considerable debate about the meaning of the "millennium." These verses in Revelation chapter twenty form the only passage in the Bible where the concept is presented in this way.[12] But whether the thousand years is taken literally or figuratively, the text itself clearly portrays a considerable passage of time between the first resurrection and the second, or general, resurrection; between the binding and release of Satan; between the battle of 19:11–21 and that of 20:7–10; and between the final destruction of the beasts and that of the devil himself (cf. 20:10 where these last two are clearly portrayed as two separate events). Within this passage the expression "a thousand years" is repeated six times, indicating that the separation of these events is strongly emphasized and deliberate. There are two resurrections clearly portrayed (cf. 20:4–6), two judgments (beasts and Satan), and two battles, each separated in the text by 1,000 years.

Then follows the "great white throne" judgment (Rev 20:11–15). The text here suggests that all of the rest of the dead—i.e., all who have ever lived who did not have a part in the first resurrection—are raised to life at this time to face judgment. This presumably is a second resurrection, as that referred to in Revelation 20:5 is called the *first* resurrection, and the text here says the rest of the dead will come to life after the thousand years. Daniel spoke of the resurrection of some to everlasting life and some to everlasting shame and contempt (Dan 12:2). Jesus spoke of the resurrection of both "those who have done good" and "those who have done evil" (John 5:28), and Paul spoke of the resurrection of both the "righteous" and the "wicked" (Acts 24:15). The writer of Hebrews referred to a hope in a *better* resurrection, which probably means a better quality resurrection (in terms of reward, see 1 Cor 3:10–15) but which may imply an alternative, undesirable, resurrection (Heb 11:35). Those who have a part in this second resurrection are judged and separated on the basis of their deeds and their inclusion or not in the "book of life" (cf. Matt 25:31–46). The final judgment of those whose names are not recorded in the book of life is "the second death," the lake of fire where Satan met his end (cf. 21:8). The text here tells us that at this time, there is an end to the physical creation in some way (Rev 20:11; 21:1). Earth and sky "flee" from the presence of him who is seated on the throne.

The second stage of the establishment of God's kingdom on the earth then begins with a renewed physical creation; there is "a new heaven and a

---

12. A good discussion of the issues involved can be found in Newton, "Time Language."

new earth" (Rev 21:1, 5). Paul speaks of the present earth being corrupted by sin (Rom 8:20–22), awaiting "liberation from decay" and Peter speaks of the heavens and "the elements" being destroyed by fire and a new earth and heavens created (2 Peter 3:10–13). He says *everything* will be destroyed in this way.[13] Peter tells us that this will happen on "the day of the Lord," again reinforcing the fact that what is presented to us in Revelation is a fulfillment of that expected day. The apocalyptic language of cosmic destruction is common to descriptions of the Day of the Lord in both Old and New Testaments, however literally or figuratively we interpret it (see Isa 13:6–10 and Matt 24:29; Joel 2:30–31 and Acts 2:19–20; Isa 34:4; Mark 13:25). The text here in Revelation appears to be talking about a literal event of judgment and re-creation. Whatever this means, it is going to be dramatic.

Human beings are created, body, soul, and spirit—created able to commune with God, but created also for this physical earth. The future destiny of human beings is in a physical existence on a renewed earth, cleansed of sin and all its consequences. Again, the defeat of death (1 Cor 15:26) has no meaning if this is not so. This is the whole argument of 1 Corinthians 15; only resurrection to life in a physical body will demonstrate that sin and its consequence—death—are defeated (1 Cor 15:16–19). I repeat again, the Bible knows nothing of the idea of Christians living with God forever in "heaven" in some kind of out-of-body state. Death is the dissolution of the divine image, the sundering of spirit, soul, and body. It is the undoing of God's very good creation. It is the antithesis of the abundant life. It is a grotesque, unnatural, evil intrusion into the realm of light and love. It is separation, sorrow, hopelessness (without Jesus). It is the ultimate enemy of human life and joy. Only if death is defeated in all of its manifestations through a physical resurrection can God's good plan succeed. The defeat of sin and death is really the essence of the Bible story. It must culminate with human beings (body, soul, and spirit) living as they were designed and created to live—in a physical body on a physical earth. Thus is death defeated, thus the image restored. The (new) earth is our eternal home, not "heaven."

Descending upon the new earth then appears the New Jerusalem, the second city of this third vision as opposed to the first city "Babylon." It is also the second woman of this third vision, the Bride of the Lamb, as opposed to the "great prostitute." This city is the subject of the fourth vision, where further details are given. The third vision closes with the declaration, "it is done!" God is seen again as the Alpha and Omega; he has brought to completion that which he began. The purpose of creation is complete with

---

13. Not destroyed totally, rather "renewed," as with the flood judgment. See 2 Peter 3:6–7.

the appearance of the heavenly city. The Day of the Lord has come. The eschatological plan of God is fulfilled. All that was prophetically declared from Genesis 3:15, through God's promises to Abraham and David, through the Psalmist, through the long line of prophets, through the messiah, through the apostles and prophets of the New Testament—all is complete. There is a new heaven and a new earth; the old order has passed away and heaven and earth have become one. The long exile of human beings is over and the people of God dwell again in the presence of God. Death is defeated. There is no more suffering. Those who have overcome have received their eternal inheritance, and all that is evil is excluded from the new creation. The kingdom of God has come on earth, the earth is covered with the glory of the Lord. It is done.

SUMMARY OF CHAPTER FIFTEEN

John's third vision continues the unfolding story of the prophetic Day of the Lord, in this part of which God's plans for the creation are brought to completion. In this second and final part of the Day of the Lord, judgment finally falls on "Babylon," the rebellious world system. It is destroyed by the beast, resulting in a complete collapse of the global economy, system of trade, politics and the worldwide entertainment industry. The beast gathers the armies of the world to fight against God's people, but he is destroyed, captured, and bound for a thousand years by the returning Jesus. The first resurrection takes place at Jesus' return also, followed by his reign on earth for a thousand years. At the end of this time, Satan is released and again gathers the world's armies for battle against Jesus and his people—a battle that this time results in his final destruction in the lake of fire. The second resurrection and final judgment take place, the earth and heavens are cleansed by fire, and a new heavens and earth created upon which descends the New Jerusalem. This is the completion of all the purposes of God in creation. It is done. However we interpret it, that's what the text tells us.

Chapter Sixteen

GARDEN AND CITY

"He said to me: "It is done. I am the Alpha and the Omega, the Beginning and the End...." (Rev 21:6)

THE FOURTH VISION (REV 21:9–22:7) reaches beyond the realm of the present order into the next, beyond the boundaries of this present creation into the realm of the realized new creation. It draws heavily on the new temple imagery of Ezekiel, the tabernacle imagery of Exodus, and the original sanctuary imagery of Genesis 1–3 (cf. Isa 54:11–14). Here in the final pages of the Bible is revealed the *end* that God had in mind for the world from before the foundation of the earth. This was the purpose of God from the beginning; this was the reason for creation.

The focus and subject of the text in this fourth vision is the New Jerusalem, the bride and wife of the Lamb. This is highly symbolic language, of course, and passages like 2 Corinthians 11:2, Ephesians 5:22–33, and Revelation 19:11; 22:17 make it clear that the metaphors of *bride* and *wife* in relation to Christ are both speaking of the church rather than a literal "city." This is imagery which has roots, in turn, in the Old Testament prophetic literature (cf. Isa 54:5–6; 62:5; Jer 3:14, 20; Hos 2:19; etc.) relating to God's special relationship with Israel.

The holy city has gates on which are inscribed the names of the twelve tribes of Israel (cf. Ezek 48:30–34) and foundations on which are inscribed the names of the twelve apostles of the Lamb. Both Old and New Testament people of God are united in the bride. God has been doing one work through all of redemptive history. There *is* a meta-narrative. Revelation *does* present the completion of the eschatological Bible story. The church (including the Old Testament people of God) was the reason for creation (Eph 1:4, 9-12; 3:10-11), and now here it is, beautiful, glorious, perfected. Heaven once again overshadows and infuses the earth as it did in Eden.

The city has a cubic measurement, reflecting the most holy place in the tabernacle and temple into which the high priest would venture once a year. In the holy city, God's presence is open to all, and *all* of God's people will dwell in his presence forever. City and temple have become one, and God's image dwells in God's sanctuary once more. The measuring of the city recalls Ezekiel 40-41 and serves to show the order, the symmetry, and the perfection of God's eternal plan. The number twelve (144 is 12 x 12) is predominant in this passage, seemingly to do again with the idea of God's governance. All of this is highly symbolic of course and to attempt to identify every little detail (e.g., who are the people outside the city?) have very little meaning or application here. This is a picture of the finished work of God.

The special garments (Rev 21:2), the pure gold, and the precious stones all recall the priestly attire of Exodus 28. Their emphasized purity contrasts with the filthiness and gaudiness of the great prostitute of chapter 17. Solomon's temple was overlaid with gold and precious stones (2 Chr 3:4-7) and the kings of Israel accumulated great quantities of both (2 Chr 9:1; 9:10; 32:27). To this city, however, the kings of the earth will bring their splendor (21:24-26). The glory that filled the tabernacle (Exod 40:34-35) and the temple (2 Chr 7:1-2), will shine forever in the holy city (Rev 21:11, 23).

The angel shows John another scene of a river flowing from the throne of God (22:1-5), which draws on the background of both Ezekiel (47:1-12) and Genesis (2:10-14; cf. Dan 7:10). Here we have a picture again of the triune God, since the river—symbolic of the Holy Spirit (John 7:38)—flows from the throne of God and of the Lamb. The "deposit" of the Holy Spirit, enjoyed by the prophets and by the prophetic community during the church age (Eph 1:14) is now given in all its fullness. The tree of life is available again to God's people through eternity, its leaves bringing health to all the nations. God's people, the royal priesthood, will serve him and worship him (22:3). "These words," said the angel guide to John, "are trustworthy and true. The Lord, the God of the spirits of the prophets, sent his angel to show his servants the things that must soon take place" (Rev 22:6).

THE GARDEN AND THE CITY

It is this final vision which brings to completion the whole Bible story. Here in the holy city in the new creation, all the threads are drawn together and all the loose ends are tied off. Without this vision, the biblical meta-narrative has no natural end. But with it the Bible story is completed. What began in the garden is brought to completion in the city.

In the Genesis account of creation, the story of humanity's beginning is necessarily contained in language, terms, and concepts familiar to the civilizations of the ancient Near East at the time of its writing. The setting is the garden sanctuary of Eden where human beings in the image of God are living as priest/kings in covenant relationship with God and enjoying his blessing. From there the man and woman are to subdue and rule over the creation and fill it with the divine image. This creation account of Genesis 1–3 is the most foundational of all stories, echoing and re-echoing through the literature, theology, folklore, and mythology of Christianity for two millennia, and of Judaism for centuries before that. It is the story of humanity's beginning in the garden in Eden, a prologue to the Bible narrative. One commentator calls it *the* text of Western civilization, central in giving meaning and content to our sexual, moral, artistic, and literary traditions.[1] It is certainly one of the world's best-known stories, and commentators have noted "the cosmic scope of its themes, the majestic imagery of its poetry, and the warm drama of its narrative."[2] It continues to inform and shape contemporary theology, being central, for instance, to current debates over women's participation in leadership in church and home, the place of human beings in the ecological system, and the question of creation versus evolution.

Major concepts and motifs arise in the Eden narratives that find echoes throughout Old and New Testaments and in fact help to shape the whole biblical narrative. The Edenic-garden motif is so prevalent throughout the Bible story that it constitutes a major thrust of the biblical meta-narrative.[3]

The garden was a familiar concept in the ancient world and would have formed a part of the shared cultural knowledge of the time. The aesthetic pleasures associated with gardens, their intrinsic value, the symbolism of the walled enclosures—all would have been widely known. The Bible often refers to gardens of various kinds—of fruit trees and timber trees, vegetable gardens, flower gardens, and vineyards. The translators of the Septuagint

---

1. Morris, *A Walk in the Garden*, 23.
2. Davis, *Paradise to Prison*, 13.
3. Clearly giving support to the idea of creation / new creation as the "center" of the Bible story.

used the Persian/Greek loanword *paradeisos* for the garden, possibly derived from the Median word pari-daeza meaning "enclosure."[4] So the picture of the garden in the ancient world was of a walled place, secure and protected, fruitfull, peacefull, and well-watered. It is a place of delight, and in the Bible such a garden is symbolically a sign of God's blessing.

However, Eden was more than an earthly paradise. There are several references in the literature of the ancient Near East to places which were associated with dwellings of deities. These frequently contain references to such things as beauty, safety, and fertility, and many of these motifs can also be found in the Genesis garden. Eden was a temple—a sanctuary, a holy or sacred place—the place where God's presence dwelt and where he met with the man and woman. We see in the later tabernacle and temple that it was God's presence in the inner sanctuary that sanctified it, that made it sacred; so Eden too was God's sanctuary—it too was sanctified by his presence. Many of the features found in the garden are also found in later sanctuaries, so Eden serves as a kind of prototype of the sacred place.[5] Both Eden and the tabernacle/temple are entered from the east, the jewels and gold of Eden find echoes in the materials used to decorate the tabernacle and the priests' garments (Gen 2:12; Exod 25:11,17; Exod 25:7, 28:9-14, 20; 1 Chr 29:2), and the trees of the garden are stylized in the tabernacle menorah. The verb used in Genesis 3:8 of God walking in the garden is the same term used to describe his presence in the later tent sanctuaries (Lev 26:12; Deut 23:15, 2; Sam 7:6-7).[6]

Cherubim (Gen 3:24) were traditional guardians of holy places in the ancient Near East. In the temple, cherubim guarded the inner sanctuary. Two others on top of the ark formed the throne of God, and pictures of cherubim decorated the curtains of the tabernacle and walls of the temple (Exod 26:31; 1 Kgs 6:29). A river flowed out of Eden (Gen 2:10-14), separating into four—the number probably being used to show totality and completeness (as in the term "the four corners of the earth"). Water becomes a powerful symbol of life throughout Scripture (Ps 46:5; Ezek 47; John 7:38; Rev 22:1). Rivers always flow from a height, and this gave rise to the concept of a holy mountain in Eden. In the mythology of the ancient Near East, the "world mountain" was an important theme. It was the highest point on earth, at the center of the earth—the point from which creation began, and thus the point where God could be encountered. It was the point where heaven and earth came together. Sacred mountains played a

---

4. Noort, *Paradise Interpreted*, 21.
5. Alexander, *From Paradise to the Promised Land*, 21.
6. See Wenham, "Sanctuary Symbolism," 400.

significant role in Israel's religious life. In the stories of the Exodus, the giving of the law, and the wilderness wanderings that followed, God's activity is often associated with mountains. Ezekiel gives credence to the concept of the "world mountain" in Eden (Ezek 28:13–16). This pervasive motif can also be traced throughout the Scripture record, both in direct references to the holy mountain, such as Psalm 48:1–3, and in the general pattern of mountains associated with divine activity—Sinai, Horeb, Zion, the Mount of Transfiguration, the Mount of Olives, Golgotha, etc. Another major element of the creation/Eden story is the concept of rest. This rest is to be seen not as a goal or consequence of human actions, but as a foundation or starting point for their lives, the natural state of affairs in the divine sanctuary. The seventh day (without an end) is the end of God's creative activity. It is his provision for the man and woman he created. Again, the concept of rest may be traced through the Bible narrative (see especially Hebrews 4).

God brought the first couple into the garden he had made. It needed their work. Creation is extravagant, rampant, chaotic, and it must be subdued, must be ordered. It provided for all the needs of the first humans, both aesthetic and practical. The man and woman were not additions to the divine plan, but central to the creation process. This is what God created for. God had made the man and woman *in his own image* (Gen 1:27). This is the central concept that needs to be grasped in order to understand all that follows in the Bible record—the very special relationship men and women have with the creator and the great lengths to which the creator is willing to go for the creature. To be human is to be made in the image of God.[7]

It is this personhood that distinguishes human beings from the animals, thus no suitable companion or helper for Adam could be found among their number. God made another *person* to be his companion. It is important to note again that human beings were made for this world, and as part of the creation they shared certain physical characteristics with the animals—all of which God proclaimed here were very good (Gen 1:31). But as God's regents, they also transcended the physical limits of the world and walked and talked with God. The climax of Genesis chapter one sees the image bearers, both *persons*—male and female—standing side by side before

---

7. There has been much debate on the meaning of this *imago Dei*. Some attempt to assign female attributes to God, reasoning that because God created both "male and female" in his own image, he can rightly be spoken of in terms of both genders. God's "image," however, has nothing to do with gender (so gender cannot be projected back on God). God created male and female "in his own image," i.e., as *persons* like himself. This is the starting point for any discussion of the value of men and women before God. This is not to say that women and men do not reflect in different measures various aspects of the divine nature, i.e., the nurturing love of the mother or the protective love of the father.

their creator.[8] This "personhood," in its God-likeness, *and thus the ability of each to know God*, is the basis of dignity for all human beings. God's express purpose and desire throughout Scripture is to develop this personhood to its fullest possible potential—through Jesus and the indwelling Spirit.[9] This *person*—this being that was fully awake to God, that could fully relate to him, could intellectually and emotionally *enjoy* him (behold God's goodness and grace) and respond to him in love, this male and female person—God brought as his regent, the priest/king, into his garden sanctuary.

The text says "the Lord had planted a garden . . ." (Gen 2:8). It was God's garden, not the garden of Adam and Eve. They were stewards and the garden was their home for only as long as they lived in right relationship with the owner. They lived in the shadow of the two trees, under the divine will—the blessing ("I give you") and commandment/curse of God ("you must not," Gen 1:29; 2:17). Of the tree of life, it seems, they could freely eat. Of "the tree of the knowledge of good and evil" they were not to eat under any circumstances. Again, much debate has centered on the meaning of this enigmatic name for the second tree. "You will be like God," the serpent said, "you will use your own will, choose your own course, please yourself."[10] The woman and the man found this an irresistibly seductive idea, so they ate and plunged themselves and their children into darkness and death.

This is the human tragedy. For the first couple, this was the negation and repudiation of the whole divine purpose, the rejection of the divine image, of priesthood, kingship, and "sonship." God knows the end from the beginning, but the consequences of human choices are largely beyond their own comprehension and largely beyond their control. It is only God who can see and form the future. It is only God who can fashion the end from the beginning. When they violated the tenancy agreement, the man and the woman were expelled from the garden and lost their close relationship with the creator and the privilege of God's presence. Because of their priestly role their disobedience affected—and began to permeate—the whole creation. Human sin, says J. T. Walsh, "has cosmic dimensions. No matter how petty or private the deed may seem, it is a violation of the sacred at the heart of reality; and it involves a rejection of the whole divinely established order

---

8. There is no suggestion here of rank or role, both are persons, both bear the divine stamp.

9. Many Christians today would say that the "gospel" is "the good news that Jesus died for my sins so I could go to heaven when I die." However, texts like Acts 2:38 tell a different story. Jesus died for forgiveness so those forgiven people could be filled with the Spirit. The question then becomes: "why are we filled with the Spirit?"

10. There are other ways of interpreting the meaning of what took place at that time, but this seems clear in context.

of creation."[11] Adam and Eve rejected their destiny as image bearers—to glorify God by filling the good earth with that image and reflect the glory back to God—so they were ejected from the garden. Choosing the tree of autonomy, they forfeited their part in the tree of life.

Eden is not often mentioned by name outside of the Genesis account (Isa 51:3; Ezek 28:13; 31:9, 16, 18; 36:35; Joel 2:3). This has sometimes led to an inadequate appreciation of its importance not only *to*, but also *through*, the biblical narrative. This paucity of specific reference belies the fundamental and foundational place of Genesis 1–3 in the whole Bible story. The concepts and motifs arising in the Eden narratives echo and re-echo through the scriptural writings until they are drawn to a conclusion here in Revelation. The garden is the backdrop against which the whole tapestry of the Bible story—shot through with the multi-colored threads which have their beginning there—is woven. Any of these threads can be profitably followed through the Scripture to reveal the intricate handiwork of the most skilled of weavers. Taking just one thread, for instance, Eden was the Garden of God, God's dwelling place, the confluence of heaven and earth, the place where God met with man. This can be followed through then to the tent of meeting, the tabernacle, the Jerusalem Temple, to Jesus, the Spirit-filled church, and on to the New Jerusalem.

ECHOES OF EDEN

The Eden story finds echoes in several familiar Old Testament passages. One commentator notes, for instance, that movement in an easterly direction (away from Eden) appears to represent "the descent of humanity into degradation," the journey away from God. Adam and Eve leave Eden from the east (Gen 3:24).[12] After killing Abel, Cain moves to the east where, in an attempt to alleviate the loneliness of his enforced wandering, he founds the first city, a walled place of safety, a parody of Eden (Gen 4:16). The founding of civilization (thus tied to man's rebellion) is contrasted with the spiritual development of the descendants of Seth who remain in the West (4:26). Babel too came as men moved eastward (11:1–9), a direct challenge to God's power leading to the confusion of language and conflict between people groups.

The similarities between the stories of Adam in the garden and that of Noah in the post-flood world are also instructive. In Noah's post-flood experiences we can see a new world, a new Adam, a new commissioning,

11. Walsh, "Genesis 2:4b—3:24," 161–77.
12. Kunin, *Themes and Issues in Judaism*, 115–48.

a new garden, even a new fall—resulting in a new conflict among the descendants of Noah—and a new judgment (dispersion at Babel). A man fails again.

The tabernacle echoed Eden, a walled sanctuary wherein dwelt the presence of God. Leviticus 1:1 is one of the most significant verses in the Old Testament when we notice where it is God speaks from—he has pitched his sanctuary/tent among the tents of Israel. He has come to dwell once more among his people, an "Eden" theme that echoes throughout the Bible. Alexander points out that the extensive use of gold and silver, of blue, purple, and scarlet yarn and fine linen, indicates that the tabernacle was a royal residence wherein the ark "functioned as a . . . throne protected by guardian cherubim (cf. 1 Sam 4:4; 2 Sam 6:2; 2 Kgs 19:15; Ps 80:2; 99:1; Isa 37:16)."[13] The king was in residence, and his presence sanctified the camp. The Jerusalem temple was a garden picture also. Birds, animals, fruit, and trees adorned its walls and furnishings. The two pillars which stood at the entrance were most probably stylized trees. It was the place of God's presence. The prophets speak of life-bringing waters flowing from the temple in Jerusalem (Ezek 47:1–12; Zech 14:8; Joel 4:18).

A NEW EDEN

So we see that the Bible is replete with recurring Edenic symbolism and allusion. In fact, so pervasive is this that we are forced to see it as a major theological thrust of the biblical narrative. "Eden" (God's image in God's sanctuary) was God's purpose and remains so throughout the Bible. Gerhard von Rad notes that the books of the Hexateuch (Genesis to Joshua) present a connected narrative which takes us from creation to the entrance of the tribes into Canaan, many stories woven together into one.[14] What God began in Eden he sets out to do again in Canaan. The promised land is a new Eden, a special place, a new sanctuary where God is to provide for and to dwell among his people. In the nation of Israel, God creates "a corporate Adam."[15]

The role of priest/king that was Adam's in the garden became Israel's in Canaan. Israel was to be a *kingdom* of priests, serving God in his new sanctuary (Exod 19:5–6). N. T. Wright notes that the Israel-Adam link was so woven into Jewish thought and writing that it emerges virtually everywhere

---

13. Alexander, *Paradise to the Promised Land*, 98.
14. Rad, *Genesis*, 13.
15. Beale, "The Eschatological Conception," 25–26.

we look.¹⁶ The stewardship given to Adam in Eden was now afforded to Israel in Canaan.

Israel's history itself echoes creation/Eden. Creation is pictured as God brings Israel out of the bondage of Egypt, through the waters of the sea, the fiery pillar giving light and the wind moving across the waters causing dry land to appear (Exod 14:19–21; Gen 1:2–9). Like Adam, Israel is created outside of the garden/land (Gen 2:8) and brought into a new creation; a finished work; a place of rest, provision, and blessing; a land "flowing with milk and honey." William Dumbrell notes that there are brooks, fountains, and springs; there are cisterns which Israel did not dig, houses they did not build, fruit trees and vineyards they did not plant (Deut 6:10–11). Fullness of life would be enjoyed, sickness removed, and every threat to Israel's security dealt with (Deut 11:11–12). "By means of such references," he says, "the concept of the land as 'Eden regained' comes through strongly."¹⁷

The tabernacle/temple was the dwelling place of God the King among them; his presence sanctified the land and transformed it into a sanctuary.¹⁸ Israel was to return to Edenic rest in the land (Exod 33:14; Deut 3:20; 12:9; 25:17–19. Cf. Jos 21:43–45). This rest was tied to God's presence—more than his merely *being there*, it spoke of relationship, of personal interaction, of provision (and thus freedom from painful toil), of lasting security, of abundance, joy, the destruction of enemies and so the absence of fear. Canaan is God's gift to Israel (Jos 1:2), who must do what Adam should have done and drive the serpent/Canaanites from God's sacred place (Deut 7:1–6). Israel was to live in the land under the blessing and commandment of God (Jos 24:1–27) and in the blessings and curses of Deuteronomy 28, we see again the reflection of the two garden trees. There in the new Eden God will build his kingdom, and from Israel the image of God would fill the earth. Here again is the world mountain. In the Israelite tradition, the mountain of God was Sinai (Exod 3:1; 18:5; 24:13), but with the growing importance of Jerusalem, Zion took over the function of the mountain of God.¹⁹ God chose Jerusalem for his dwelling place, Mt. Zion for his palace/temple (Ps 78:68; 132:13). Zion is identified with Mt. Zaphon (Ps 48:2 "in the far North"), theologically understood to be the highest point on earth (cf. Ps 2:6; 68:18; 87:1; 99:9). Those who dwell in Zion shared the blessings

---

16. Wright, *The New Testament and the People of God*, 266.
17. Dumbrell, *End of the Beginning*, 134.
18. Ibid., 39.
19. Noort, *Paradise Interpreted*, 27.

of God's presence (Ps 48:12–14; 132:13–18; 133:1–3; 147:12–20).[20] Jerusalem became the new world center.[21]

But again, as with Adam and as with Noah, Israel failed. The image of God was rejected as Israel fell again and again into idolatry, until finally Israel too was expelled from the land for their continued breaching of the covenant. Again human beings were driven from God's sanctuary, driven forth from the presence of God into exile, without temple, land, or rest. Fortunately, that was not the end of the story. God's wisdom, love, and power are again greater than human weakness and failure.

THE NEW JERUSALEM—EDEN RESTORED

In the New Testament the garden is not mentioned by name at all, but Eden/garden imagery and allusion permeate its pages nevertheless. Some of these are direct references—to Adam, to "the beginning," to the creator, etc.,[22]—but the New Testament is replete with indirect garden imagery also. From the all-embracing emphasis on "fruitfulness" to the many references to vines and vineyards, trees, husbandsmen, abundant life, joy, living water—and most poignantly, the "tree" on which Jesus died—the New Testament narrative echoes the garden where the story began. As with Adam, Jesus too had an encounter with the divine will in a garden. He too stood before the tree of autonomy, where he—last Adam and second man—this time chose the Father's will (Matt 26:39). As a result of his choice, the full force of the judgment for the first man's disobedience, "you shall surely die," finally fell on him. Hung on that tree (Acts 5:30; 10:39; 13:29; Gal 3:13; 1 Pet 2:24), he forever broke the power it had wielded for so long over the image-bearers. And in his death and resurrection he became the gate (John 10:9), the way back past the flaming sword and the cherubim, back to the garden sanctuary, back to the tree of life, back to the Father's presence. All of these themes find their full and final expression in the obvious Eden references and comparisons in the city of Revelation 21 and 22.

---

20. Gowan, *Eschatology in the Old Testament*, 7.

21. See Dumbrell, *Search for Order*, 76.

22. See Luke 3:38; 1 Cor 15:22, 45; 1 Tim 2:13; Jude 1:4; 2 Cor 11:3. See also Matt 19:4–6; 10:6; John 1:1; 1 John 1:1; etc.

SUMMARY OF FOURTH VISION

In this vision, God's presence is restored to his people (or God's people are restored to God's presence). Humanity's long exile comes to an end. Cast out of God's sanctuary in Eden, and cast out again from the restored sanctuary in Canaan, the people of God now *form* the sanctuary in which God dwells by his Spirit. God's great power, wisdom, and love are now apparent to all, and God now openly reigns over a new creation from which all evil is banished forever. God will dwell among his people living on the new earth.

Final Word

EVERLASTING JOY

The conclusion of the book of Revelation is found in chapter 22:8–21. In contrast to the instructions received by Daniel when he was given visions of the time of the end (Dan 12:4), John is instructed *not* to seal up the words of the prophetic revelation he has received because "the time is near." This sense of urgency is emphasized twice more in this passage when Jesus declares, "I am coming soon!" He is the alpha and omega; what he began he will bring to completion. He will bring about the "end" that he had in mind from the beginning, and the end, like the beginning, is very good. Thus, in reading the text of Revelation and allowing it to tell its own story, it is clear that the book claims to be a prophecy (a revelation through the prophet John) that presents to us the events of what the prophets called the Day of the Lord, the cataclysmic upheaval that will be the final dividing line between this age and the age to come. In highly symbolic language drawing extensively on the Old Testament, especially the prophetic literature there, it details the final judgment and the final salvation that brings the creation to its God-intended fulfillment. It is a book about the end of the world in every sense.

We started this book with the Old Testament prophets, seeing that they served as God's advisors to the kings of Israel and Judah and brought to the people of God the messages they received from him. Primarily, those messages addressed the historical situation in which they lived together. Israel had made a covenant with God but was not living according to the covenant terms. Their living in breach of the agreement was likened to a wife who was being unfaithful to her husband. The prophets warned the nation of Israel, and later Judah, over and over again to repent and return to a right relationship with God. When this failed to eventuate, they then began to proclaim that inescapable judgment was coming. This took the form of a violent end to both nations at the hands of foreign invaders and the deportation of God's people to captivity and exile in foreign lands. The prophets also promised that after judgment had fallen and the exile was completed, God would restore the fortunes of Israel and Judah. There were many and varied aspects to this promised restoration, the outworking of which can be summarized under the two interrelated categories of the kingdom of God and the Day of the Lord. The promises surrounding the kingdom of God began to be fulfilled with the coming of Jesus and are covered in the prophetic literature of the four gospels and Acts.

Prophecies, promises, and warnings surrounding the Day of the Lord concept began to be fulfilled at that time also, but in a typical prophetic "telescoping" effect, they await a further and more complete fulfillment in the events surrounding the return of Jesus and the end of the present age. At that time everything the Old Testament prophets proclaimed and predicted will finally come to completion. We have seen that the book of Revelation claims to be a record of those final events. As predicted by the prophets (including Jesus), a period of great distress will come upon the earth, brought about by a final and climactic satanic attempt to destroy God's people and thwart his intentions and by the final judgment of God upon the unrepentant. This will be accompanied by a great spiritual revival that will result in "a great multitude . . . from every nation, tribe, people, and language" becoming followers of Jesus. The great commission given to the church by Jesus will be completed.

These events will usher in the end of the age and the beginning of the age to come, when all of God's good and wise purposes for creation will be finally fulfilled. There will be a new heavens and a new earth where King Jesus will reign in righteousness and justice forever. God's people, in resurrection bodies, filled with God's Spirit, will form God's sanctuary on the new earth, enjoying God's presence, and the glory of the Lord will cover the earth. What God will do then is not recorded, though it is hinted at in places like Ephesians 2:6; 3:10 and 1 John 3:2. After the end will come the beginning of something wonderful in every sense—the new creation, in which God's image will reign with him over the earth and worship him for his beauty, power, wisdom, and love.

> *Behold I will create new heavens and new earth. The former things will not be remembered, nor will they come to mind . . . But be glad and rejoice forever in what I will create, for I will create Jerusalem to be a delight and it's people a joy.* (Isa 65:17–19)

Finally, after talking about the return of Jesus, the final judgment, the creation of the new heavens and new earth, and the descent of the New Jerusalem where God's Spirit-filled people will dwell in God's presence forever, we have still not arrived at the "end." The end of all things for the people of God, as Isaiah prophesied above, is joy in God's presence forever.

Joy is one of the hallmarks of the kingdom of God (Rom 14:17) and attends the presence of the Holy Spirit (Acts 13:2; 1 Thess 1:6). It is a gift of the Spirit (Gal 5:22). This is, and always has been, God's intention, his planned and purposed "end" for the creation. It was very good to begin with and it will be very good when it is renewed. Isaiah prophesied again: "Those the Lord has rescued will return. They will enter Zion with singing; everlasting joy will crown their heads. Gladness and joy will overtake them, and sorrow and sighing will flee away" (Isaiah 35:10; 51:11).

In God's presence—as the musicians sang before the Ark of the Covenant—are strength and joy: "Splendor and majesty are before him; strength and joy are in his dwelling place" (1 Chr 16:27). The psalmist agreed. "You make known to me the path of life," he wrote, "You will fill me with joy in your presence" (Ps 16:11).

Isaiah said that the day of salvation would be marked by great joy. "With joy you will draw water from the wells of salvation . . . In that day you will say: 'Give praise to the Lord, proclaim his name . . .'" (Isa 12:3–4).

It was the promise of joy that motivated Jesus to endure the cross (Heb 12:2) and this great and everlasting joy will be shared by those who appear finally in the presence of God when all other things are completed, "To him who is able to keep you from stumbling and to present you before his glorious presence without fault and with great joy—to the only God our Savior be glory, majesty, power and authority, through Jesus Christ our Lord, before all ages, now and forevermore! Amen" (Jude 24–25).

The end of all things is joy—great joy, *exceeding* joy, unspeakable joy; everlasting, eternal, unending joy; unbreakable, unstoppable, unbearable, uncontainable joy; joy worth any cost; joy in the presence of God and the Lamb and in the fullness of God's Spirit.

This then, is the end of the prophetic eschatology of the Bible: for those who receive that grace and choose to follow Jesus, great and everlasting joy with him forever.

> *"Lift up your heads, O you gates; lift them up, you ancient doors, that the King of glory may come in. Who is he, this King of glory? The Lord Almighty—he is the King of glory."*
>
> —Ps 24:9–10

BIBLIOGRAPHY

Aland, Barbara, et al., eds. *The Greek New Testament*. 4th rev. ed. New York: United Bible Societies, 1983.
Alexander, T. Desmond. *From Paradise to the Promised Land*. Grand Rapids, MI: Baker, 1995.
Barker, Joel D. "Day of the Lord." In *Dictionary of the Old Testament: Prophets*, edited by Mark J. Boda and J. Gordon McConville, 132–43. Downers Grove, IL: InterVarsity, 2012.
Barker, Kenneth, ed. *Zondervan NIV Study Bible: New International Version*. Grand Rapids, MI: Zonderzan, 1985.
Bauckham, Richard. *Gospel Women: Studies of the Named Women in the Gospels*. Grand Rapids, MI: Eerdmans, 2002.
Beale, G. K. *The Book of Revelation: A Commentary on the Greek Text*. Grand Rapids, MI: Eerdmans, 1999.
———. "The Eschatalogical Conception of New Testament Theology." In *Eschatology in Bible & Theology: Evangelical Essays at the Dawn of the New Millennium*, edited by Kent E. Brower and Mark W. Elliott, 11–52. Downers Grove, IL: InterVarsity, 1997.
Beasley-Murray, George R. *John*. 2nd ed. Word Biblical Commentary 36. Nashville: Thomas Nelson, 1999.
Brown, Michael L. *Israel's Divine Healer*. Grand Rapids, MI: Zondervan, 1995.
Brown, Raymond E. *The Gospel According to John*. 2 vols. Anchor Bible 29–29A. London: Doubleday, 1996.
Casey, Michael. *Toward God: The Ancient Wisdom of Western Prayer*. Melbourne: Collins Dove, 1990.
Chilton, David. *The Days of Vengeance: An Exposition on the Book of Revelation*. Fort Worth, TX: Dominion, 1987.
Cunningham, Loren, David J. Hamilton, and Janice Rogers. *Why Not Women?: A Fresh Look at Scripture on Women in Missions, Ministry, and Leadership*. Seattle: YWAM, 2000.
Davis, John J. *Paradise to Prison*. Salem: Sheffield. 1998.
Dodd, C. H. *The Interpretation of the Fourth Gospel*. London: Cambridge University Press, 1965
Dumbrell, William J. *The End of the Beginning*. Grand Rapids, MI: Baker, 1985.
———. *The Search for Order*. Grand Rapids, MI. Baker, 1994.
Dunn, James D. G. *The Christ and the Spirit*. Grand Rapids, MI: Eerdmans, 1998.

———. *The Theology of Paul the Apostle*. Grand Rapids, MI: Eerdmans, 1998.
Faxon, Alicia Craig. *Women and Jesus*. Philadelphia: United Church, 1973.
Fee, Gordon D. *God's Empowering Presence*. Peabody, MA: Hendrickson, 1994.
Fee, Gordon D., and Douglas Stuart. *How to Read the Bible for All It's Worth*. Grand Rapids, MI: Zondervan, 1993.
Fosdick, Harry Emerson. *The Meaning of Prayer*. London: Collins, 1960.
Giles, Kevin. *The Trinity & Subordinationism: The Doctrine of God and the Contemporary Gender Debate*. Downers Grove, IL: InterVarsity, 2002.
Gowan, Donald E. *Eschatology in the Old Testament*. Edinburgh: T. & T. Clark, 2000.
Gundry, Robert H. *The Church & the Tribulation*. Grand Rapids, MI: Zondervan, 1973.
Howell, Don N. "The Centre of Pauline Theology." *Biliotheca Sacra* 151 (January-March 1994) 50–70.
Kunin, Seth D. *Themes and Issues in Judaism*. London: Cassell, 2000.
Ladd, George E. *A Theology of the New Testament*. Rev. Ed. Grand Rapids, MI: Eerdmans, 2001.
———. *A Commentary on the Revelation of John*. Grand Rapids, MI. Eerdmans, 1972.
Lewis, C. S. "The Efficacy of Prayer." In *Subject and Structure: An Anthology for Writers*, 6th ed., edited by John M. Wasson, 442–47. Boston: Little, Brown, 1978.
———. *Miracles: A Preliminary Study*. London: Fount, 1998.
Morris, Paul, and Deborah Sawyer. *A Walk in the Garden*. Sheffield: Sheffield Academic, 1992.
Moyise, Steve. *The Old Testament in the New: An Introduction*. London: Continuum, 2001.
Newton, Jon. K. "Time Language and the Purpose of the Millenium." *Colloquium* 43, no. 2 (November 2011) 147–68.
Noort, Ed. "Gan-Eden in the Context of the Mythology of the Hebrew Bible." In *Paradise Interpreted*, edited by G. P. Luttikhuizen, 21–36. Leiden: Brill Academic, 1999.
Paige, Terence P. "Holy Spirit." In *Dictionary of Paul and His Letters*, edited by Gerald F. Hawthorne et al., 404–13. Downers Grove, IL: InterVarsity, 1993.
Petersen, David L. *The Prophetic Literature*. Louisville, KY: Westminster John Knox, 2002.
Rad, Gerhard von. *Genesis*. London: SCM, 1972.
Rea, John. "Abraham in the New Testament." In *Wycliffe Bible Encyclopedia*, edited by Charles F. Vos Pfeiffer et al., 12. Chicago: Moody, 1975.
Robertson, O. Palmer. *The Christ of the Prophets*. Phillipsburg, NJ: P&R, 2004.
Snodgrass, Klyne R. *Stories with Intent: A Comprehensive Guide to the Parables of Jesus*. Eerdmans, Grand Rapids, MI: Eerdmans, 2008.
Spivey, Robert A., D. Moody Smith, and C. Clifton Black. *Anatomy of the New Testament: A Guide to Its Structure and Meaning*. Minneapolis: Fortress, 2010.
Stagg, Evelyn, and Frank Stagg. *Woman in the World of Jesus*. Philadelphia: Westminster, 1978.
Stein, Robert H. *An Introduction to the Parables*. Philadelphia, PA: Westminster, 1981.
Tenney, Merrill C. *Interpreting Revelation*, Peabody, MA: Eerdmans, 2003.
Thompson, Alan J. *The Acts of the Risen Lord Jesus*. Downers Grove, IL: InterVarsity, 2011.
Walsh, J. T. "Genesis 2:4b—3:24: A Synchronic Approach." *Journal of Biblical Literature* 96 (1977) 161–77.

Watts, Rikk. "Jesus and His Mighty Deeds." Lecture, Harvest Bible College, Melbourne, July 10, 2003.

Wenham, David. *Paul: Follower of Jesus or Founder of Christianity?* Grand Rapids, MI: Eerdmans, 1995.

Wenham, Gordon J. "Sanctuary Symbolism in the Garden of Eden Story." In *I Studied Inscriptions From Before the Flood*, edited by Richard S. Hess and David T. Tsumura, 399–404. Winona Lake, IN: Eisenbrauns, 1994.

Wilson-Kastner, Patricia. *Faith, Feminism, and the Christ*. Philadelphia: Fortress, 1983.

Witherington, Ben. *Revelation*. New York: Cambridge University Press, 2008.

———. *Women and the Genesis of Christianity*. Cambridge: Cambridge University Press, 1990.

Wright, N. T. *The Challenge of Jesus*. Downers Grove, IL: InterVarsity, 1999.

———. *Creation, Power and Truth*. London: SPCK, 2013.

———. "Gospel and Theology in Galatians." In *Gospel in Paul*, edited by Ann L. Jervis and Peter Richardson, 22–39. Sheffield: Sheffield Academic, 1994.

———. *How God Became King*. London: SPCK, 2012.

———. *Jesus and the Victory of God*. London: SPCK, 2001.

———. *Kingdom New Testament*. New York: HarperOne, 2011.

———. *The New Testament and the People of God*. Minneapolis: Fortress, 1992.

———. *The Resurrection of the Son of God*. London: SPCK, 2003.

———. "The Servant and Jesus: The Relevance of the Colloquy for the Current Quest for Jesus." In *Jesus and the Suffering Servant: Isaiah 53 and Christian Origins*, edited by William H. Bellinger Jr. and William R. Farmer, 281–297. Harrisburg, PA: Trinity, 1998. www.ntwrightpage.com/Wright_Servant_Jesus.htm.

www.ingramcontent.com/pod-product-compliance
Lightning Source LLC
Chambersburg PA
CBHW070315230426
43663CB00011B/2132